# Chicken Soup for the Soul.

# Food *and* Love

*Chicken Soup for the Soul: Food and Love*
*101 Stories Celebrating Special Times with Family and Friends... and Recipes Too!*
Amy Newmark. Foreword by Catherine Cassidy. Introduction by Chef John Doherty.

Published by Chicken Soup for the Soul Publishing, LLC    www.chickensoup.com
Copyright © 2014 by Chicken Soup for the Soul Publishing, LLC. All Rights Reserved.
No part of this publication may be reproduced, stored in a retrieval system or transmitted in any form or by any means, electronic, mechanical, photocopying, recording or otherwise, without the written permission of the publisher.

CSS, Chicken Soup for the Soul, and its Logo and Marks are trademarks of Chicken Soup for the Soul Publishing LLC.

The publisher gratefully acknowledges the many publishers and individuals who granted Chicken Soup for the Soul permission to reprint the cited material.

Front cover photo courtesy of iStockphoto.com/fertnig (© Chris Fertnig).
Back cover photo courtesy of Juan Montenegro. Interior photo courtesy of iStockphoto.com/bluestocking (© Uyen Le). Interior illustration courtesy of iStockphoto.com/hellokokoro (© Jeremiah Simpson).

*Cover and Interior Design & Layout by Pneuma Books, LLC*
For more info on Pneuma Books, visit www.pneumabooks.com

Distributed to the booktrade by Simon & Schuster. SAN: 200-2442

**Publisher's Cataloging-in-Publication Data**
*(Prepared by The Donohue Group)*

Chicken soup for the soul : food and love : 101 stories celebrating
  special times with family and friends... and recipes too! / [compiled
  by] Amy Newmark ; foreword by Catherine Cassidy ; introduction by Chef
John Doherty.

   pages : illustrations ; cm

  First issued 2011 with compilers: Jack Canfield, Mark Victor Hansen and Amy
Newmark; reissued 2014 with added foreword and introduction.
  ISBN: 978-1-935096-78-8

  1. Food--Social aspects--Literary collections.  2. Food--Social aspects--Anecdotes.
3. Cooking, American--Literary collections.  4. Cooking, American--Anecdotes.  5.
Anecdotes.  I. Newmark, Amy.  II. Cassidy, Catherine, 1959-  III. Doherty, John, 1958-
IV. Title: Food and love : 101 stories celebrating special times with family and friends...
and recipes too

GT2853.U5 C455 2011
394.120973      2011937663

PRINTED IN THE UNITED STATES OF AMERICA
on acid∞free paper
20 19 18 17 16 15 14                    02 03 04 05 06 07 08 09 10

# Chicken Soup for the Soul.

# Food *and* Love

## 101 Stories Celebrating Special Times with Family and Friends... and Recipes Too!

**Amy Newmark**
**Foreword by Catherine Cassidy**
**Introduction by Chef John Doherty**

Chicken Soup for the Soul Publishing, LLC
Cos Cob, CT

Chicken Soup for the Soul
www.chickensoup.com
for the Soul

# Contents

**❶**

## ~Learning to Cook~

**❷**

## ~Just Like Mom's~

**❸**

# ~Table for Two~

**❹**

# ~Comfort Food~

**❺**

# ~Little Helpers~

**❻**

# ~In Memory of...~

**❼**

# ~A Bite of Fun~

**❽**

## ~The Taste of Tradition~

**❾**

## ~Life Lessons in the Kitchen~

## ⑩
## ~Always Room for Dessert~

# Foreword

My good friend Ardyth was a great lover of food. The simpler the better. A slice of sweet, juicy watermelon. Steaming corn on the cob dressed with butter and salt. A hot dog with spicy sauerkraut. "I can't cook and don't want to," she told me once. "But I love to eat and I love the people who feed me."

That sentiment is the essence of this book and the stories that fill it. As you read, you'll discover how food nourishes us in ways beyond sustaining our bodies. The gathering, caring and bridge-building that results from the preparing and sharing of food makes it a veritable love potion.

And its magic knows no bounds. It spans generations, connecting us with our past and helping us create new traditions and powerful memories. Think of some of your own family's most cherished experiences. I bet most if not all of them involve food—a family reunion, cookie baking for the holidays or even dinner in front of the TV. Food provides us something that little else can: the opportunity to come together and share a part of our lives with each other.

At Taste of Home, we gather and share recipes from home cooks across the country. And as important as the recipes are the stories behind them, stories filled with love and laughter and hope, laced with tears and reminiscences of times past. The oatmeal jam bars 102-year-old Warren makes in his toaster oven to share with the Vermont nursing home community where he lives. The foods Michele was given by her neighbors and friends when her home in Michigan was destroyed in a fire. The cookies Liz bakes every week for veterans in California. The homemade marshmallow recipe Lindsay's dad used to make and that she makes as gifts each year to honor his memory. As the editor-in-chief, I'm humbled every day to be the steward of this incredible family recipe box.

Like Taste of Home, this book tells the stories of how food brings people together and helps us to celebrate our triumphs and cope with our tragedies. In the reading of it, I hope you will find comfort and inspiration, and the encouragement to create your own food love story.

My food-loving friend Ardyth passed away four years ago after a hard-fought battle with ovarian cancer. During her many chemotherapy treatments, she had trouble keeping food down. So I made gallons of chicken noodle soup for her, the only food, she told me, that she felt like eating. Making those pots of soup for my dying friend was profound for me. It gave me the chance to share my heart with her and helped me say goodbye in a very personal way. I still make that soup, and when I do, I think of Ardyth. And I smile.

~Catherine Cassidy

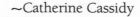

# Introduction

As the front door opened, before I even got the best hug in the world, I could smell the roast duck in the oven. Even as a young boy, memories of dinner at Grandma's are not just embedded in my mind but my soul. Roast pork with mashed potatoes and creamy sauerkraut with caraway, not to mention the pan gravy... what a cook!

We looked forward all year to having Grandma's peach dumplings. I can remember her wrapping fragrant, juicy peaches in a dough made from potatoes and then waiting for these softball-sized dumplings to bounce to the top of boiling water, which is when she'd scoop them out onto a platter. What happened next was magical — melted butter and cinnamon sugar. Dessert you're thinking? Heck no! We had this for dinner and we ate them till we couldn't move.

If you were lucky, Grandma would let you sleep over and that meant one thing... a trip to the pond to feed the ducks! Well, it was a little more than just feeding the ducks, which was fun, but what really mattered was lunch. At the crack of dawn, the milkman had already dropped off glass bottles of ice-cold milk, eggs and soft semolina sandwich bread with sesame seeds on which Grandma would spread butter and egg salad with a little mayonnaise, salt, pepper and a few drops of cider vinegar. After feeding the ducks, we would sit on a bench in a sunny spot next to the pond and eat our sandwiches together — just my grandma and me. Today, whether it be elegant tea sandwiches or a quick lunch, I make them just the way she did.

When I think of being at home as a young boy, I remember the sound of a pressure cooker. My mom would be cooking a pot roast, with tender carrots, potatoes and soda dumplings. At the table, we all shared much more than pot roast. We shared our stories of the day. They may have been funny, sad or angry, but we always shared them, and our love. And that's where we made new stories too, those great stories that became part of family lore and were told again and again through the years. Although we each had our own little universe in which we lived, we all seemed to settle into one place for that brief amount of time, a time when we made sure that we got to know each other and share our lives.

None of these fond food memories inspired me to become a chef or to even get a job as a cook at a local restaurant. I became a cook because I wanted to go to a rock concert and my parents said I had to earn the money myself for the ticket. So I did. At fifteen, I got that job and I loved it because I got a free bacon cheeseburger and root beer soda every day!

What happened next took me by surprise. I stood in amazement in this open kitchen and watched as the husband-and-wife team served each meal with such care because they truly loved each customer walking through the door. That's when I learned that love is the magical ingredient that makes everything taste better. Mom's, Dad's and Grandma's food tastes so good because of the love that they put into it.

I learned years later that home wasn't the only place where people gathered to share their thoughts and lives around the table. When President Ronald Reagan hosted a dinner commemorating the 40th Anniversary of the United Nations, he broke bread with the prime ministers of Canada, Great Britain, France, Italy and Japan, and the Chancellor of Germany. This gathering could have easily been a meeting at the UN, but President Reagan understood that the dining table was the one place that leveled the playing field. No matter where we're from, what language we speak, or what beliefs we hold, we can find some common ground as human beings to build more meaningful relationships around the table. It's hard to imagine that sharing a meal wouldn't improve any relationship. After preparing that meal and receiving a personal and sincere gesture of gratitude from the President, I couldn't help but think that I had some small part in making the world a better place.

Through my years as Chef, having fed more than 3,000 people a day, I know all too well how stressful getting a meal on the table can be. That's why I can attribute much of my success to keeping menus and recipes familiar and simple, relying on quality ingredients and a balance of flavor and texture. In fact, some of the recipes I prepared for world events with Presidents and heads of state were the same meals I prepared at home, like my Crispy Chicken with Truffled Grape Salad and Port Sauce, a favorite of my daughters.

I applied that same philosophy to creating the Chicken Soup for the Soul line of products, which are designed to make it fast and easy, even for busy moms, to get dinner on the table. From my own personal experience, the fewer steps in getting a meal on the table, the more likely it is that people will have that quality time, sharing food with family or friends... and with a host or hostess who is relaxed, not stressed!

Some of my own recipes appear in the back pages of this book, and you'll also find family favorites from many other writers attached to the stories about food and love that fill this volume. There's nothing I like better than reading about my two favorite topics—food and love—and I hope you'll enjoy these stories too and find new inspiration to bring your own family and friends together around the table.

~Chef John Doherty

Chapter
1

# Food and Love

## Learning to Cook

*Cooking Rule... If at first you don't succeed, order pizza.*

*~Anonymous*

# Becoming a Cook

*Cooking is like love. It should be entered into with abandon or not at all.*
*~Harriet van Horne*

"Do you like Hamburger Helper?" my soon-to-be-husband's twelve-year-old son, Austin, asked me the first time I met him. "I hope so because it's the only thing my dad knows how to cook."

"It's okay, honey, I can cook," I assured him without even thinking.

He eyed me suspiciously. "What do you know how to make?"

I shrugged and then plunged into the abyss of deception. "I know how to cook lots of things. What do you like to eat?"

He shrugged back. "I like pretty much everything. Well, except Hamburger Helper." He wrinkled his nose. "I'm kind of tired of that."

I laughed. "If you like pretty much everything, we should be just fine in the food department."

He grinned and looked at his dad. "Marry her tomorrow, Dad. Seriously."

Eric and I followed Austin's suggestion and got married just five months after we met. I quit my job and moved the two hundred miles from my apartment in the Chicago suburbs to Eric's farmhouse in southern Indiana. His kids and my kids got along the way blood siblings do—loving each other one minute and fighting the next.

And Eric, well, he was practically perfect in the husband department. Things were going exactly according to plan.

Except for one thing. That little white lie I'd told. I'd said I could cook. Talk about the mother of all exaggerations! Yeah, I can cook—if calling the pizza delivery boy qualifies as cooking! Saying I could cook was like saying I could fly. It hadn't happened yet, but who knew? But maybe I could figure it out and then I'd never have to fess up to my little fabrication.

The pressure was on. I could practically hear Rachael Ray's voice taunting me, "Did you tell that poor kid you know how to cook? How could you do such a thing?"

But Emeril, the angel on my other shoulder, responded, "It's all right. She'll learn." And then he added a "Bam!" just to encourage me.

For the first few months, I faked it with easy stuff like spaghetti and tacos. We grilled hamburgers and brats on the grill at least once a week. It was summer, so nobody expected me to spend a lot of time in the kitchen. But I knew winter was coming and that meant the grill—my new best friend—would soon be going into hibernation.

I panicked, but not for long. I soon found a new favorite appliance—my crock pot. You can throw practically anything in that thing and it turns out all right. At first, I made sure I had a recipe and I followed it exactly. But after a while, I got creative and started throwing in whatever I had on hand. One day, I tossed in some boneless, skinless chicken breasts, a packet of onion soup mix, and a can of cream-of-whatever soup.

When Eric got home from work, he took a bite of my creation, which I'd mixed with egg noodles. His eyebrows went up and he nodded. "This is pretty good. What's it called?"

"Um, let me check," I said. I reached for a cookbook, flipped through to the section of chicken recipes and read the first one I saw. "Perfect Breasts," I said.

Eric grinned. "Excellent. Be sure to make this one again. Maybe just for me next time." He wiggled his eyebrows suggestively.

Chalk one up for me and my "cooking" skills.

After I mastered my crock pot, I discovered some really great cooking websites. One site's specialty was recipes that required just five ingredients.

Even I couldn't mess that up. I printed some of the more appealing ones and tried them out. They were really good. Even my oh-so-picky daughters asked for seconds.

I was getting pretty good at faking the cooking thing.

And then the real test came: my husband's birthday. In his family, birthdays are a huge deal. The whole family comes over to celebrate, but no one serves just cake and ice cream. No, these people come hungry and ready for a good, home-cooked meal.

Did I mention my husband is one of eight children?

Yeah, so about forty people — including my new mother-in-law — came over to our house, expecting food that was not only edible, but actually tasty. I was beyond overwhelmed by it all.

I filled two crock pots with chicken, boiled some egg noodles, fixed some bread — the kind that comes in the tubes — heated about a dozen cans of green beans, and hoped for the best. If the food were terrible, there would always be cake. It was store-bought, so I couldn't mess it up.

I watched closely as my mother-in-law took her first bite of the chicken I'd made. Her eyes lit up and she quickly took another bite.

Holy cow, she liked it. I had pulled it off after all.

When my husband's sister asked me for the recipe, I picked up my jaw from the floor and stammered, "Oh, you don't want this recipe. It's so easy, it's embarrassing."

She smiled. "But those are the best kinds of recipes."

I rattled off the five-ingredient recipe, ashamed that now everyone would peg me for the fake I was.

"Diane, that chicken was delicious," another sister-in-law said. "The fact that it was easy to cook only makes me like it more."

"But I'm really not a very good cook," I insisted.

"Did you make the meal today?" my mother-in-law asked.

"Well, yeah," I said.

"Then you're a good cook."

I looked into the smiling faces of the women in my new family. And I realized that becoming a good cook was a lot like becoming a member of their family.

It didn't matter how I'd gotten there. But I was sure glad I finally had.

# Cream Cheese Chicken

4 boneless skinless chicken breasts
1/2 cup butter
1 package Italian seasoning mix
1 (8 oz.) package cream cheese
1 (10 3/4 oz.) can cream of chicken soup
Cooked rice or pasta

Cube chicken into bite-sized pieces.

Combine chicken pieces, butter and Italian seasoning mix in a crock pot and cook on low for 6 to 8 hours.

Then add cream cheese and soup, and cook on high until cheese is melted.

Serve over rice or pasta.

~Diane Stark

# Hockey Pucks

*A hundred hearts would be too few*
*To carry all my love for you.*
*~Author Unknown*

My husband had only two culinary skills—coffee and tuna salad—and although he did those both very well, he was terrified to take things any further.

He broke into a cold sweat if I so much as asked him to take something out of the oven. He required detailed instructions when asked to pick up an onion or a dozen eggs. The good news is that cooking was such a complete mystery to him, he thought I was brilliant because I could transform raw chicken into dinner. The bad news is that left at home with a little girl to feed, he was utterly helpless.

But early on, my husband committed a deed of culinary derring-do, when he set aside his fear of anything involving food preparation because he loved me so much.

I had just returned from the hospital with our new baby girl. She was not sleeping and neither was I, and between hormones and sleep deprivation, I was a wreck. The baby cried. I cried. I was also hungry and not up to doing anything about it. He looked on, worried and desperate to help.

"What would you eat if you could eat anything?" he asked, nervously. We both knew that unless it was take-out, whatever "anything" was would be beyond his capabilities, probably involving an oven or stovetop and baffling ingredients from little jars. But even his wanting to try helped. I dried my eyes and considered.

"If I could have anything I would want some whole grain applesauce muffins," I said, with no hope that there would be any until the baby permitted me fifteen minutes to bake them. (I figured sixteen years, give or take.) He sat on the edge of the bed for a moment, thinking hard, and then vanished into the kitchen.

An hour of banging cabinets and refrigerator doors later, he walked in, flushed and sheepish, carrying a steaming mug of perfect decaf... and a plate of hockey pucks. I bit into one. They were warm and cinnamon-y and odd. I am not sure why they turned out that way—the recipe is foolproof—but they were half an inch tall and rubbery. "They're awful, aren't they?" he said, defeated. He didn't get it.

I started to cry again, because of hormones and sleep deprivation, but also because I had a plate full of the most wonderful muffins that I would ever eat, a husband who loved me so much that he would crack raw eggs for me, and the baby I had dreamed of. I was the luckiest girl on earth.

People like to say that food made with love tastes better. We know that's not necessarily true. We've all choked down Grandma's stringy pot roast or Aunt Rachel's parsnips and prayed for a reprieve. What is true is that sometimes food is made with so much love that the taste is irrelevant. When my husband made the applesauce hockey pucks he overcame fear and insecurity because he wanted me to feel better.

Sometimes the best dish that you ever had is a transcendent blend of tastes and textures and beautiful presentation. And sometimes it is an even more transcendent blend of courage and dreams and love.

# Whole Grain Applesauce Muffins

2 cups of multigrain flour (whole wheat works fine too)
2 eggs
1 cup of milk (soy or rice milk works fine too)

1 cup applesauce
1/2 cup vegetable oil
1/2 cup sugar
2 teaspoons baking powder
1 teaspoon cinnamon
1/2 teaspoon salt
1 cup raisins, walnuts, or a combination of the two (optional)

Preheat oven to 400 degrees.

Combine dry ingredients with the exception of the optional nuts/raisins in a large bowl.

Beat the eggs lightly and stir in the milk and oil. Quickly stir together the two mixtures until just combined and then add the nuts and/or raisins in a few quick strokes.

Spoon into greased muffin cups and bake 15-17 minutes.

~Jacqueline Rivkin

# The Inside Story

*I was 32 when I started cooking; up until then, I just ate.*
*~Julia Child*

I stared at the chicken section in the grocery store, trying to figure out why there were so many options. There were legs, thighs, whole organic chickens, split breasts, breasts with skins, skinless breasts, fryer chickens and roaster chickens. The choices seemed endless. At least I knew I wanted to make a whole chicken. But which one? Should it be the fryer or the roaster?

I had never cooked a chicken before in my life. I had just moved into my new home with the man of my dreams and I had a baby on the way. The tears started stinging my eyes. My only option was to pick up my cell phone and call my mom. I told her where I was and what my great dilemma was. There was a familiar sound on the other end of the phone. Still staring at the chicken choices in front of me I sighed, "Mom, are you laughing at me?"

I believe she hiccupped and erupted into another fit of hysterics. At that point I hung up. Yes, I hung up on my mother. Here I was, young and ambitious, willing to showcase my love for my family through food, and the chicken was defeating me. And all my mother could do was laugh at me? I almost stormed out of the grocery store and ordered pizza for dinner.

Instead, I called her back, "Are you done yet?"

Gasping for breath she replied, "Yes," and then started laughing again.

I stood in front of all that chicken while my mom tried to catch her breath and I struggled with the great chicken debate.

"You... should... get... a... roaster..." she replied between gasps of breath.

"Thank you, Mom," I said, with an attitude that said I wasn't playing around, and hung up.

I grabbed my roaster chicken, paid for my other groceries and went home. I took the chicken out, grabbed a pan, gathered some spices and was getting ready to cook that bad boy up when my phone rang.

"Yes?" I said.

It was my mom again. She had taken control of herself.

"Are you cooking the chicken?" she asked.

"Yes," I said.

"Did you take the innards out?" she said softly.

"The what?" I pulled the phone away from my ear and stared at it like she could see me.

When I put the phone back to my ear she was saying, "...inside the chicken. You have to take that stuff out."

I looked at the chicken. I saw the little opening where its head used to be. "I'm not sticking my hand in that."

She snickered into the phone, "Oh yes you are, if you're cooking that chicken and not trying to kill anyone. You need to take the plastic bag with the innards out before you cook it."

I believe at that point I made a sound that was something akin to, "blechhhgrossill-ick-ick-ick!"

My mom's voice went soft in my ear. "I'll tell you a story while you take the insides of the chicken out."

"Okay, I'm listening," I said while having an internal conflict about sticking my hand inside the chicken.

"I didn't always know how to cook." I could hear the smile and whimsy in her voice. "And, I can still remember the first meatloaf I tried to cook for your father. I was so young. All I wanted to do was make a home-cooked meal for my family. So I gathered all my ingredients, mixed up that meat, added eggs, breadcrumbs, seasoning and then I flattened it as I put it in the pan."

"Why?" I might not have been the best cook around but I had never heard of flattening a meatloaf.

"Well, my dear, I thought that my meatloaf would rise in the oven just like bread rises. It turns out, it doesn't."

"You didn't!"

"I did. I'll never forget that meatloaf. Just like you'll never forget your chicken. Did you get the insides out?"

I had not noticed but I was holding a dripping bag filled with neck, liver and who knows what else in my free hand. I had just plunged my hand right in, grabbed that bag and pulled it out while my mom told me her story.

"Yes, I got it," I said into the phone.

"Just throw them away for now. I'll tell you how to use them on your next chicken," she said with a slight hitch in her voice. I think she was about to laugh again.

"Thanks, Mom," I said, and suddenly I was reassured that it was okay. It didn't matter if my chicken didn't come out perfect or if my mother's meatloaf never rose. It only mattered that I wanted to do something for my family and was making the effort to do it. That was the whole concept of food and love that my mother had taught me growing up.

"Don't forget to give the chicken a good butter massage before putting your spices on it," she said and hung up.

"What?" Wasn't sticking my hand inside it enough? Now I had to give the bird a spa treatment before eating it. I was never going to cook a chicken again. Never. Ever.

It has been ten years since my first chicken. I've grown quite experienced in the art of cooking a chicken. I have cooked hundreds of chickens over the years—some fryers, some roasters, each one better than the last. I'm no longer grossed out about sticking my hand inside a bird or having to feel it up before cooking it to a tender juicy crisp. And, I know that one day I'm going to have to tell my son the story of the first chicken I tried to cook for his father when he calls me up to complain that my future daughter-in-law doesn't know the difference between halibut and flounder. I may have to tell him about Grandma's meatloaf too.

~Linda St.Cyr

# Unlikely Gourmet

*Recipe: A series of step-by-step instructions for preparing ingredients you forgot to buy, in utensils you don't own, to make a dish the dog wouldn't eat.*
*~Author Unknown*

My dad has never been a gourmet cook, a follower of trends, or a television devotee, but by chance all three came together in a surprising way. By profession he is an electrician, but can fix anything—albeit sometimes on a "temporary" basis. Like the time I dropped my eyeglasses down the well where we got water for our horses. It was astounding that my dad actually duct-taped a flashlight to his head and lowered himself into the well on a rope attached to an apple tree to retrieve them. I was utterly embarrassed when I had to wear them to school for weeks after that, held together with copper wire. But in a family of eight kids, you kept your glasses as long as you could see your hand in front of your face.

When the rare occasion called for my dad to prepare a meal, his menu was always predictable. If it was before noon, we had pancakes and eggs. If it was after noon, we had fried potatoes, hamburgers and baked beans. Then, by chance, my dad was introduced to the world of gourmet cuisine. After years of a wire antenna on the television barely picking up a "local" channel, my parents relented and got satellite television. Suddenly, they were exposed to a myriad of new experiences ranging from hunting to travel to fashion and food.

After preparing three meals a day for more than fifty years, my mom became fascinated with all the Food Network shows. She watched them for hours and seemed oblivious to one very unexpected spectator beside her on the sofa... my dad.

Dad was fascinated with the male chefs on the shows, urging my mom to try different recipes. After a few barely edible attempts at the show recipes, my mom concluded it was impossible to make these dishes in their rural area because you couldn't find all the special ingredients, in particular the spices. My dad, who never gave up on anything, kept watching, and one day he took action that surprised us all.

Home for the weekend, I found my mom sitting at the kitchen table with a baffled expression, staring at my dad—who was surrounded by books. Not the electrical parts catalogs he was always poring over, but cookbooks! I couldn't imagine what was going on, but he looked up with a big smile and announced he was going to make braised short ribs like the ones Bobby Flay prepared on his show.

He explained he didn't have the actual recipe Bobby had used, but had settled on a recipe from the Assembly of God Women's Cookbook that he had found. Dad said it was the closest recipe to what he remembered from Bobby Flay on TV, and lots of the ingredients were right there in the kitchen. If not, he could "make them." And if I had any doubt that he was actually going to attempt this, there were a dozen packages of venison ribs thawing in the sink. Dad explained that venison would be the same as beef, but it was free.

When Dad gets an idea, it's best to remain quiet and get out of the way. After all, he single-handedly built a plywood camper for our Ford pick-up truck and took us on a magical journey across the United States when we were little. As we crossed the country, eating cereal out of little boxes at roadside rest stops, my dad consulted maps and crossed places off his list. Later, when these places came up in our history classes, we were the only kids in our class who had actually seen them. It was this kind of determination that set the course for his life, and luckily had seeped into mine. So my mom and I left him to his rib project and went shopping.

After a few hours of distracted shopping we couldn't stay away any longer. When we returned, the kitchen was a disaster. Every pot and pan in my mom's inventory was somewhere on a counter, stove or table and they were all used. Empty ketchup bottles were strewn about, and every spice from her cabinet was open and lying around in disarray. Bowls, utensils, cookie sheets, colanders, skillets, measuring cups and spoons were all covered in some strange red-brown sauce. Flour, brown sugar, maple syrup, mustard, hot peppers and jelly spotted the counters... and in the middle of it all was my smiling dad, wearing a sauce-smeared apron, sitting at the cluttered table with a big plate of some sort of meat on bones. The wonderful aroma in the kitchen was almost enough to make you overlook the horrendous mess. Jazzie, my dad's Sheltie, was licking her empty bowl, but she eats anything so that wasn't as reassuring as you might imagine.

My dad jumped up and started pulling out chairs, making room at the messy table for us to sample his masterpiece. We sat down warily, me on top of some sticky sauce and my mom after brushing cookbooks off her chair. My dad scurried around the kitchen filling our plates with his concoction. His hands were slathered in sauce and the paper towels he tried to hand us stuck to his fingers. No amount of sauce could hide the obvious delight he felt for his epicurean creation.

Despite the flavorful aroma, what he placed in front of us didn't look fit for human consumption. I was sitting too far from Jazzie's bowl to surreptitiously give her my portion, so I just dove in. After all, if you eat anything fast enough, don't chew, and swallow quickly, it's not too bad. But something very unexpected happened when the first bite hit our tongues. This dish was delicious! Saying that it melted in our mouths seems inadequate. Just like the television chefs always promise, "layers of flavor" were revealed at every bite. What those flavors were actually comprised of, I didn't want to know, as I scanned the ingredients scattered around the kitchen.

My dad was beyond proud. "That Bobby Flay really knows what he's talking about," he said with delight. I couldn't burst his bubble and say this was probably as far away from Bobby's recipe as anything could ever be.

We pitched in to clean up the kitchen, which took hours. Somehow, the mystery sauce had congealed on every surface. As Dad helped dry the endless number of dishes, he mused, "I think I'll see what Bobby Flay is up to tomorrow and give it a try." My mom and I both groaned. Our only comment was that next time he wanted to cook for us, hamburgers and baked beans would be just fine, thank you.

~Patti Lawson

# Cooking with Mom

*A recipe has no soul. You, as the cook, must bring soul to the recipe.*
~Thomas Keller

I'm four years old. Mom is always busy working, but she pulls down the big heavy mixing bowls and chooses the huge yellow one. It's a baking kind of day. She gets out the amber jar full of flour and lets me pack the brown sugar. My favorite part is when it all slides into the bowl in the shape of the little, copper measuring cup. She shows me how to carefully separate the eggshell so no pieces fall in. We make the best chocolate chip cookies. We eat a few chips together while we're mixing them, and she makes half with no nuts just for me.

She teaches me that sugar is a wet ingredient and how to multiply fractions and that if you pull the mixer out of the batter before you turn it off, batter splatters everywhere.

I'm six. Mom gets me up in the middle of every night and carries me to the car. It's time to make the donuts. She lays me in a lawn chair in the back of the donut shop and covers me with her jacket before she gets to work with Dad. There, under her jacket and in the midst of all that hustle and bustle, I feel completely safe, secure and loved. I get up and try to talk customers into playing *Candy Land* with me before I catch the bus for school. I get to take donut holes for snack time. I'm everyone's favorite snack-bringer.

I learn about friends and eighties music and that the way to anyone's heart is through his or her stomach.

I'm seven. Mom teaches me to scramble an egg and how to be careful with the gas when I light the burner. How to keep stirring so the eggs won't stick and burn on the bottom. And not to use metal in a Teflon pan.

I learn to get up before my mom to make my own hot breakfast and watch the news, cause that's what grown-ups do. And I learn that when I fall asleep in my chair, Mom will pick up my dishes and clean whatever mess I left in the kitchen without ever saying a word to me about it.

I'm ten. Mom takes me to the grocery store every day to get the ingredients for endless casseroles, meat loaves and fried chicken. I complain a lot. I learn about budgets, Green Stamps, and that all that stuff tastes better than I would ever let on.

I'm eighteen. I make my first solo fried chicken, mashed potatoes and gravy, all from scratch of course, and I start a fire in the kitchen. My date offers to help from the living room, but I save the chicken and he's none the wiser about the fire.

I learn that no matter how old and wise I get, my mom is never more than a phone call away when I realize I'm out of my depth. And, later, that they actually make mixes for things like mashed potatoes and gravy, but that that would be cheating and it probably wouldn't taste as good anyway.

I'm twenty-eight. For my birthday, I ask my mom to finally show me the trick to her famous pies for which there is no recipe. She shows me how to mix the ingredients for the crust, just as her mother showed her. She tells me that we'll pre-bake these for cream pies but that you don't do that for custard-style pies. We whip egg yolks and double-boil pudding for hours.

I learn that, regardless how detailed your notes, nothing can replace practice and an inherent knack, and that using my great-grandmother's rolling pin, my maternal grandmother's recipes and my paternal grandmother's pie pan while cooking with my mom creates a feeling of connection I can't explain.

I'm thirty. I finally pin my mom down on her homemade dressing and giblet gravy. Like the pies, she learned from her mother, and there is no recipe. She can't tell me any specific measurements, but she can go on forever with that dreamy look in her eyes about how special it was for her mother to impart to her these same skills.

I learn that I really can pull together an entire holiday meal.

I'm thirty-one. I'm standing in my mother's kitchen with her and my sister, my memories so thick I can hardly breathe. I'm helping her weed through a lifetime of collected utensils and appliances for their imminent downsize. Throw that away, sell this, keep that. Yes, sell all the new-fangled, modern plastic stuff. But I will never part with those multi-colored glass mixing bowls, the copper measuring cups, the old pie plates and baking dishes and cookie jars from my childhood in the kitchen. With my mom.

I learn that sooner or later, we all have to let go of the things, because the memories are now a part of who we are. But I also learn why my mom was always so happy in the kitchen. With her mom.

And now, no matter what happens, I've learned that my mom will always be with me in mine.

~Kimberly Noe

# Smoked Salmon

*I'm not saying my wife's a bad cook,*
*but she uses a smoke alarm as a timer.*
~Bob Monkhouse

The day after I moved into my first apartment, my mother called. "Do you want me to bring over some cooked meals? I don't want you living on toast and cheese."

Staring at the remains of my toasted cheese sandwich, I wondered if mothers really did have X-ray vision. I shook off the thought. "I'm a grown woman. You don't have to feed me." A sigh followed by silence on the other end of the phone told me my mother disagreed. As I imagined her showing up on my doorstep, arms laden with food, my gaze fell upon my calendar. September fourth was just a few days away. "To prove I can manage, I'll make you and dad an anniversary dinner. How does Saturday at seven p.m. sound?"

"It sounds like a lovely idea. Can I bring anything?"

"Nope, just yourselves." I kept my voice cheery, but even before I hung up I was having second, third and fourth thoughts. Since my cooking skills were limited to boiling water and making toast, my kettle, toaster oven and can opener were my best friends. Not exactly a great basis for a gourmet meal. Maybe I could get takeout and pretend I had cooked. As long as I hid the containers, I'd be okay.

But that was silly. How hard could it be to make dinner? I was a university graduate. I knew how to read. I even had a cookbook, a gift from my mother, along with a set of pots and pans. With four days to prepare, I'd ace my first dinner party the same way I'd aced my courses.

I sat down to plan a simple meal, with the emphasis on simple.

Tomato juice for starters. A salad with bottled dressing. But what about the main course? Roast beef was too ambitious for me. I couldn't stand the look of raw chicken. Salmon, on the other hand, was possible. Even better, my father liked it. Salmon it was. I flipped through my cookbook until I found a recipe even a domestically challenged diva like me could handle.

I added rice and canned peas to the dinner menu, as my father's taste in vegetables was limited. For dessert, I would definitely buy something — maybe a fruit flan.

On Friday morning, my mother called again. "Are you sure you don't need anything? If making an entire meal is too much, we could always go out for dinner instead."

"Come on, Mom, have a little faith in me."

"Of course I do, but your father is very fussy about his food. Everything has to be cooked just right. No sauces. No broccoli. No Brussels sprouts. And absolutely no liver."

I sighed. "Trust me, he'll eat everything on the menu. Gotta go. See you tomorrow night."

Early the next morning I was at the grocery store, complete with a detailed shopping list. Returning home, I put the food away, checked my cookbook again, wrote out a battle plan for each step of that night's dinner, including prep and cooking time, and taped it to the fridge. Then I set all the pots, bowls, pans and utensils I'd need on the kitchen counter, like a general lining up her troops.

Satisfied that I had everything I needed, I rechecked my schedule — six hours before I'd have to start the prep. Easy. I spent the rest of the morning and afternoon reading and watching TV.

When it was time to start Operation Anniversary Dinner, I marched into the kitchen and got to work. I assembled the ingredients for the salad, prepared the glaze for the salmon, measured out the rice and water in one pot, and put the canned peas in another.

Twenty minutes later I had ticked off everything I needed to do before my parents showed up.

By the time they arrived, the rice was simmering, the peas were heating, the tomato juice was poured, with a lemon slice for each glass, and the salad was dressed. As they sat down to dinner, I looked at my watch, calculating five to ten minutes for the juice and salad course, maybe a bit longer. My one-inch salmon steaks would need eight to ten minutes. "Be back in a second," I said, dashing to the fridge to get the main course and put it in the oven.

Since my cookbook had warned me that every oven cooks a bit differently, halfway through our salad course I got up to check the salmon. When I opened the oven door, there was no rush of hot air. I glanced at the oven controls to make sure I had turned it on. I had.

"Anything wrong?" my mother asked.

I stared at the raw fish, unable to speak. When the lump in my throat dissolved enough for me to talk, the only thing I could think of saying was "Anyone for sushi?"

"What?"

"The oven isn't working." My gaze darted around the kitchen as I wondered what else I could serve. All I had was cereal, eggs, cheese and toast. Toast. Of course. The other half of toaster oven is oven. I breathed a long sigh of relief that dinner could still be saved. "Give me ten minutes and I'll be ready." I crammed the salmon in the toaster oven and cranked it up to its highest setting.

Eleven minutes later, after I opened the windows to let the smoke dissipate, my parents and I dined on "blackened" salmon that was more blackened than salmon. Accompanying the main course was hard, dry rice that I scraped off the bottom of the pot, and soft, mushy peas. My oven might not have worked, but the burners did.

"I'm really sorry," I said, pushing peas around my plate. "I've ruined your anniversary dinner."

My parents smiled. "No, you didn't," they said in unison. "It was a lovely thought and really, the food was..." my mother paused, "surprisingly good for your first attempt."

My father winked at me as he slowly chewed on a piece of burnt salmon.

I winked back. "The good news is I bought the dessert, so it should be fine. Now a toast," I said, raising my glass. "Happy anniversary. May your lives be filled with love, happiness and good food—preferably not cooked by me."

~Harriet Cooper

"Thank you for the anniversary dinner, sweetheart. If we can survive this, we should be able to make it another 25 years."

# Stepping Outside My Comfort Zone

*There is no sight on earth more appealing than the sight of a woman making dinner for someone she loves.*
~Thomas Wolfe

When Shaun and I were first married, he half-jokingly said I was not allowed in the kitchen. He would do all the cooking, he assured me. I didn't argue. We both knew my cooking skills were limited at best.

At twenty-two years old, my culinary repertoire consisted of grilled cheese sandwiches and cereal and milk. Don't get me wrong, I could follow a recipe—as long as it had no more than five ingredients and they could easily be found in the kitchen cupboard.

Unfortunately, I had high expectations for my married self: I would be an expert chef and the stereotypical wife of yesteryear, with a hot meal on the table every evening.

In reality, those expectations created a barrier between my kitchen and me. In my desire to excel, I found it easier to avoid cooking, as opposed to preparing a meal that ended up in the trash.

Shaun, on the other hand, was completely at ease in the kitchen and could throw together a delicious meal with random ingredients he plucked from the cupboards. Luckily, he was aware of my apprehension and, as we cooked meals together, gently guided me through the ins and outs of boiling, broiling and baking.

But two and a half years later I finally realized that, for my husband, a home-cooked meal meant love. And while we frequently cooked meals together, "Food always tastes better when someone else makes it," he once explained. He also hinted on occasion: "To properly woo a woman, you can't do it on an empty stomach."

Taking his sentiments into consideration, I decided it was time for me to try it on my own. We were sitting in the living room watching TV when I first broached the subject.

"Shaun," I said during the commercial break, "I'm cooking dinner Thursday night."

"Oh?" he asked, raising an eyebrow.

"But what if it doesn't turn out well?" I added hastily, becoming panicked as visions of charred meatloaf and soggy biscuits flashed through my mind.

With a reassuring grin, he said, "Then we'll have the Chinese restaurant on speed dial!" And that's what we did. There was no pressure to make the "perfect" meal because I knew there was a back-up plan.

When Thursday evening arrived, I prepared a simple chicken dish with a side of green beans and potatoes. While it wasn't on the table as soon as Shaun walked in the door (my unrealistic expectation), it was ready shortly thereafter. We said a brief prayer asking God to bless the food—and make it edible—and then began to eat.

After a few tentative bites, Shaun began to chow down. "Heather, you did a great job," he said between mouthfuls. "Thank you for dinner; this is delicious."

But what made the dinner delicious wasn't the taste of the food—although it was edible. It was the acknowledgement and appreciation that I was stepping out of my comfort zone (and overcoming my perfectionism) to show my husband that I loved him.

I try to cook at least one night a week; that's usually all I can manage with a busy schedule. As I prepare those meals, Shaun keeps his distance from the kitchen, allowing me the space I need to feel relaxed and confident.

Now I find that I want to cook, and I enjoy experimenting with new recipes. I also cherish the appreciation in my husband's eyes when he enjoys a home-cooked meal. Sometimes the meal turns out well, other times not, but it's almost always edible. We've only had to order take-out a few times. Granted, Shaun still cooks dinner for both of us several times a week, and we make many of our meals together, but he knows that once a week he'll get a meal made especially for him... except on Mondays. I don't cook on Mondays—the local Chinese restaurant is closed that day!

~Heather Brand

# Honoring Our Love

*It's the company, not the cooking, that makes a meal.*
*~Kirby Larson, Hattie Big Sky*

"Hey Sallie, what do you want for lunch?" my husband Paul would call out to me.

"Oh, is it that time already? Well, let's see... I'd like an egg salad sandwich with lettuce and tomatoes, pickles and onions, and toasted lightly, please," I would reply.

At dinnertime we would repeat this scenario.

"Hey Sallie, what do you feel like eating for dinner?"

"Oh babe, whatever you want to cook is fine with me, but orange chicken with jasmine rice sure would be yummy. Maybe artichokes with lemon butter on the side?" I would reply.

Paul and I had developed this routine. He never seemed to mind that I asked for exactly what sounded good to me and he was always willing to comply with my requests. Paul delighted in making my palate sing. He loved to cook and I hated it. We were nicely matched. We often laughed about our younger years when the children were still living at home. I said, "The children grew up in spite of my cooking." He would just laugh and nod.

A few years after the kids moved out, Paul took on the cooking and I was thrilled. I would rather be in my studio writing or doing artwork. He also loved to grocery shop, always bringing home new food items he found that he thought I would like.

I took the love he poured into this chore for granted until Paul passed away suddenly last December. My world crumbled. My sweetheart of forty-six years was never coming back. I found myself lost, broken-hearted and alone.

Everyone keeps telling me to keep up my strength and eat healthy. Not only do I not have an appetite, but I have no clue how to cook anything.

I buy all the wrong items at the grocery store. I am still shopping for two but there is only one of us now. I want to have some friends over to keep me company on the lonely Sunday nights but I can't even make them a decent meal.

I'm overwhelmed with the long list of things to learn to do for myself, like when to take the car in for a tune-up, how to invest my money and how to file my income tax. Now I also have to learn to cook.

I bought a simple cookbook and I'm happy to say I'm feeling my way with mixed results. I've had some catastrophes, like burned biscuits and tough rice, but I'm not giving up. I keep trying and have mastered a couple of simple dishes. I even served my sister-in-law, Joan, a halfway decent Sunday dinner.

I can still hear Paul humming in the kitchen as he cooked my favorite meals. I remember his daring way of just throwing in seasoning, while I have to measure everything. I think of his kindness in the little touches, like adding parsley to a plate. So I make myself sit and eat each meal at the table, not on the run, or standing at the counter. I set a full place with a fancy napkin and plate.

My husband showed his love by cooking my meals, so I can honor his memory most by learning to cook. He would be so proud.

~Sallie A. Rodman

# Excellent Stock

*When you are sorrowful look again in your heart, and you shall see that in truth you are weeping for that which has been your delight.*
*~Kahlil Gibran*

My husband is Scottish. Not "American of Scottish descent" Scottish, but "born and raised over there and talks with an accent" Scottish. So, after we were engaged, we planned a trip to Scotland to introduce me to his family. Now, I am a native Texan, and I can sometimes, on the rare occasion, when extremely provoked, use some interesting vocabulary words. On the plane, my well-intentioned fiancé gave me a rundown of all the words I wasn't to use in front of his mother. "Even though nice girls say those words in America," he added—looking as if he were trying to convince himself I was truly a nice girl and worthy of meeting his Mum—"nice girls in Scotland don't."

I remember biting my tongue. I loved this man, and I would not scream obscenities at his mother when we met, no matter how tempting he had just made it seem.

When I met her, a five-foot-two, ash-blond sixty-year-old, she asked how I felt after my trip. I very carefully considered my vocabulary, and replied with one of the new Scottish words I had often heard my husband use.

"Well, Liz, I'm happy to be here, but I'm totally knackered."

My husband turned bright red. My mother-in-law raised one eyebrow and very politely offered to make me a cup of tea. My brother-in-law wasted no time telling me that the cute expression I had just used meant exhausted, yes. But exhausted as in "weary from too much conjugal bliss."

Ah, first impressions.

Those early years were not smooth sailing for Liz and me. She was the epitome of Scottish womanhood. "If Napoleon had had a Scottish wife," my father-in-law said, "we'd all be speaking French now." It was true. Liz was frighteningly competent, and at twenty-four, I knew I was nowhere near her league. She could do it all—cook brandy snaps from memory, whip up a four-course meal every night, sing in the local operatic society, serve as headmistress of the primary school, raise three ambitious and intelligent sons to adulthood, and keep an immaculately clean household.

On the other hand, I was a Texas girl, a child of divorced parents, who swore, drank margaritas, cleaned only when the toilets got too disgusting, and could cook any recipe as long as it started with a can of cream of mushroom soup.

We grew closer when I gave birth to my son, her first grandchild. Even though she had knitted a closet-full of tiny pink wool sweaters (as if the gender of my baby could be determined by how many pink winter garments she sent), she loved my red-faced, colicky boy and spent a month with us after his birth. She filled my freezer that month. The first day home from the hospital, I wandered blearily downstairs around ten a.m. to find her in my kitchen with a casserole, a giant pot of ratatouille, and a sponge cake already made. She did this every day for a month—cooked two or three meals in double batches, and froze enough dinners that I didn't turn on the stove for three months after she left.

I remember sitting on a kitchen chair, watching while she made stock. "First stock is best," she told me, meticulously picking the last pieces of meat from a roasted chicken and placing them in a bowl. "But during the war, we made first, second, and sometimes third stock." She broke the bones down, and added onion, carrots, garlic, salt and pepper. I had never seen stock made before; I thought it came in cans. As I watched, she turned the scraps I had always thrown away into the most delicious soups and stews, sharing stories from her life as she worked. I was in awe of her.

As we were the possessors of the sole grandchild, my in-laws came to stay with us, for a month at a time, every nine months or so. We made each other crazy. We learned not to let it show.

When I was pregnant with my second—another boy who could have worn a different hand-knitted pink sweater every day for two weeks—we found out that Liz had cancer. Not breast cancer, or skin cancer, or one of those kinds of cancers that people recover from and live for decades longer. She had ovarian cancer—they call it the silent killer—and it was in stage four. I didn't know what stage four meant then. After about ten minutes on the Internet, I discovered it usually meant "hopeless."

She wouldn't talk about it, and never acknowledged how bad it was. She died when my second son was eight months old, after a long visit two months before. I remember the day I reached into my freezer, three months after the funeral, finding a shepherd's pie she had made and frozen, knowing that was the last dish anyone would ever eat that she had cooked.

It was delicious, of course, but we all cried through dinner.

When Liz was alive, I would call my sister to vent. "She unpacked my linen closet this morning, and ironed all the sheets," I would shout into the phone. "What the heck is that about?" My sister was always appropriately sympathetic.

"What a witch," she would murmur, "to iron your clothes for you without even asking. How rude."

Now, with a closet full of linens that have more wrinkles than a thousand grandmothers, I regret those complaints. I miss Liz, and wish I could have her back, so she could see her grandsons learning to walk, to read, to ride their bikes. So I could thank her again for all those meals, and the stories. So I could show her that she was one of my life's great blessings.

I am a mother of boys, like she was, and I hope someday to be a mother-in-law. I pray I will be like Liz, teaching my sons' brides how to put together a meal, how to hold a colicky baby, how to fold a fitted sheet, and biting my tongue when they do it all wrong. I have learned a hard truth: the mother-in-law you feared and loved can disappear, in a heartbeat, in a day, leaving you with a heart full of longing.

But if you are very lucky, like me, you may realize you have something of her left to pass down. A skill to teach your own daughters-in-law. A recipe for making the best out of what you have—for holding on to every bit of goodness you can—like the one I learned from my magnificent mother-in-law: the secret to making truly excellent stock.

## How to Make Liz's Excellent Stock

After a turkey or chicken dinner, place in a large soup pot the remaining bones, skin, and any small bits of meat. Add a chopped onion, a teaspoonful or so of salt, a dash of pepper, some sliced carrots, celery, a bay leaf, and a clove of garlic if you like. (Liz would use whatever sad, withering vegetables I had in the fridge. Of course, she never commented negatively on the state of the veggies, only smiled and said they were "perfect for stock.")

Add enough water to cover it all and bring to a boil. Immediately turn the heat to low; simmer for two hours. Strain the liquid into a large bowl and refrigerate for four hours or more. Skim the fat off the top. Use the remaining stock as a base in soups, or to replace canned broth in any recipe.

~Nikki Loftin

# Food and Love

## Just Like Mom's

*Now, as always, the most automated appliance in a household is the mother.*

~Beverly Jones

# Jess's Legacy

*No one ever really dies as long as they took the time to leave us
with fond memories.*
~Chris Sorensen

In the dedication of one of my books, I labeled my mother Jess as "the woman who made me what I am today... a diabetic with a weight problem." Of course, it was written with humorous affection, but that doesn't make it untrue, right? My mother historically showed her love through a beautiful evening meal, a batch of warm cookies, or a Southern breakfast buffet that inevitably spilled over to a second table, and I've been battling the resulting weight problem for most of my life. But did I inherit the same penchant for cooking? Not a chance. I am sorry to report that I've actually ruined Jell-O more than once and, although I do still give it the good old college try now and then, creating edible meals is a task I've only marginally mastered.

I suspect that young homemakers of today know Betty Crocker only as the name on boxes of cake and brownie mix, and I can't help but think my mother shifts a bit in her grave at the thought. She learned to cook from two sources: high school cooking class and a beautiful red-and-white, photograph-filled Betty Crocker cookbook from the 1950s. On many afternoons, she would pull that same cookbook out and flip through the worn pages, index cards with other treasured recipes filed between them, as she told me stories about a most memorable meatloaf, a special soup, or the creamy white icing recipe from cooking class.

In the late 1990s, a particularly bad Florida storm caused flooding at my mom's house. She lost some family photos, a few boxes of delicate linens, and a shelf filled with books. She only cried over the loss of one item: That red-and-white Betty Crocker cookbook. We tried blow-drying the pages, but it was just never the same, and parting with it broke my mom's sweet elderly heart. Not that it could ever be replaced, of course, but I began looking into locating another copy for her; before I got around to it, she passed away.

When I finally got ready to go through her belongings after losing her, I came across one recipe box after another! A long wooden box filled with handwritten recipe cards and folded tear sheets from magazines... a small plastic card file jammed with appetizer recipes only... even a Skechers shoe box held together with a thick rubber band and marked across the top with bold letters: Desserts.

One rainy Sunday afternoon, I began cleaning out Mom's desk, and I noticed a metal box in the bottom drawer. Inside were a few photos that brought me to tears, some letters she'd left behind, and a curious red and white notebook bound with a red plastic spiral. Although the cover was very different, I couldn't mistake the similarity to that old Betty Crocker cookbook Mom had loved so much.

I turned over the cover and there, on the first page, her recognizable wobbly writing from the latter days of her life greeted me.

*For my daughter, Sandie.*

On the next three pages, I found a handwritten table of contents listing everything from appetizers to desserts. Knowing that the end of her life drew near, my sweet mother, the one with the daughter who couldn't figure out Jell-O, had spent those final days creating a legacy just for me, an inheritance of the most loving gift she could dream up: A handwritten book of her favorite recipes.

I alternated between weeping and laughing as I flipped through the pages, remembering that favorite meatloaf of hers, and those scalloped potatoes my father loved so much. When the table of contents promised that the next entry would hold my mom's prized twelve-egg torte with the dreamy filling, I drew in a sharp breath. The page was blank. In fact, except for the shaky page numbers written in at the bottom corner of each of them, the next dozen or so pages were all blank.

That's when I realized she'd died before she could complete her project. While I was procrastinating, never quite getting around to locating that replacement Betty Crocker cookbook for my mom, she was fighting the effects of Parkinson's disease to write out another type of cookbook for me.

One of my friends recently described a beautiful piece of jewelry she'd inherited from her grandmother, appraised at more than twelve thousand dollars. I'm happy for her that she has such a wonderful, tangible memory of her gram, but a mere twelve thousand dollars? Really? Too bad she doesn't have what I do: A priceless cardboard notebook with red plastic spiral binding that proclaims "Jess's Legacy" every time I glance at it.

~Sandra D. Bricker

# Mom's Biscuits

*The sweetest sounds to mortals given*
*Are heard in Mother, Home, and Heaven.*
*~William Goldsmith Brown*

I don't remember just when I realized that my mother's biscuits were special. They were big, puffy things that she formed with her hands in a bowl she kept on a shelf in the side cabinet, pinched off with floured fingers, and placed gently on a black biscuit pan with a starburst pattern. Mornings before I went to school, she stood in the kitchen patting them out while the oven heated. By the time I was dressed and had my books gathered up, they were done. I ate one with oatmeal before heading out the door, across the creek, and over to the road, where I stood with my brother and sister beside the mailbox and waited in the early gloom for the school bus.

On Sundays, those same round biscuits filled a bowl next to fried chicken and mashed potatoes in our sunny kitchen. Sometimes when there were biscuits left over, Mom broke them into pieces, layered them with applesauce and cinnamon, and baked them till they were steaming hot. This concoction would be dessert on a winter evening. That was the way I loved them, but they didn't seem like anything unusual to me—just biscuits with a peculiar starburst pattern on the bottom. Whenever we had company, however, people always remarked on them, and it eventually occurred to me that I needed to learn to make those biscuits myself.

The summer before I got married, Mom took time to show me

her secrets. I stood beside her as she added a little more flour to the bowl that was always at the ready. She hollowed out a hole with the back of her hand and poured in some milk. With her other hand, she scooped out a generous portion of Crisco, and confided, "The secret to good biscuits is plenty of shortening." After some practice, I could make a decent pan of biscuits, but in my mind they would never measure up to Mom's.

Once my husband and I had our own home, I could not figure out where, in my small efficiency kitchen, to keep a bowl always ready for making biscuits. I was in school, space was limited, and somehow, it just wouldn't work for me. Maybe there's another way to make biscuits, I thought, and started searching the cookbook. Feeling almost guilty, I tried out recipes and methods until I found what worked for me.

My husband and I eventually moved to another state and began raising our own family. In the midst of a busy life with four young children, I didn't have a lot of time to regret my shortcomings in baking. One day, hurrying to get breakfast ready, I stooped by the cabinet trying to find what I needed, and realized that it was my mother's black biscuit pan I was looking for. With a wry smile, I pulled out my own shinier pan and placed on it the biscuits that I had stirred with a spoon and cut out with a yellow Tupperware circle.

As time passed, Mom's health deteriorated and she was no longer able to stand. The job of cooking for family gatherings fell to my sister Sharon and me. Though we missed Mom's special touch, we could only be ourselves; it had to be good enough. When our mother died, we gradually sorted out her belongings, but most of the kitchen things stayed at the house, which had become my brother Steven's.

One summer day, years later, Steven, Sharon, and I sat on his porch. The children had all grown up and moved in different directions. Big family dinners were rare. Without saying anything, Steven got up and went into the house. He came back carrying the black biscuit pan that hadn't been used in some time. It was a little bent and in need of a good scrubbing, but the familiar starburst pattern was still apparent.

"Who wants it?" he asked. After a short negotiation, the pan became mine. I took it home, cleaned it up, and put it into the cabinet alongside my other pans.

In a few weeks, my oldest daughter Sarah was coming for a visit. I wanted our time together to be special, like the times I remembered with my own mother.

"Is there anything you'd like to have while you're here?" I asked.

"I just want biscuits at least once," she replied.

On the day her dad went to pick her up from the airport, I got things ready for Sarah's arrival. I put clean sheets on the extra bed, made sure her bathroom was fresh and clean, swept the leaves off the walkway, and went into the kitchen. I placed on the counter everything I would need to make biscuits: a medium sized mixing bowl, a spoon, a knife, flour, shortening, baking powder, salt, milk, my yellow Tupperware biscuit cutter and Mom's black pan. Turning the oven to 450 degrees, I tied on my apron and began measuring out the flour for biscuits as only my daughter's mom can make them.

# Mom's Biscuits

2 cups all-purpose flour
3/4 teaspoon salt
2 teaspoons baking powder
4 large dollops of shortening (about 4 tablespoons)
a little milk

Put the dry ingredients into a medium-sized mixing bowl.

Use a table knife and cut in the shortening. (A little more shortening won't hurt.) You want the shortening evenly distributed and in small bit — smaller than peas.

Pour in some milk — no more than 2 tablespoons. Stir this in. Keep adding milk and stirring until you have a good doughy consistency.

Turn out onto a floured surface and knead until the dough is smooth—but not overly so.

Pat out the dough to the desired thickness. (Thinner biscuits have a nice crust.)

Cut out with round Tupperware cutter—or whatever you like to use.

Place biscuits on an ungreased pan.

Bake at about 425 until done to desired brown-ness—about fifteen minutes.

You will smell the biscuits when they're about ready.

Makes approximately eight—Recipe can be doubled.

~Sherry Poff

# Midnight Grace

*A mom forgives us all our faults,*
*not to mention one or two we don't even have.*
~Robert Brault, www.robertbrault.com

**M**om and I stood in the hallway, nose to nose. Her hands were on her hips and her feet peeped out from her long robe. Even her toes looked curled and angry.

"I think you'd better go to bed now," she said. "I'll be talking with your dad when he gets home. He'll be in to give you your consequence."

I spun around and stomped to my bedroom. Then I yanked the curtains shut, flipped the light switch, and plopped down on my bed. 10:15. The green digital numbers reported that my dad would be home from second shift soon. Dad was a gentle man, but I knew that I'd be in trouble. Worst of all, I deserved it.

I'd had the worst day at junior high school. My best friend, Mary Ellen, decided to join forces with cool-girl Regina. So there was no room for me at the lunch table. I ate my turkey-on-wheat alone, in the library, pretending to be immersed in a book. Then we square danced in P.E. class. I was nervous about holding hands with a boy. The boy was unkind, refused to hold my cold, clammy hand, and called me Trout for the rest of the day.

Of course, none of this had anything to do with my mom, except that I'd been terrible to her that afternoon. Years later I'd learn the terminology—misplaced anger—but on that day I'd just been hurt and mad and Mom was the retaliation target.

I watched the numbers morph until 10:30. "Might as well lie down," I muttered. I pulled back the comforter and slid between flannel sheets. As I lay there, I replayed the day's events through my mind.

Mom had baked cookies and they'd been fresh, piled on a plate, when I got home from school. Peanut butter. Sprinkled with sugar and imprinted with the tines of a fork.

"Couldn't you have made chocolate chip?" I said.

Mom looked up from the table where she helped my sister with her homework. "I could have," she said. "But I made peanut butter. Why don't you pour a glass of milk?" Then she smiled.

Later that night, when she pulled chicken from the oven, I balked again. Never mind that Dad was at work and Mom still put a nice meal on the table. I wanted hamburgers. "No one even likes that kind of chicken, Mom. Why didn't you make hamburgers?"

Mom breathed deep and ran her fingers through her long blond hair. "I made chicken and I've never heard anyone complain about it before," she said.

And it went downhill from there. I growled and complained until Mom hit her limit, lost her cool, and we had a shouting match in the hall.

By the time I heard the garage door open, I felt pretty bad about the whole thing.

I lay in bed and listened. The creak of the door. Dad's boots squeaking on the tile. Muffled voices in the kitchen. Then silence.

I wondered what my consequence would be. After soaking in the dark for a while, I didn't really care anymore. I'd hurt my mom. I'd seen it in her green eyes.

Why had I taken my troubles out on Mom? I knew that if I'd come home and shared what had happened, Mom would've listened. She would have offered encouragement and compassion. Then she would've said something funny and we'd have ended up laughing.

But I hadn't done that.

Before long, I heard Dad's quiet, bootless footfalls pass back down the hall. Then I heard the bathroom door shut. Then the rush of water. "Why is he taking his shower first?" I wondered.

The longer I waited, the heavier my heart felt. I considered getting up to apologize, but Mom didn't want to see me. I decided it was better to wait for Dad.

The sounds of the night were exaggerated in the dark. The rumble of the heater. The wind outside my window. Then a strange sound. A whirring from the kitchen. The clank of dishes. "What's going on?" I wondered.

The minutes stretched long, but finally my bedroom door creaked open. A shaft of light stretched across the room and stung my eyes. Soft footsteps to my bedside. Mom's hair slid past my cheek as she leaned over to whisper in my ear. "Why don't you come down to the kitchen?" she said.

I shimmied out of my bed and followed Mom through the bedroom and down the hall. As I passed the bathroom, I noticed the door was open. Dad had gone to bed. I was halfway to the kitchen when I smelled the thick, juicy scent of hamburgers.

I rounded the corner, puzzled, confused, and wondering if I'd fallen asleep and was dreaming. The kitchen table was set for two. "Have a seat," Mom said. She bent to lift a tray of French fries from the oven.

I sat.

Mom scooped the steamy fries to our plates and then poured thick, vanilla shakes into the tall glasses she'd set on the table. Then she slid two burgers from the griddle onto rolls and placed them on our plates. Then she sat down, too.

"Ketchup?" she asked. She tilted the bottle in my direction.

I reached out to grasp the bottle, but I couldn't. My eyes turned to my pajama-clad lap. "Mom, I've been awful to you today. I had a bad day at school and I came home and took it all out on you. You didn't deserve it. And I don't deserve this," I said. "I'm sorry."

I looked up.

Mom put the bottle down. She stretched her hand across the

table. "You're in a tough spot, Shawnie. Halfway to being a woman. Halfway from being a girl. I remember those days." She smiled and tears welled in her eyes. "And I forgive you." She stretched her fingers toward me.

I reached out and took her hand, soft and comforting.

"Now," she said. "How about some ketchup for that burger?"

I wiped my own tears and nodded.

Mom and I sat in the kitchen and munched burgers while the night wrapped around our house. We slurped shakes, crunched fries, laughed and cried.

And I learned a lot about grace.

It's now twenty-seven years later, and I'm the mother of five sons. They are good boys, but there are many, many times when a hefty consequence is laid out for one of them. And rightly so.

But then there are the other times. The times when I remember that night. The silence of the dark broken by Mom's laughter. The warmth of her hand around mine. The sizzle of the burgers and the salty, crisp fries.

The night when I should've been served a consequence.

But instead, my precious mom pulled out the griddle, wiped the dust from the blender, and dished up a hearty portion of grace.

~Shawnelle Eliasen

# She Tricked Me!

My mother tricked me. And not just me. She tricked my sister and brother as well. In the midst of three children and an additional half dozen or so in an at-home daycare, she had the nerve—the audacity—to absolutely fool us into leading healthy lives.

Sure, we were allowed two cookies after dinner. But she had us convinced that we didn't need the Sugar-Frosted Chocolate Krispie Gems calling out to us from the cereal aisle. We had something better.

We had "fruit plates."

Arranged on a brightly colored plastic plate would be a yogurt, an apple and a peach, sliced and rationed among the troops, and a handful of crackers or pretzels. Sometimes there'd be toast or half of a sandwich. And man, were we thrilled.

Fruit plates offered a brief respite from the "well-balanced" healthy meals we were forced to enjoy as a family at roughly 5:12 p.m. every single day. Fruit plates could be enjoyed at 4:30 p.m. when an elementary school open house beckoned at 5:30 p.m., or even after 6:30 p.m. on the days when soccer ran late. Fruit plates were the rebellion against the norm.

It wasn't until I tried to pass off a bagel, a handful of raspberries, and an apple as dinner for my ravenous husband that it hit me like a brick wall.

Fruit plates were the result of a woman who, once in a blue moon, didn't have time to cook a full meal in the midst of running a household, running a daycare, and running after three kids. One last-ditch effort to pull together a meal that satisfied the food pyramid.

And that woman made us think it was a treat.

Sneaky.

She probably even made us go to bed before ten so we'd be awake in school and stay on the honor roll. I wouldn't put it past her.

My mother probably knew what was best for me all along, and what's worse, she probably did what was best for me every day.

And here I am now, making fruit plates. And turning into my mom in other ways too. When I remind my sister to write down all her credit card numbers and phone numbers in case her wallet's stolen, I get it. After telling my collegiate brother to be careful at a party, the response taunts me: "Thanks, Mom."

Anyone who has ever met my mother has been let in on the secret mantra, which they then joyfully recite for their own entertainment: "You are your mother's daughter."

It's worse, though, and I don't know if anyone but me and my all-knowing mother know the extent of just how bad it is.

I am my mother.

I already type up lists of emergency phone numbers—and laminate those lists before posting them on the refrigerator. I can't stand crossing out dates on the calendar and instead take the extra seventeen minutes to locate the Wite-Out. I worry when my husband or siblings are out late and forget to call. Christmas isn't complete without a tree in every single room.

And the prognosis? Incurable. My affliction will only get worse.

Someday, I'll hang every hand-drawn picture on the fridge, and a framed drawing of a stick-people family will sit on my mantle long after the artist has gone off to college. I'll feel the need to sit in the bleachers at every basketball game and hang up posters for every school play.

Someday, I'll trick innocent young children into believing that crackers, a cut-up apple, and a peach yogurt is a treat.

Someday, I'll be the sneaky mom I was blessed to have.

~Caitlin Q. Bailey O'Neill

# Just the Way I Like It

*It isn't so much what's on the table that matters, as what's on the chairs.*
~W.S. Gilbert

I was excited! I was going home to visit Aunt Marge. Marge lived in Kansas and I lived in Seattle so although I called her every week, I hadn't been home to visit her in years.

I'd been a neglected child from a broken home and the happiest memories of my childhood were the brief visits I spent with Marge. Spending a few weeks with Marge in the summer was an oasis in my life and I always thought of her as my "real" mother. She was cheerful and kind and patient and fun to be with and she was a fabulous cook. Every meal was delicious and even after all the food had been eaten, no one was anxious to leave the table, so we'd often sit and talk for an hour while the food dried on our plates and the ice cubes melted in our sweetened tea.

When I knocked on her door, I hollered, "Mom, I'm home!"

It was a happy and tearful reunion.

"I cooked all your favorite foods," Marge said.

She had cooked a meatloaf that was burned and crusty around the edges and she made lumpy mashed potatoes and half-cooked corn on the cob. She had sweetened iced tea, and she had sliced tomatoes and cucumbers and doused them in vinegar. For dessert, she had baked a chocolate cake that had fallen in the middle and was evened out with extra frosting.

It was the exact meal she'd cooked for me many times when I

was a child. It was perfect, and she was right—it was my favorite meal, because Marge was my favorite person.

At Marge's table, burned meatloaf and lumpy potatoes were a banquet, because she loved me. I told her everything was delicious and perfect because I loved her. We sat at the table and talked about the old days, family, friends, and a hundred other things because when you had a meal with Marge, you were never in a hurry to leave the table.

The next morning she fixed my favorite breakfast, coffee with cream and extra sugar and burned toast. She scraped most of the black crumbs off the toast and she covered the toast with extra butter and jelly to hide the burned parts.

We sat at the kitchen table watching the birds come and go at the birdfeeder outside the window.

"I like..." I started.

"Meadowlarks," Marge said, "When you were eight, you liked meadowlarks."

"I still do," I said. There wasn't another person in the world who knew or cared that I liked meadowlarks. Marge knew me better than anyone else and she was the only person beside myself who remembered my childhood.

That evening we sat on the front porch and listened to the locusts in the elm trees. I felt eight years old and although Marge's hair was now white, I remembered when it was dark auburn.

"Do you still have Suzie?" she asked.

"No, she got lost a long time ago," I said. Suzie was a doll with a cracked head and one missing eye. The rubber band holding her arms onto her body had rotted and her arms had fallen off, but she'd been my favorite doll when I was five.

"Too bad," Marge said. "I've really missed you. I wish you didn't live so far away."

"I've missed you, too," I said. I hadn't realized how much until now. "I'll come home more often, I promise."

The sun went down and we went inside to watch television.

"We should have a snack before we go to bed," Marge said. She went into the kitchen and returned a few minutes later with a bowl of ice cream for each of us. When I was a child, we always had a bowl of ice cream before we went to bed. Tonight it was strawberry ice cream with broken potato chips sprinkled on top because that was how I liked it the summer I was seven.

I knew the next day, and every day of my two-week visit, would be the same. The meals would only vary by which foods would be burned and which foods would be half-cooked. We'd scrape the black crusts off the meat, potatoes, rolls or toast. We'd reheat undercooked vegetables. We'd laugh and do whatever we needed to do to make it edible, whether it was just scooping out the middle and leaving the black edges stuck to the pan or if it meant covering something with gravy that was either as thin as water or thick enough to cut with a knife. When she accidentally dropped a hot pad into a boiling pot of chicken and dumplings she dug the hot pad out with a spoon and asked, "Do you think that will affect the flavor?"

I told her no, I didn't think so, and it didn't matter—it would taste like a feast to me.

Because with Marge, it was never about the food, it was about the love.

~April Knight

**15**

# I've Got That Tupper Feeling

*All women become like their mothers. That is their tragedy.*
*No man does. That's his.*
*~Oscar Wilde*

While other kids my age were listening to Disney songs, the songs I knew by heart were Tupperware jingles. My mom was a "Tupperware Lady" throughout my childhood. As a child, I often despised Tupperware and what it represented. Having a mother who sold Tupperware meant she was gone most weeknights holding parties. She drove a wood-paneled station wagon, sang corny Tupperware jingles and talked Tupperware and food freshness—all the time. While other kids were picking out cool themed lunchboxes or were able to carry a brown bag that could be thrown away to allow for more playground time, I was given the Tupperware lunchbox complete with sandwich holder and mini cup. That cup, as I remember, barely held a sip of juice. I hated that lunchbox!

Our meals were created from recipes she learned in the Tupperware training classes or newsletters. We were the guinea pigs... testing the recipes prior to the parties so she could demonstrate the containers. Casseroles with cream soup or Jell-O molds were a constant menu item. Homemade play dough was made from kitchen ingredients and ended up an ugly color because the food coloring ran together. As each holiday rolled around there was always the kooky themed recipe such as Dinner in a Pumpkin.

As my teen years approached, I made some crazy affirmations: I vowed I would never cook with cream soup, never drive a station wagon and never, ever have a piece of Tupperware in my house. The years passed quickly and I believed I was on the path to keeping my vows.

Then... I moved out, bought a house of my own, got married and started a family. Before I knew it I was cooking meals with cream soup and had multiple cupboards containing Tupperware and matching lids. As if all of this was not bad enough, when my son's first Halloween rolled around, I didn't even think twice. I started shopping for the ingredients for Dinner in a Pumpkin!

As an adult working to help support my family I realized that my mom being gone at night and holding Tupperware parties was not necessarily something she wanted to do, but rather something she had to do to help support her family. Sure it seemed to me she loved her job and all things Tupperware, but selling Tupperware afforded my sisters and me ballet lessons, softball, family vacations, birthday parties and the latest fashions. Through food containers, recipes to demonstrate them, and many nights out earning a living, she showed us how much she loved us.

I think back now to my childhood and all the things Tupperware made possible for us and I am grateful that my mom worked so hard. As a busy mom myself, many of my recipes have cream soup in them, but my favorite recipe comes around once a year when, to my son's horror, I can hollow out the pumpkin and sing, "I've got that Tupper Feeling."

# Beef Dinner in a Pumpkin

2 lb. lean hamburger
1 (8-12") diameter fresh pumpkin
3 garlic cloves, minced
1 medium onion, chopped

12 small mushrooms, sliced
1 medium bell pepper
1 1/4 cup uncooked rice
1 1/4 teaspoons salt
1/2 teaspoon pepper
5 tablespoons butter
1 can stewed tomatoes
2 cups beef broth
1/4 cup grated Cheddar or Longhorn cheese
Parsley sprigs
8 to 12 cherry tomatoes

Wash the pumpkin and cut the top stem out to create a lid. Scoop out the seeds and stringy fibers.

Melt two tablespoons of the butter. Take a plastic sandwich bag and dip it into the melted butter to grease the inside of the pumpkin. Turn the pumpkin on its side and sprinkle inside with 1/2 teaspoon salt.

Sauté onion, mushrooms, bell pepper, and garlic in the remaining 3 tablespoons butter.

Add the 2 pounds lean hamburger, brown, and drain.

Then add the rice and stir until thoroughly mixed.

Add the remaining salt and pepper, the stewed tomatoes, and the beef broth and bring to a boil. Boil for 2 minutes then fill the pumpkin with this mixture.

Replace the pumpkin lid and place the pumpkin in a shallow greased baking pan. Bake approximately 1 to 1 1/2 hours at 350 degrees. Pumpkin is ready when tender and should remain firm enough to hold the filling without danger of collapsing.

If necessary, more beef broth can be added.

When baked, remove from the oven, lift lid and sprinkle inside with the 1/4 cup cheese.

Return pumpkin to oven without lid until cheese is melted. Remove from oven, replace lid and garnish around the bottom of the pumpkin with fresh parsley and cherry tomatoes. Serve from the pumpkin, scraping some of the pulp into each serving.

~D'ette Corona

# Mother's Secret Journals

*The act of putting pen to paper encourages pause for thought, this in turn makes us think more deeply about life, which helps us regain our equilibrium.*
~Norbet Platt

A s a child, lured by the mystery of a keyhole, I peered into my mother's bedroom, observing her form as she sat crouched over a writing desk. An old-fashioned teapot and mug rested on a nearby warmer. With my left eye squeezed shut, I spied on her through the hazy nighttime shadows flickering across her comforter and walls. Scanning the room, I saw a small lamp illuminating an antique bureau draped with a lace scarf. Numerous framed photographs of my two sisters and me lined the top.

I watched as my mother stopped writing, glanced at those pictures and poured herself another cup of hot tea. After sipping the warm brew, her eyes sparkled. Mom turned back the page and reread her notes, then smoothed a new blank sheet. I longed to view the words Mom secretly scribbled in her private journal.

On my tenth birthday, Mom and Dad presented me with a miniature one-year diary. Attached was a gold lock and key. I clutched the book to my chest and my heart leaped with joy.

"Happy Birthday, Suzanne," Mom and Dad said. That year Mom baked a batch of my favorite almond raspberry cookies, and introduced me to hot tea in a porcelain cup and saucer. I celebrated my first birthday tea party.

The silver tongs clinked when I plopped in two blocks of sugar. I added a dash of milk, stirred and sipped. A steamy mist rose from the warm cup and tickled my nose. I giggled and dipped in a cookie. The combination of almond raspberry and Earl Grey tea made me crave more. Mom smiled and refilled my teacup and plate. Dad grinned. I savored each swallow and surrendered to the distinct flavors.

That night, I jotted "Happy tenth birthday to me" and penned an entry in my new diary. I described the day as the best birthday ever. Besides receiving the journal, I had tasted black pekoe tea enhanced by Mom's almond raspberry cookies. I locked the diary and slipped the key on my neck chain.

The next few months, instead of spying on Mom writing in her own diary, I retired early to the sanctuary of my bedroom. Facing a blank page, I mulled over the highs and lows of my day. My pen glided across blue lines, revealing my inner feelings. The diary soothed me. I reread some of my previous entries. Finally, confessing in ink, I wrote that I harbored a secret desire to read my mother's journals.

Every February on my birthday, we had almond raspberry cookies and tea. It became our traditional family tea party. While the cold snow decorated the landscape outside, inside I was cozy and warmed by love.

Five years passed, and by age fifteen, I had received five yearly diaries. That birthday, I talked my mother into letting me help bake the almond raspberry cookies.

"Mom, where's the cookie recipe?" I asked.

"Honey, I haven't actually written the ingredients on paper. I made them so many times with Grandma that I remember them by heart. The recipe's been passed down for many generations."

I helped by whisking flour, baking powder, egg and butter together, while Mom ground almonds with brown sugar. She sprinkled them in and I continued to beat the dough. The cookies were cut with a two-inch round cookie cutter and placed in neat rows on a parchment-lined baking sheet. Once in the oven, our kitchen air wafted with almond. After cooling, we topped them off with raspberry jam and dusted on confectionary sugar. Everyone loved the cookies and I matured a little more having helped prepare them.

During my high school years, activities and dating became important, and I no longer wrote much in my journal. When I met Alex, I tossed the diary in my drawer and forgot about it. Three years later, we were married and before long I had my own daughter and son. On my thirtieth birthday, Mom gave me a new journal and I renewed my nightly writing.

I'll never forget the phone call from my mother a month before Mother's Day.

"Suzanne... your dad left me. He packed his suitcase and walked out to another woman," she said sounding breathless.

"What... who?" Shocked, I couldn't believe my ears. He never returned. Mom needed all the attention I could give her. Mother's Day came and she complained about not feeling too well. I assured her it was all the stress. The doctors proved me wrong. By July she had passed away. I was devastated. Somehow, I survived the funeral and returned to my normal life.

All I had left of her were my memories and those secret journals. I discovered them nestled in the bottom of that old desk drawer. One evening, I curled into my recliner with a fresh pot of hot tea and opened the first diary. I took solace in reading her private thoughts. I started to see the world through Mom's eyes.

In the very last one, I found a special note she had written for me. When I turned the page there was a hand-printed copy of the almond raspberry cookie recipe. It was a gift from her heart that would keep us forever connected. Chills traveled through me. Mom mentioned how much she loved me and my sisters in those journals. Her unconditional love revealed itself on each line. She wrote about the sweetest moments in her life, her courage and sorrow after Dad left, and how she carried on as her health deteriorated. Tears welled in my eyes.

Now, when I bake those special almond raspberry cookies for a birthday tea party, the house fills with an almond scent and I can almost visualize Mom sipping tea with me. I'll always treasure her secret journals. Every personal handwritten line keeps her memory alive. Through her inspiration, I'm writing about my own experiences. Perhaps someday my children will find mine.

# Mom's Almond Raspberry Cookies

2 1/2 cups sifted all-purpose flour
1 teaspoon vanilla extract
1/2 teaspoon baking powder
1/2 cup 10X confectioners' sugar
1/2 teaspoon salt
1 jar (12 oz.) raspberry jam
1/4 teaspoon ground cinnamon
2/3 cup sweet almonds
1 cup (2 sticks) unsalted butter, softened
1/2 cup light brown sugar
1 large egg

Preheat oven to 350. Spread almonds on a foiled cover baking sheet and toast them for 6 to 7 minutes. Let cool. When completely cooled, grind almonds in a rotary hand grinder until well ground, add 1/4 cup of brown sugar and mix together.

In a medium bowl, whisk together the flour, baking powder, salt, and cinnamon.

In another bowl, beat the butter with a wooden spoon until creamy and then add in 1/4 cup of brown sugar, beat together with at least 100 strokes or more, for 2 to 3 minutes. Next, beat in one egg and the teaspoon of vanilla. Slowly add the almond mixture, the flour mixture and stir until the dough is evenly blended.

Split dough into two halves, knead and form two long rolls, wrap tightly in a couple of layers of wax paper and chill well in a refrigerator until they become solid or firm. Usually takes 3 hours. Keep well wrapped.

Preheat oven to 350. Using your rolling pin, flatten each piece of dough to 1/8-inch thickness on a floured section of wax paper. Using 2-inch round cookie cutters, cut out dough rounds and place on cold, well greased (preferably sweet butter) baking sheets, spacing cookies an inch apart. Knead and roll remaining dough scraps flat. Cut out a few more cookies.

Bake 10 to 12 minutes, till edges are golden. About halfway through remember to reverse the baking sheets. When done, let the cookies cool two minutes and then spoon a 1/2 teaspoon of raspberry jam on the center of each cookie. Let cookies finish cooling. Lastly, dust the top of each cookie using a confectionery sifter with 10X confectioners' sugar. Store the cookies in an airtight cookie tin.

Makes about thirty-six cookies.

Hint: To soften hardened or dry cookies, put them with a piece of bread into a tightly closed container.

~Suzanne Baginskie

# 17

# A Mother's Son

*There are so many things in life which link me to my past,*
*but few have been more lasting than Mama's soup.*
*~Leo Buscaglia*

"Have you had your lunch yet?" I ask my son after talking with him on the phone for less than five minutes. The answer is always, "Yes, Mom, I did."

"What did you have?" I probe further. "Did you make it yourself or did you buy it? Do you have enough food in your refrigerator?"

I miss my son. On the days I want to have lunch with him, I have to travel several freeways to get to the Big City. When I arrive at the quaint, outdoor restaurant where we are to meet, I can hardly wait to see him. I never get over that empty feeling that grabs me when I see him walking up the street toward me. Dressed in a shirt and tie, smiling through blue-tinted sunglasses, I see that he has grown up. And my heart skips a beat. When did all this happen? What's he doing in the Big City all by himself? When did he let go of my hand?

Sharing a vegetarian pizza, I can see that he is happy—and that makes me happy. I recall the dozens of times that I made pizza for him in my own kitchen. And now I find myself sitting here at a sidewalk café in a busy city, listening to a voice within me that says, "Let him enjoy his new world."

Before we leave the restaurant, I tell him to order something to go, so that he will have something for dinner when he gets home from work. "And make sure you order enough," I call after him, as he enters the restaurant with a to-go list in mind. When he returns with his dinner in a Styrofoam box, I hand him a grocery bag filled with applesauce, oranges, avocados, and a homemade batch of his favorite Italian cookies—pizzelles. My contribution to his dinner and beyond.

On my way home, I think of my mom and how she must have felt when my brother left home for the first time. When he was twenty-one years old, my brother walked out the door in his white Navy uniform on his way to the plane that would take him to a faraway land. Mom missed her son terribly. She cried a lot and couldn't sleep. No one could console her. One of the ways she coped with his absence was to make his favorite cookies—pizzelles—and ship them thousands of miles to Da Nang, Vietnam, where he was stationed.

Helping her out, I would sit for hours in our garage (where the gas stove was), making those anise-flavored, snowflake-like cookies one at a time on a press that resembled a miniature waffle iron. This old-fashioned pizzelle press had a long, iron handle with a decorative design at the end. When one side of the cookie was done, I would flip the iron over and bake the other side. But I didn't mind spending my afternoons this way, as I had my little blue radio to keep me company—and I, too, missed my brother terribly.

When the cookies were ready for packing, Mom would stack the pizzelles in a large tin, placing popcorn in and around the delicate, crispy cookies so that they wouldn't break. Then she was off to the post office, visualizing that big, silver bird in the sky carrying her love to her son in another part of the world. And I'm sure if Mom could have included a grocery bag filled with everything from applesauce to avocados, she would have.

Today, four decades later, I still remember my brother's homecoming. And I'm so grateful that he is now living just a couple of blocks from me. I call him often.

"Can you come over for a cup of coffee?" I watch for him as I stand on the sidewalk in front of my house, waiting for him to come flying around the corner on his bike.

I set the table with cups of hot espresso and a heaping plate of pizzelles. I can now make two cookies at a time on an electric pizzelle maker.

After the coffee pot is empty and the anise-flavored, snowflake-like cookies are gone, I go to the closet where I keep a big, gold can brimming with more pizzelles and make a to-go bag for him.

"Take care of yourself," I call after him, as he and his bike and the pizzelles disappear up the street and around the corner.

When my son comes to visit, I always make sure that big, gold can is filled to the top. I can hardly wait to see him. The moment he enters the house, I ask him, "Did you have lunch yet?" I don't wait for his answer. Lunch is already on the table. And for dessert... a heaping plate of pizzelles. We sit and talk for hours, enjoying our conversation and the anise-flavored treat.

When it's time for him to head back to the Big City, I stack a batch of pizzelles in a large tin, sometimes stuffing popcorn in and around them so they won't break.

"I love you," I say, handing him the cookie tin and a grocery bag filled with everything from applesauce to avocados. "We'll have lunch soon." I hug him tightly... and my heart skips a beat.

"Take care of yourself," I call after him, as I watch him round the corner on his way to the several freeways that will take him back to his new world.

~Lola Di Giulio De Maci

# Mom Didn't Play Fair

*A man loves his sweetheart the most, his wife the best,*
*but his mother the longest.*
~Irish Proverb

I checked my watch. Yeah, I had time to catch a quick breakfast at IHOP. So I exited my car, slammed the door shut, and leapt up on the curb. As soon as I pulled open the door, it hit me.

I flashed back forty-two years. During the cold Ohio winters of my youth, the last thing that I wanted to do was crawl out of my toasty cocoon and go to school. I remember being snugly curled in the fetal position beneath a mound of blankets. If I happened to awake, then I would intentionally flip the pillow over to get to the cold side, and curl up again. Mmmm... there was no way that I was getting up!

But my mom didn't play fair. She knew how to get my brothers and me up without the use of an alarm clock.

And Mom did so with a minimum of effort. She didn't stand in the bedroom doorway and yell. She didn't rudely turn on the bedroom lights and walk away. She didn't violently jostle the sleeping lumps under the blankets.

No, Mom would depart the kitchen to silently trudge down the long hallway of our single-story, ranch-style home. Upon arriving at my bedroom, she would simply open the door. Then Mom would turn around and silently traipse back down that hallway to the kitchen.

In a matter of minutes, I'd start sniffing. I'd roll over and face away from the open bedroom door. I'd place my pillow over my head. It was no use.

My brothers and I would kick off our blankets and roll out of our beds. Then we'd race down the hallway to the kitchen to find Mom's primary weapon: bacon that was perfectly fried—not too floppy and not too crispy.

From that effort, Mom always saved the bacon grease in an empty can of Maxwell House coffee. Placing it in the refrigerator, she would use it to fry the next day's eggs. Or she would use it to prepare her homemade mush on a giant griddle. Little more than fried cornmeal batter, those orange slices of mush were slathered with butter and then drenched with hot syrup.

That's right—Mom even heated the syrup. Yeah... Mom didn't play fair. And I love her for it.

~John M. Scanlan

# The Potato Salad Rule

*Tradition simply means that we need to end what began well
and continue what is worth continuing.*
~José Bergamin

When I was a young girl, my family attended a church that frequently hosted potluck suppers. Each family brought a large dish of food they were happy to share. There were carrot and raisin salads, chicken casseroles, homemade breads, Jell-O molds with fruit suspended in them, cherry pies, a cake with cat hair in the frosting. And of course, many dishes of potato salad.

My mother took a large bowl of potato salad to every church potluck. She was proud of her potato salad. She diced potatoes, eggs, onions, sweet pickles, dill pickles, and celery. She mixed in pickle juice, salt, pepper, and paprika. Her recipe seemed to go on and on. As a child, I thought these things belonged in potato salad. It was a rule.

When all the ingredients were mixed in, my mother would take a clean spoon from the drawer and taste a bite.

"It's not tart enough," she would declare. "I need to add some pickle juice." Then she would take another clean spoon and taste it again and again until she had it just right.

"Will there be any left for the potluck tonight?" my older brother, Steve, would tease.

When it was time to leave for the potluck, my mother would

spoon the chilled potato salad into a pretty serving bowl. She never served it in the same bowl she mixed it in because the edges would look sloppy. She did not decorate her salad with sliced eggs. She did not sprinkle the top with paprika. She never garnished it in any way, as some ladies did. My mother's potato salad spoke for itself.

When she placed it on the table next to the potato salads of the other ladies who attended the church, she did so with a pride nearing sin. Then my mother would put a small spoon of the other potato salads on her paper plate, just to taste and compare.

"Why do you want to eat more potato salad after you just ate all that at home?" I asked her.

"You need to know what other people are up to," she said. "Remember that. It's good advice."

Then we would sit down together, and I would listen to her running commentary on all the other potato salads. Sister Hillard didn't bother to taste hers before she brought it. It didn't have enough salt. Sister Lynch didn't use the right kind of onions. There wasn't enough bite. Sister Guthrie didn't use pickle juice. Hers was too dry. Sister Shelton cooked her eggs too long, and they turned gray. Church potlucks were fraught with complications such as this.

When I grew up and started buying my own groceries, store-bought potato salad just seemed easier. A little tub, a couple of dollars, and a spoon. But I always felt like I was cheating, and it never tasted quite right.

I developed my own running commentary. This store put a funny tasting preservative in theirs. That store's potatoes were too rubbery. Another store allowed human hair as an ingredient. I started making my own, using my mother's recipe.

I didn't like onions, but no one would know. It was my potato salad, so I left them out. Pretty soon I was leaving out a lot of things. And I really liked dill, so I added a lot of that. But, somehow I felt like I had broken a rule. It was terrible what I had done to my mother's recipe. I kept it a secret for a long time.

Over the years, with my husband's taste in food as a good excuse,

I got over the guilty feelings and just started making and taking my potato salad to family gatherings as needed.

My mother never said anything critical, never suggested I add anything. She never reminded me what really went in a potato salad. Still, I knew what I made was very different than the dish she had taken such pride in all those years. What I made could hardly even be called potato salad by her standards.

In my memory, my mother had been so vocal about those church ladies. Where were her comments to me? I had nearly braced myself for "Where are your onions?" but it never came.

It began to irritate me that my recipe was not important enough for her to comment on.

That summer, my irritation was replaced by anxiety over my mother's heart attack. When she recovered from a quadruple bypass, I began to sense a handing down of the crown. My mother was making me the keeper of important things.

"I thought you might like my big mixing bowls," she said. "I don't need them anymore, and you'll use them." She gave me her rolling pin, because she knew I always loved it and would keep it in the family. Shoeboxes full of family photos began appearing at my house, for safekeeping. She did not give me her recipe box.

That autumn, my brother Steve's house burned down.

"How can I help?" my mother asked him.

"You don't need to. We already have a bunch of friends coming tomorrow to salvage things and start the clean-up," Steve said.

Newly recovered from open-heart surgery, my mother could not clean up a burned and gutted house. But she could make potato salad to feed the crew.

My mother bought all the ingredients herself, and then she asked me to bring her mixing bowls back. Side by side, we chopped and mixed everything. Onions and pickles, perfectly cooked eggs. It was the rule.

I helped her taste and taste until it was just right. The sharp oniony taste of childhood was a relief after the recent events.

She bought ten pretty plastic serving bowls to spoon it into, and she did not garnish it. Her potato salad still spoke for itself. It fed a huge clean-up crew, and everyone there loved it. Of course, everyone there was dirty and tired, and a lot of people were crying, but she was sure they were comforted by her recipe.

Just recently, my mother came to my house for dinner, and I served my version of the dish. Without hesitation, she took a big bite and said, "You always have made the best potato salad I have ever tasted. I don't know why I didn't make mine just like this all those years."

Every time she hands down the crown, a little more of my heart breaks.

"You can't stop making yours, Mom," I said to her. "What would we do without you and our family traditions?"

"Family traditions? My potato salad is not my mother's recipe," she said. "It's something I figured out on my own, just like you did. That's the rule."

## Mom's Potluck Potato Salad

6 medium potatoes, peeled and quartered
6 hard-boiled eggs, diced
1/2 cup minced yellow onion
1 cup minced celery
1/2 cup diced dill pickles
1 cup diced sweet pickles
1 tablespoon sweet pickle juice
1/2 cup mayonnaise
1 teaspoon yellow mustard
1 1/2 teaspoon salt
1/2 teaspoon paprika
1/4 teaspoon pepper, optional

Boil potatoes in water until tender. Cool and dice.

In large bowl, toss together potatoes, eggs, onion, celery, dill pickles and sweet pickles.

Add sweet pickles, juice, mayonnaise, mustard, salt and paprika. Mix Well.

With clean spoon, taste. Add pepper if desired.

Chill and spoon into pretty serving bowl. No garnish needed. Serves 6

Mom says readers can adjust any of the ingredients to their own taste — that's the rule.

~Carrie Malinowski

# Food and Love

## Table for Two

*We should look for someone to eat and drink with before looking for something to eat and drink, for dining alone is leading the life of a lion or wolf.*

*~Epicurus*

# The Rescue

*Chains do not hold a marriage together. It is threads, hundreds of tiny threads which sew people together through the years.*
~Simone Signoret

It had been one of those days. My three-month-old son, Tate, had not napped all day and now lay with his head on my shoulder, sobbing. Laundry waited by the washing machine, oatmeal was hardening in the breakfast bowls, and dirty diapers were emitting a smell from the trashcan. I surveyed my chaotic little world. Exhaustion washed over me, leaving me lightheaded. When would this day end?

For the last couple of weeks, I had managed to have the house cleaned and dinner well under way when my husband Jim got home from work at the end of the day. He worked all day and I got to stay home with the baby. It seemed like a fair trade. Jim had been very impressed, which made me very happy with myself.

This week, however, Tate was not his normal, happy self. He was getting his first tooth. Nothing seemed to relieve his pain for long.

Now Jim was on his way home during his short lunch break. I heated leftovers while holding my whining little guy. As Jim came in he surveyed the mess in the kitchen. "Not a good day?" When he turned to me he didn't need an answer. He could see I was still in the sweats I had slept in. When Tate let out an earsplitting cry, Jim picked him up. "I've got him. Take a break." I ran upstairs and cleaned up, got dressed, and did the minimum of my make-up routine so I felt more human.

Later that afternoon I managed to start the laundry and do some cleaning but then Tate started screaming again. Dinner would not be ready.

When Jim walked in, he took Tate from my arms, gave me a smile and threw his son playfully in the air. Tate squealed with delight. "Why don't you go up and take a break? Tate and I can handle things down here." He shooed me upstairs, telling me not to worry about anything. Lying on the bed, I briefly wondered what he was up to, but only for a minute. The next minute I was fast asleep.

I awoke two hours later. Jumping out of bed I ran downstairs. "Shhhhh." Jim pointed to Tate who was asleep. I walked into the kitchen and found that the love of my life had made one of my favorite meals. Coming from Italian roots, my husband knew how to create a very delicious spaghetti sauce. Before we met I had never been a huge spaghetti fan. But the combination of spices my husband used to make his sauce from scratch had me hooked from that first romantic meal he had made for me. It was all arranged—the meal, the light smell of vanilla candles, the soft music in the background. The oven even boasted dessert yet to come. Peeking in, I realized my husband had somehow made a trip to Applebee's and bought my favorite dessert ever—a Maple Butter Blondie.

"I thought you needed a night off." My husband smiled as he came into the kitchen. "You have been doing way too much around here. I can see you need a break." He escorted me to my seat and served me. We ate the savory spaghetti, tossed garden salad, mouth-watering, buttery garlic bread and enjoyed each other's company. As he served the blondie we grinned at each other. We shared it on one plate with two forks clinking together. And when Tate let out a loud cry from his crib upstairs, Jim said, "You stay right there. This will only take a moment and we will finish the rest of dessert."

The rest of the night consisted of foot rubs, long talks, and romance. Even to this day when we have spaghetti or blondies from Applebee's we always feel a little more romantic. My now six-year-old son knows when we have this meal we will act a little more "smooshy," as Tate puts it. And it always reminds me I am blessed to have such a thoughtful man who can turn a bad day into delicious perfection.

~Jami Perona

# Knight in Shining Armor

*To find someone who will love you for no reason, and to shower that person with reasons, that is the ultimate happiness.*
*~Robert Brault, www.robertbrault.com*

Ted was a friend of my very best friend, Barb, who often told me hysterical stories about Ted's escapades. One day, I agreed to meet Barb at the establishment where Ted bartended on a part-time basis. Ted and I were introduced and shared many a laugh. That was not when I fell in love—although Ted would tell you that it was exactly the time that he did!

Since we had shared so many laughs and so much fun, Ted and I began dating. At that same time, I had just switched jobs. Unfortunately, after starting with my new employer, I came down with an atrocious head cold.

I got up for work one morning, feeling more like the walking dead than someone heading off to a workday full of challenges. I realized that having been at my new job less than a month it probably wouldn't be a brilliant decision to call in sick, so I persevered and forced my sneezing, feverish body into my office.

Ted was working the night shift at a local manufacturing firm. He would be finishing his workday as I was beginning mine. He called me before he went to sleep to see if I would like to meet him for dinner.

Ted immediately understood why I declined when he heard my voice, with my scratchy throat and tremendously congested nose, along with frequent coughing. I replied, "I'll be lucky to make it through this day and if I do, I'm planning to collapse under a warm blanket on my couch." I thanked him for the kind invitation and said I'd talk to him later.

I assumed that Ted would go to sleep while I continued my struggle to make it through my workday. But shortly after midday I received a call from our security downstairs. "Lil, you have a visitor." He didn't even give me the chance to question who my "visitor" might be. I had no idea if, in my clogged and muddled state, I had forgotten an appointment.

I dragged myself to the stairway to open the door, and as I walked onto the landing, I looked down and there was Ted, charging up the stairwell. I immediately envisioned the movie *Pretty Woman* when Miss Vivian speaks of dreaming of her knight charging up on a white stallion to save her from her imprisonment in a castle tower.

Okay, he was not riding to my rescue, but he did have a crock of homemade chicken noodle soup. He was taking every step ever so carefully so as not to spill a drop. It was somewhat difficult not to laugh aloud at the intense concentration on Ted's face.

Not only had Ted foregone his sleep, he had gone to the store, purchased groceries, and toiled in the kitchen making this soup from scratch. To make it even more incredible, my office was forty minutes from Ted's home through a fair amount of traffic. Yet, he made the journey balancing this hot soup in the car. He even brought crackers.

That was the moment I fell in love.

Over nearly twenty years of marriage, there have certainly been times when I have wanted to pour chicken soup over Ted's head, but then I think back and remember that special day in the stairwell. Homemade chicken noodle soup has become not only a comfort food, but also a dear symbol of my husband's love for me. I've made what seems like millions of meals for us over the years, from traditional mashed potatoes and meatloaf to glorious holiday feasts. Yet none can surpass my knight coming to my rescue with steaming hot chicken soup. That was truly a recipe made entirely with love.

~Lil Blosfield

# 22

## Mango Love

*When I am with you, the only place I want to be is closer.*
*~Author Unknown*

It was our first date. He'd asked me to a movie, and I had suggested we each bring some food and have a picnic first. I was pretty excited; it had been a while since I'd been out with anyone, and I could tell this guy was special. Besides that, he was gorgeous.

It was a warm summer evening so I chose to wear my new sundress and sandals. I gathered some food, nothing special: half a loaf of bread, a block of Vermont cheddar cheese and I was just about to throw in some apples when I glanced at the fruit bowl. Oh yeah! A few days ago I had bought a mango. When we buy mangos in Vermont they're hard as a rock, and you have to wait forever for them to ripen. Even then you never know if they'll be any good, and they are expensive to begin with, so it's rare I would even buy one. This mango had gone from green to a beautiful yellow/orange with reddish streaks. A gentle squeeze showed me that it was ripe so I added it to the paper bag and headed out the door.

We met by the movie theater and walked to the river. I had that little heart-poundy thing that happens if I'm excited, nervous, and extremely hopeful. We found a grassy spot to sit by the water and started to unpack our picnic. While he pulled a green pepper from his backpack I noticed how far away I had sat down from him. I tried to be nonchalant as I inched closer, pretending I needed to brush some pine needles off my dress.

"This is from my garden," he said. His hair had this way of parting on his forehead in just the right way to make him look, well, dreamy. "I thought we could slice the pepper and dip it in this." He took out a container of hummus. His hands were so big. He pulled out his pocketknife and sliced up the pepper. He carries a pocketknife, I thought, and inwardly swooned.

"There's more," he said, "but let's see what you have first."

What I have? I had gone into a teenage daze even though I was in my thirties. The guy was so darn handsome! "Oh, yeah. What I have." I pulled out the bread and cheese.

"Is that the Cabot extra sharp?" he asked. He reached out to take it and his hand touched mine. It sent a spark through my whole body. I'm sure I turned bright red. Pretending to look for something, I stuck my head into my picnic bag, trying to hide my pink face. I realized I never answered his question about the cheese.

"Yeah," I said from inside the bag. "It's the extra sharp." I was feeling lightheaded from the way his eyes sparkled and I thought maybe it was a good thing I was inside the bag. Isn't that what you're supposed to do if you are about to faint? Stick your head in a paper bag? Breathe, silly, I told myself. He's just a guy. "Oh, here it is!" I said pulling my head out and retrieving the mango. Could he possibly believe I had to search that hard for a mango inside the now empty paper bag?

"A mango?" he said. Uh oh. What if he doesn't like mangos? What if they make his tongue go fuzzy or his throat seize up? "Yum," he said and he smiled.

Oh no! That warm thing was happening again and I was afraid I would have to dive back into the bag. Deep breath, I told myself.

"Maybe we should eat," I somehow managed to say, trying to swallow tiny little gasps.

He sliced the green pepper, cheese and bread with his pocketknife. We drank from his water bottle and ate our picnic while a duck family swam up and asked to be included in the feast. The river quietly flowed by, the wind whispered through the leaves above us, and my heart flip-flopped inside me as I began the journey of falling in love with this gorgeous man. Quietly we sat next to each other, letting the grassy smell of July fill the space between us. Andy picked up the mango, and said, "Shall I?" All I could do was nod.

He peeled and sliced the perfectly ripe mango and placed the whole thing in his massive hand, offering me a piece. The combination of his hand and the juicy mango made me unbalanced. I reached out and grabbed a slice, but then ended up jostling his hand, which made him drop the rest of the mango onto the sand and ant-covered grass. Our eyes met and I was amazed that in deep crisis he could still take my breath away. We turned our gazes to the mango slices. They were a loss. There was no way to get the sand off them. The duck family looked at us as if to say, "We'll eat it! We love sand and ants!"

I didn't know if I should laugh, cry or stick my head back into the paper bag. Andy nodded toward the slice in my hand. "Go ahead," he said, a twinkle in his eye.

"No, no, it should be for you! I'm the one who knocked it all to the ground. Here." I handed the mango piece to him. He took it from me and bit it in half. Then he reached out and brought the other half to my mouth. Oh lord, help me stay alive for this, I silently prayed. He placed the mango slice in my mouth and I tried really, really hard to leave his finger alone. The mango was perfect. Sweet, juicy, tender.

Maybe we should get going, I thought, and I started packing up our little picnic.

"Not so fast," Andy said. He reached into his bag and pulled out... a mango! He had brought one too! It was yellow, orange and red. He peeled it, he sliced it and in an incredibly trusting move, he offered me a slice from his giant hand.

Slice by slice we ate that mango, the sweet juice dripping through Andy's fingers. The duck family sat close by and watched us eat and fall in love.

Today, whenever we eat a mango, the kids ask us to tell the story about the time Mom flung the mango out of Dad's hand onto the sandy, ant-covered ground.

~Lava Mueller

# 23

# Love and Lattes

*I orchestrate my mornings to the tune of coffee.*
~Terri Guillemets

When I first met my husband Geno, he lived in a garage. You may be thinking that he lived in a garage that had been converted into an actual room with real walls and some proper insulation, but that wasn't the case.

It was just a regular old garage, the only modification being a large gray carpet scrap on the ground to keep the concrete from feeling quite so cold. The "room" was furnished with a bed, topped by several colorful striped Mexican blankets, and a worn dirty-looking off-white sofa obtained at a yard sale. A very old, very ugly, solid dark wood dresser stood in one corner.

Despite the lack of luxury accommodations, I would spend the nights with him there in the garage, huddled under the blankets, completely smitten. In the mornings, we would wake up and enter the actual house. We'd go into the kitchen where, with lavish attention to detail, Geno would make me coffee.

In the early years of our dating—before we got married, before the careers, before our two kids, and before illness ever touched our lives—back in the days when we both seemed to have a lot more time and energy, the act of Geno making my morning coffee was quite elaborate.

First, Geno would grind the espresso beans fresh. Then, he would carefully pack them into a European style stovetop espresso maker, which was a complicated contraption of filters, seals, and various parts that I never could seem to put together properly. As we waited for the coffee to percolate, he would separately heat up two mugs of milk in the microwave. When the coffee had bubbled and brewed, he added it to the steaming milk, creating delicious homemade lattes.

Back then, Starbucks wasn't around, and to find a good latte wasn't as simple as driving to the nearest shopping center. Geno's lattes were the best in town, and I started my days feeling satiated by my coffee's warmness.

While drinking our morning coffee, we would chat with his various roommates who lived in the house proper, eat some cereal or toast, and then go back to the garage.

As time went on and our overall lives became more complicated, the coffee routine simplified.

After we got married, my parents gave us a fancy Italian espresso machine. We loved it, but who had time to actually use it? So after a while, we bought a regular old Mr. Coffee coffeemaker. We replaced the glass pots when we broke them, which was frequently. Sometimes, we even bought the beans pre-ground.

After fifteen years of sharing our morning coffee and our daily lives, we temporarily uprooted our family and moved to Spain. This was a result of Geno having achieved a six-month sabbatical from his university position.

When we arrived in Spain, we were charmed when we opened the kitchen cabinets of our furnished apartment. "Look at this!" Geno exclaimed, holding up a tarnished espresso maker. It was a stovetop European-style, the exact same type that Geno had used when he first started making me coffee fifteen years earlier.

While in Spain, on sabbatical from our "normal" lives, we lived in a state of constant escapism, and it was blissful. The external pressures of our typical day-to-day existences simply vanished and we went back to the essence of our relationship.

And each day, as he had throughout our lives together, Geno made my coffee.

He once again made my coffee slowly and elaborately—just as

he had when we were in our early twenties. There was no Starbucks in Granada, the city in which we were living, and while Spanish espresso is generally quite good, Geno's lattes were still the best.

When we left Spain, we returned home—and we returned to reality. We also returned to our regular old Mr. Coffee coffee-maker—which these days boasts an unbreakable stainless steel pot.

Our lives have changed throughout our years together, but one thing has always remained constant.

Every morning, as Geno makes my coffee, I am reminded of my husband's exceptional richness, warmth and love.

~Lisa Pawlak

24

# Honeymoon Muffins

*When love is not madness, it is not love.*
*~Pedro Calderón de la Barca*

For a teacher, summer vacation is a welcome reward for the many hours devoted to the needs of children. The last day is bittersweet indeed—with joy and anticipation of time off mixed with the sadness of saying goodbye to those who were one's school family for the past year.

At the end of my seventh year in the profession, I decided to leave my first school, a place where I had forged strong relationships with students, parents and the community. I truly loved my work in that small town so the farewell was especially difficult.

But love does strange things to a man. I had spent each weekend that May transporting my belongings to what would become home for me and my soon-to-be wife, some seventy miles north of that little community. By the last week, all that remained was a cot, a few clothes, paper plates, a towel and a toothbrush. The last day of school, I said my goodbyes at school amidst hugs and tears and then quickly went to surrender my keys to the landlord. I loaded the last few items, hopped in my truck and headed toward my wedding rehearsal dinner.

A few days later we were married, and then off to a little getaway in the Arizona mountains for a week. Alas, we had to return to the real world at the end of the week and begin figuring out this new thing called marriage.

My wife soon returned to her work at the bank, having only received two weeks of vacation. I, on the other hand, still had the better part of my three-month sabbatical. Each morning, she arose at six to prepare for her work as a teller. As much as I hated pulling myself from bed, I got up as well in order to prove my husbandly devotion to my beloved bride. We ate breakfast together and shared the morning paper. Then she was off to work, and I was left to the domestic duties of a vacationing groom.

I washed the dishes, straightened up the house, read a few chapters of the latest book borrowed from the library and then gravitated to the kitchen where I scoured the Betty Crocker cookbook—a wedding gift still in pristine form—for something easy yet impressive for each night's romantic dinner. My wife was not fond of my bachelor diet of ramen noodles and hot dogs despite the many delicious variations I had concocted using these two delicacies.

Ms. Crocker soon convinced me that with a little patience, practice and creativity, I could transform a few common ingredients into a gourmet dinner. I was extremely cautious throughout the training. My mother's words from my adolescence helped guide me: You make it, you eat it... no matter what!

Soon my tired wife was being treated to grand meals of baked pork chops and stuffing, homemade lasagna, rice and chicken casseroles and broiled steak with potatoes. I'm sure that a little ramen would have been a tasty addition, but I respected my new bride's wishes.

One morning, I happened upon a recipe for muffins. Dinner would now be complete. We could even have them for breakfast! The recipe was simple, and I followed it just as Betty prescribed. I added chopped apple pieces to the ingredients, poured the mix into the individual muffin cups and baked for twenty minutes. Finally golden-brown and aromatic, my first desserts were pulled from the oven. I bit into one and found it to be fairly bland. But I did not disobey my mother... I ate four for a morning snack.

I went right back to the mixing bowl. I tripled the required amount of sugar and added an additional cup of chopped apples.

When the timer rang, I sampled a muffin from batch two. It melted in my mouth. I was so excited—I baked two more dozen and piled the morsels high on a serving plate.

When my wife arrived home, she complimented me on the inviting bakery smell. I took her to the kitchen and proudly showed off my morning's work. She looked at the muffin mountain and then at me before rolling her eyes. "Well, at least, we have breakfast for the next couple of weeks," she said.

Encouraged, I elatedly ran to the kitchen each morning after hearing her car pull away. She liked my muffins!

As any great chef will do, I soon began experimenting with my new recipe. Within minutes another twelve apple muffins were born, this time with brown sugar and cinnamon sprinkled on top. The next day I made peach muffins... three dozen. Then there were raisin muffins and blueberry muffins and cranberry muffins—even pear muffins. Two dozen each.

My confidence bolstered, my courage strong, I ventured away from fruit. There were marshmallow muffins and chocolate chip muffins and gum drop muffins and mint muffins. A dozen each. I even considered ramen muffins—but reconsidered.

After a week of indulging my out-of-control culinary compulsion, my wife took me aside and counseled me. "What in the world are we going to do with all of these muffins? Get under control, dear. Read a book! Get another hobby!"

Dejectedly, I looked at the piles of muffins filling every flat area of our tiny kitchen and then back to her. "But I did it for you," I whimpered.

She kissed me and then grabbed a blueberry muffin and stuffed it in her lunch box. "Thanks. I love you, but please, no more muffins!"

I wrapped up several packages and delivered my treats to my parents and siblings. Then I took more packages out and delivered muffins to my wife's family. My mother-in-law rolled her eyes, but I have learned over the years that this is what mothers-in-law do. However, she graciously accepted the gift from my kitchen.

Several dozen muffins remained in our refrigerator and kept us from worrying about what we would have for breakfast all that first month of our marriage. Now, many years later, with life a little more hectic, I often turn to store-bought mixes and whip up a dozen muffins every now and then. But they just don't taste the same as those early honeymoon muffins.

~Tim Ramsey

# Best Restaurant in Town

*When love and skill work together, expect a masterpiece.*
*~John Ruskin*

The dinners my husband so lovingly prepares each night are mouthwatering delights, from braised Chilean sea bass, to salmon bathed in sesame ginger sauce, to luscious chicken cordon bleu. He marinates filet mignon till it is fork tender, or he tops ultra thin pork chops with an apricot sauce that melts in your mouth. The aroma of rosemary and thyme that cover a lamb roast is a hint of a delicious feast ahead.

Almost every night he makes his signature salad of baby spinach leaves, blueberries, sliced strawberries, chopped walnuts, and thin strips of Dubliner cheese, topped with raspberry vinaigrette dressing.

He bakes petite Idaho potatoes or sometimes sweet potatoes and tops them with margarine or sour cream. Verdant asparagus or broccoli round out the plate, sometimes covered in homemade Hollandaise sauce.

As if all this isn't mouthwatering enough, you should taste what he does with the leftover meat or fish! He makes what I lovingly call a pizza. He places a large whole wheat and virgin olive oil soft wrap on a pizza stone, and brushes an appropriate sauce on it. Then he finely chops salmon, filet mignon, chicken, lamb, or whatever is left over, and sprinkles it on top, followed by baby spinach leaves, and then tops it with shredded Colby-Jack cheese. He bakes it on the pizza stone, and then he cuts it into wedges. This luscious pizza is served with freshly made guacamole. I almost love the leftovers more than the original dinner!

As if all this isn't sweet enough, he keeps a supply of my favorite ice cream in the freezer: white chocolate raspberry. However, after such scrumptious dinners, I hardly ever have room for dessert.

We've been to many restaurants. A few years ago we went out to a highly recommended new one on my birthday. As delicious as the Chilean sea bass was, it couldn't compare to what my husband serves me at home. I went to Michael's and bought a frame, matting, and sparkling letters. With the blue letters I spelled out "Best Restaurant in Town," and hung this framed piece between the kitchen and the family room — rooms where masterpieces are lovingly created and enjoyed every day!

~Virginia Redman

# Pane Rustica

*Good bread is the most fundamentally satisfying of all foods;
good bread with fresh butter, the greatest of feasts!*
~James Beard

Bread rules my life. Personally, I can take it or leave it, but for my husband, Prospero, it is truly the staff of life. Therefore, each day begins with procuring the perfect loaf for his meals.

Now, I did not set Prospero on this path; I'm simply an enabler. His love of bread—good bread—began back in a small town in the region of Apulia, Italy. His mother, in an effort to feed seven children on limited funds, created two large rounds of pane rustica—rustic bread—that she then took to il forno, or the local ovens, to bake in a wood-burning brick oven. This she did every other day, supplying her family with crusty bread that became the staple food at mealtime.

Prospero often tells me stories of how he satisfied a sweet tooth as a child. "I had to sneak the sugar," he would begin, "and I'd sprinkle a little on a piece of bread. But I was afraid that the wind might blow it off, so first I'd spread a little olive oil on the bread to make the sugar stick. Then I'd run out of the house so I wouldn't get caught." If he had enough lire to buy a small square of chocolate he would let it melt and spread it carefully over a slice of bread, letting it ooze into the deep yeasty tunnels.

After I met my husband, I would enjoy this homemade bread

with meals, but it was never more special than when we dropped in to visit his mother for a quick lunch. During the warm summer months, Mamma Lucia would pick ripe red tomatoes and cool green leaves of basil and make a salad slick with olive oil that she would toss over chunks of rustic bread soaked with water—panzanella. On cold days she would make steaming bowls of white beans garnished with dollops of green olive oil—smuggled into the country—and diced garlic. We would scoop up the beans and sop up the broth with her fresh baked bread. It was a feast.

Then Prospero decided to marry me, a third generation Italian-American raised on Wonder Bread, and the baking stopped. Fortunately, we lived in an Italian section of the city and I was able to buy some excellent bread from any number of Italian bakeries in the neighborhood. Eventually we moved to the suburbs and the loaves of supermarket "Italian" bread didn't measure up. So I had to search the stores and by trial and error learn where I could go to buy bread with the correct taste and texture. None were as good as my mother-in-law's bread, but they would have to do.

Bread continues to present a challenge. If Prospero happens to be home for lunch I have to buy fresh sub rolls to make a panino with Italian cold cuts. Bologna on sliced bread simply won't cut it. And his royal highness, the Italian prince, loves a nice grilled American burger but—you guessed it—it has to be on a crusty hard roll. Packaged soft buns will not do. There's no getting around it; meals require a daily trip to the market.

The only time I begin to panic is when there's snow in the forecast. How will I get to the store? And what if all the bread is gone? Luckily I found a good quality take and bake loaf and I stock my freezer just in case. There's also the extra bonus of the scent of baking bread wafting through the air. But shopping for bread during snowstorms is not only difficult, it can be downright dangerous.

"Where did you get that bread?" demanded a woman pointing to my cart one snowy morning.

"Over in the bakery department," I confessed with a gulp. "But it's the last one." I'm not sure why, but I was actually afraid. What if she snatched it from my cart while I was sifting through the escarole?

About now you may be wondering why I don't simply break him of this habit. It's because, in some small way, I feel like buying fresh bread each day is the way I show Prospero how much I love him and how special he is to me. It's also my way to show respect for who he is and where he comes from. By making his traditions mine, we truly bonded as a married couple.

There is a bright side to all of this. As long as Prospero has good bread and a nice bottle of wine, dinner can be as simple as a good imported cheese, some prosciutto or sopresata, and olives, or "picky stuff" as my husband likes to call it. He's not fussy in that department. All that really matters is that bread and wine are on the table.

Bread and wine on the table... now where have I heard that before? Next he's going to tell me he has to eat it — it's his religion.

~Lynn Maddalena Menna

# Life's Simple, Sweet Pleasures

*Chocolate is the answer. Who cares what the question is.*
~Author Unknown

I know there are couples out there who toast one another with champagne and truffles on special occasions. I know there are those who dine on chateaubriand at the latest fabled restaurant. And then there are the rest of us.

When I was a bride, I experimented with what I regarded as "gourmet" fare. My older, wiser friend, Alice, taught me how to make Beef Wellington, a project that took endless hours and caused lots of frustration. I quickly reverted to baked chicken anointed with bread-crumbs, and my husband, and later our kids, loved it.

Another friend taught me how to stretch a meatloaf into eight servings, and I greedily welcomed it into my repertoire.

And then there was the simple marinated salmon that seemed to find its way onto our table on summer nights when "light" was right.

So these simplest of dishes became the standard at our house, and as my writing career grew more and more demanding, our meals stayed simple. Every now and then, I'd stun my family with slightly more elaborate dishes, but I never returned to that Beef Wellington.

Life propelled us past the usual stages: full house, emptying nest, empty nest.

Sometimes, the silence seemed to crawl up the walls as I set a table for two, and our simple dinners went from routine to—well, boring.

I never did take the cooking course I'd vowed I would. I never did invest in a full library of gourmet cookbooks. And I can say with absolute certainty that I never perfected the strawberry shortcake that I swore I'd master after tasting it at a neighbor's house.

But I did yearn to find a dessert that would be a special treat when the world was too much with just us, and days tumbled onto other days with a kind of relentless sameness. So I experimented.

I made a lemon meringue pie that ended up in the garbage disposal. It was just plain awful. I found a recipe for a torte that I foolishly sprang on a few friends at a dinner party, only to note that there was more left on the plates than consumed.

I was not destined to be a brilliant gourmet cook. Yet I still had that longing to find my special gift, the dish that would make my husband smile after an arduous day, and that would ignite my own taste buds.

I didn't have far to look. One day in the supermarket, I walked down the pudding aisle. I'd done it a thousand times without even pausing. Pudding was... well, boring. Pudding was an after-school snack for kids.

But I reached for the instant variety—just stir in milk—and put it in my cart. That was not a roaring success. Nothing is thrilling about placing a small bowl of vanilla pudding on the table.

My husband mentioned that chocolate might be a better choice. So the next week, into my cart went instant chocolate pudding. And it tasted... well, instant.

Then, on a winter day when the wind was howling, I reached for cook-and-serve pudding. Hardly a giant step. But standing at the stove that day, stirring and stirring the pudding and the milk brought a strange sense of contentment. It was just that little saucepan, country music on the kitchen radio, and me.

Weird as it sounds, my husband and I devoured that pudding as if we'd discovered manna from heaven. It was rich, chocolate and somehow seemed home-cooked.

Over the months, and now the years, cook-and-serve chocolate pudding has marked our tiny milestones: a story finished and accepted by a tough editor, a car repair that doesn't break the bank, an unexpected mini-vacation.

Out comes the little red pot, the wooden spoon, and the bowl with the border of flowers. It's such a modest, simple pleasure in a complicated world. It's so affordable.

And every single time chocolate pudding appears on our kitchen table, with its view of the once-tiny tree just beyond the window, now grown tall and strong, there is a certain simple joy in the lives of a very married couple that's easier felt than explained.

And invariably, one of us will scamper back to the kitchen later that night to have the ultimate pleasure: A smidgeon of icy cold chocolate pudding just before going to bed.

Who needs Beef Wellington anyway?

~Sally Schwartz Friedman

# And So I Made Soup

*There is nothing like a plate or a bowl of hot soup, its wisp of aromatic steam making the nostrils quiver with anticipation, to dispel the depressing effects of a grueling day at the office or the shop, rain or snow in the streets, or bad news in the papers.*

~Louis P. De Gouy, The Soup Book

We'd been treating David's follow-up appointments as dates—first seeing the doctor, then sharing lunch and shopping afterwards. After all, with four of our eight children still living at home, time alone together was always at a premium. But on that particular day our eight-year-old daughter Katie seemed to need some one-on-one attention, so we'd brought her along.

While I'd always been in the exam room as the doctor checked inside my husband's throat, this time I stayed in the waiting room with Katie. I wasn't sure she could handle the sight of the doctor putting tubes down her father's nose. She and I talked animatedly until I fell silent after a good half hour had passed. I was starting to get nervous. These check-ups usually lasted less than twenty minutes.

After forty-five minutes, I got a sick feeling in the pit of my stomach. As my daughter read a book she'd brought, I clutched my hands, silently praying for my husband. Fifteen minutes later, when the nurse came out and said the doctor wanted to speak to me, I already knew why. When I entered the exam room I first glanced at the doctor's serious expression, then David's ashen complexion.

"Is it back?" I asked, and David nodded. My stomach lurched, and I felt like throwing up.

On the screen that showed the inside of my husband's throat, the doctor pointed out a growth on the epiglottis and said he was ninety-nine percent certain it was cancer. In the stunned quiet of the room, I thought I heard the unmistakable sound of the other shoe dropping.

It had been less than two years since my spouse had faced a diagnosis of oral cancer and undergone an invasive surgery that left him with a tracheotomy and a feeding tube. Surgery had been followed by a grueling six-week regimen of radiation and chemotherapy.

The day after the doctor's pronouncement that the cancer had likely returned, our son Dan found me in the kitchen, stirring two huge pots of homemade soup. The table was littered with more than a dozen single serving containers that I ladled soup into for storing in the freezer. Dan didn't even have to ask me why I was making mass quantities of soup, he instinctively knew. You see, he and I had been down this road already, a team united in support of his dad. Two years before, when I'd become David's caregiver, Dan had been a crucial support for both of us. He'd put his own life on hold to run errands, visit David daily in the hospital for an eleven-day stretch, and take him to appointments. He basically became a rock for me to lean on.

Dan knew exactly why I was making soup. It was one of the few things I could do. Despite our best intentions in providing a support system for David, in the end, cancer is a lonely fight. It would be David who would have to experience another surgery and additional chemotherapy, David who would be fighting for his life. I could hardly bear the thought.

So I made soup.

David hadn't been able to eat at all after his surgery. I'd fed him liquid food through a tube in his abdomen, gradually introducing soft foods. Foods like soup. Then during radiation and chemotherapy treatments, with his throat raw and sore, soup was the one food he could still manage to swallow. Even after his recovery from treatment his throat was narrowed, swollen with scar tissue. Soup remained the single food he could consume without coughing or choking. When we went out to eat, the soup of the day was the first thing he asked about. I'd gotten lazy, though, relying on canned soups. Making homemade soup was a tangible way to show David I would be there for him, whatever lay ahead. Homemade soup was love.

When the doctor's office called a week later to report that the surgical biopsy was benign, I got to experience the heady feeling people must have when they win the lottery. For months afterward, each time I pulled a single serving of soup from the freezer, I was reminded of our good fortune. With my husband waiting patiently at the table, I'd pop the container in the microwave and serve it piping hot with little oyster crackers floating on top. Then I'd kiss the top of David's head as I served it, silently thanking God for the blessing of my husband.

That was three years ago. David is now a five-year cancer survivor and our marriage is the best it has ever been. The few times that we have disagreed or exchanged harsh words I have made sure to dredge up the memories of that fateful doctor's appointment when we were certain that David's cancer had returned.

Then I head to the stove to make soup.

## Mary's Oven Stew

2 lb. stew meat
6-8 potatoes, peeled and cubed
6 carrots, sliced
1/2 cup chopped celery
1 large can of tomato juice and 1 small can of beef broth
1 bag frozen peas
1 bag frozen corn
2 tablespoons minced onion or chopped onion, to taste
Pepper to taste

Mix all ingredients except for corn and peas in a roasting pan.

Cook for 4 hours at 200 degrees.

Add 1 bag frozen corn, 1 bag frozen peas.

Cook another hour.

~Mary Potter Kenyon

# I'll Have Fries with That

*The cardiologist's diet: If it tastes good, spit it out.*
*~Author Unknown*

While my husband and I sat in our lounge chairs watching TV, I read an article out loud that promoted the benefits of proper eating. Ignoring me, he cranked up the volume on the football game and cheerfully crunched on Doritos.

When I persisted in sharing the dietician's suggestions, he turned to me and said, "You know what your problem is? You believe all that bologna."

Lord knows I'd harped at him constantly about losing weight. Our golden years were just around the corner, and I wanted to spend them together in good health. But nothing I said or did changed his poor eating habits. He continued to scarf down chips and dip while watching me count calories and carbs. As far as he was concerned, salads were rabbit food. Vegetables? Only if I found a way to fry them. Skim milk—why bother? Exercise was a sore subject—a waste of time. He had real work to do.

One day, I asked what he wanted for supper.

Out of the blue, he said, "A salad sounds good."

Where'd that come from? I asked him to repeat himself.

I smiled while I prepared a spinach salad, thinking my nagging had finally paid off. Later, I found out the real reason for his change of heart.

Fear.

Earlier in the week, he'd gone for his annual check-up. His blood pressure was sky-high, stroke level off the charts. The doctor gave him an ultimatum—lose weight or else. No ifs, ands, or buts. He warned my husband to go straight to the hospital if he felt tingling in his arm or tightening in his chest.

The next morning, my pork sausage, biscuits and gravy man fixed himself a bowl of Special K with skim milk. At first, I was elated he'd decided to change his ways. He even helped plan low-fat nutritious meals. We switched to grilled foods, whole-wheat spaghetti, and pita bread. Dessert was a no-no.

Pounds melted off him—not me. He lost five, then ten, then twenty. Soon he needed a smaller pant size and complained his belt was too big. Friends and family commented on his weight loss. I was happy for him, of course. But come on, I'd been exercising and eating healthy for years. Why hadn't the scale rewarded me?

The final straw came one day when I caught him standing with the refrigerator door open muttering about the yogurt I'd purchased. "What's the matter?" I asked.

He shook his head and turned to me. "Honey, this brand has nineteen grams of carbohydrates."

Puhleease! There's nothing worse than a rehabilitated junk food junkie. I kept my mouth shut until it was time to restock the pantry.

In a soft, innocent voice, I asked, "Sweetie, would you mind doing the shopping from now on? I'm not sure what foods will work for you."

He surprised me by asking, "Why don't we both go?"

As long as I'd known him, the man had never set foot inside a grocery store. We each grabbed a cart and parted ways with our separate lists. Ten minutes later, I rounded an aisle and stopped in my tracks. There stood my husband reading the nutrition label on the back of a package. I couldn't stop snickering.

Sheepishly, he looked up and grinned. "What?"

The next evening, I didn't feel like cooking so I suggested dining out. But no matter what restaurant I chose it wasn't on his diet. It took all I had to refrain from pointing out the numerous times he'd sabotaged my weight loss plan—tempting me with a deluxe pizza or an ice-cold Bud on draft. Never mind the warm Krispy Kremes.

Fast food was out. By the time he made a decision, my stomach growled loudly. My husband ordered first. Naturally, he chose baked chicken, steamed broccoli and mixed vegetables.

My turn. It's true there's nothing quite as sweet as revenge. His eyes opened wide when I ordered a deluxe double cheeseburger with the works. So what if the scale climbed higher the next day? It was worth every calorie-laden morsel to watch his reaction.

When the waitress turned to leave, I added, "and I'll have fries with that."

~Alice Muschany

"French fries on a salad? I guess we could do that. Should I see if we can throw some ice cream on there, too?"

# The Taste of Joy

*Our wedding was many years ago. The celebration continues to this day.*
*~Gene Perret*

I was seventeen years old when my young soldier and I eloped at the end of World War II. It didn't take long for him to discover that my culinary skills were extremely limited and for me to find that his food choices were even more so. To complicate the problem, I had to prepare our meals on a three-burner hotplate.

In our little basement kitchen with the hotplate, sink, freestanding cupboard and table with two chairs, I struggled unsuccessfully to find recipes that appealed to him. Anxious to please him, and beginning to feel like a failure, I tried to find something he would eat. "I can make macaroni and cheese. Would you like that?"

He shook his head and said, "No. I don't like any kind of pasta."

Still hopeful, I told him, "I found what looks like an easy recipe for Spanish rice. Shall I try it?"

He pulled me onto his lap and kissed me soundly before he replied, "I don't like rice, but I want you to quit worrying about it. Just fix me a couple of fried eggs. I can always eat eggs." Almost as an afterthought he added, "I like them with the yolk soft and the white firm."

This wasn't good news to me as the egg and I weren't on friendly terms. I couldn't turn one without the yellow seeping out all over the pan. "How about scrambled?" I hopefully asked.

He shook his head before he said, "Honey, I didn't marry you because I wanted a cook. I fell in love with you the first time I saw you, and I could eat eggs every day if it meant being able to spend the rest of my life with you."

Though the prospect of eggs every day didn't appeal to me, to make this man I loved happy, I would try anything. I enlisted the help of our landlady to work with me until I could flip an egg like an experienced cook. I couldn't have been more proud if I had produced a Monet.

Then my mother, who had listened to my cooking woes, came to my rescue with a shower gift of a shiny new sandwich grill. Tired of fried eggs, I was anxious to introduce a new treat to our limited menu. Even with my scant ability, I was able to slather butter on two slices of bread, place a thick slice of cheese and a pimento between the slices, slide it onto the grill, close the lid and in a few minutes gaze at my golden creation. When I offered him the grilled sandwich, a string of melted cheese oozed from the side. As he took the first bite, his eyes popped open and a look of pure pleasure crossed my young groom's face. Success at last!

Many things changed over the sixty years from those days in our little basement kitchen. We moved into a house with a fully function-ing kitchen. I learned to cook and the kitchen was soon filled with the aroma of foods that tempted his palate. We raised a family, became grandparents, and both had interesting careers. One thing that never changed, though, was our love and caring for each other.

Then, illness struck my husband, and we were told by the hos-pice doctor and nurses that, at this stage of his life, he was no longer able to eat. I refused to accept that verdict. They didn't know or love him as I did. They saw him as a sick old man while I still saw him as the young man in our little basement kitchen. Since I wouldn't give up when we were young, I wasn't going to now. After several days of taking food to tempt him, though, and sadly having to take it home untouched, I was almost ready to admit defeat.

"One more try," I told the nurse one morning when I arrived in his room. "He loves fruit so I brought chilled peaches today." She wished me luck as she swished through the door. After she left, I sat beside his chair and spooned a little of the chilled peach juice into his mouth, and, as with the grilled cheese sandwich sixty years earlier, it was as if the flavor had exploded on his taste buds. As I looked on in awe, I saw that same look of pure joy spread across his face. He smiled and squeezed my hand. That precious, joyful moment was one of our last together.

Now while I am trying to adjust to life without him, the memory of that look of pleasure stays with me and comforts me. I will treasure it always.

~June Harman Betts

# Food and Love

## Comfort Food

*Worries go down better with soup.*

*~Jewish Proverb*

# Feeding the Heart

*The hunger for love is much more difficult to remove*
*than the hunger for bread.*
~Mother Teresa

I t reminded me of a scene from the movie *Oliver*, those two chubby little hands holding his bowl out in my direction. He never said, "More please," like Oliver, but his pleading eyes made his case in a language I clearly understood.

I had never seen anyone eat like this. It didn't matter what I put on the table; Monday Night Mystery Meal, Saturday Night Surprise or Mother's famous tacos—this kid could eat. Thoughts of juvenile diabetes and the accompanying ravenous appetite ran through my mind. But that didn't show up in the lab. I just sat back and watched him.

We adopted Kurtis when he was twenty-three months old. He came into our lives with a number of disabilities that resulted from being hit over the head with a chair, seated on hot stove burners, and dunked in scalding water. The results of the abuse were easily identifiable. Scars, braces and multiple types of therapy accompanied each type of abuse.

The signs of neglect were subtler. Kurtis was a gorgeous child. His golden hair and his caramel colored eyes set him apart. His face had been spared during the bursts of rage he had endured and the skin on his cheeks was as smooth as cream. After sitting down to a family meal, Kurtis would eat every crumb on his plate. He would hold his plate out in my direction. I would give him second helpings. He would again eat every morsel of food, after which he would once more hold his plate out. I would continue filling his plate until I had scraped the pots and pans clean. Even meals I threw together after a raid on the pantry were eaten with gusto. His father and I would not take second helpings so there would be more for him. When there was nothing left on his plate, we lifted him down from his highchair. He would cling to the edge of the table, pulling himself along on his disabled legs, picking up any small particles of food that might have dropped from our forks while eating.

I had no doubt that Kurtis had been hungry. Hunger had not left Kurtis with a visible scar. It had left him with a subconscious fear of not getting enough to eat—of never knowing whether there would be a next meal. He was eating to prepare himself for doing without. One more heartbreak to add to the tragic devastation that this innocent youngster had endured in his short life.

I silently vowed, "In this forever family, Kurtis will never miss a meal."

For months, Kurtis continued to consume food like he had a hollow leg. As we loved him with a consistency he had never known, he gradually gained confidence in his new family and realized there would always be another meal. He learned to trust us to provide for his needs. After a while, he began to reject any food that was white. He refused mashed potatoes, rice, vanilla ice cream, white frosting and whipped cream. Then the vegetables were pushed aside. No tomatoes, and certainly nothing green for Kurtis. He would only eat raw carrots. Our love had changed Kurtis from being the boy who ate everything to a finicky eater. When we had to implement a new rule, "everybody must eat something green every day," our best friends would serve green Jell-O. Good friends are such a blessing.

Eventually, Kurtis began eating like the rest of our family, with one exception. He shunned dessert. Even his own birthday cake did not appeal to him. His one sweet indulgence was pumpkin pie, and for many years we lit birthday candles fixed in the orange-brown spicy custard filling. I justified all the pumpkin pies as eating yellow vegetables.

Over time, Kurtis began to have favorite foods. Hungarian noodles, ham, eggs—cooked any way, but especially deviled—were all on his list of favorites. Kurtis's all time, number one favorite, to-die-for meal, what he wanted to eat if he was sick, disappointed, sad, discouraged, or to celebrate great accomplishments and special occasions, was macaroni and cheese. I tried to teach his independent living skills teacher to make this favorite dish so she could teach him to make it himself. She could never get the sauce to thicken.

Many years have passed since Kurtis was that little boy pathetically holding his dish out in my direction. His life has changed in many ways, but his love for my macaroni and cheese has not changed. We know each other very well, and I can tell when it is time. I pull my largest ovenproof dish from the cupboard, send my husband to pick Kurtis up and just sit back and watch as Kurtis enjoys, once again, the piping hot, creamy orange succulence of the macaroni and cheese only his loving mom can make. Greens are optional.

~Karen R. Hessen

# Boeuf Bourguignon

*For some moments in life there are no words.*
~David Seltzer, Willy Wonka and the Chocolate Factory

Tuna casserole. Spaghetti and meatballs. Pork chops with sautéed mushrooms, and classic fried chicken. Towards the end of my first pregnancy, my mother began to fill my freezer with all of these and more. Several times a week she would drop off a portion of their dinner from the night before, a foil container neatly labeled with the contents, the date, and reheating instructions. I was to keep these containers in our rapidly filling deep freeze until after the baby came.

"Why on earth do I need so much food?" I was astounded by the sheer volume of frozen dinners waiting to be consumed. "I'm just having a baby, you know. It's not like I'm getting a limb amputated."

To this my mother shook her head, obviously in possession of some knowledge that I wasn't privy to, and simply brought over more food. Though I really thought that she was going overboard, I kept on rearranging my freezer, knowing that each of these containers had been filled with love—even those with the spaghetti, which after twenty-seven years I still wasn't able to convince my mother I hated.

Two weeks before Julie, our baby girl, was due, the unthinkable happened. Sitting in a hospital bed after delivering a stillborn infant, the words on everyone's lips were, inevitably, "You have to eat."

I didn't want to eat. What was the point? Not to mention that the very smell of the food that was delivered on a plastic tray to my bedside made me ill, saturating the air as it did with scents that were full of life.

"Eat something. Even if you don't want to, you have to eat something." These words came from my doctor as we prepared to leave the hospital, to go home and try to make sense of our lives.

"Yeah, right." The frustration that I felt at everyone's insistence that I eat — in effect, that I go on living when I didn't want to — threatened to boil over.

The doc wasn't the only one. We arrived home to find a pantry stocked by a well-meaning aunt. Deli meat, crusty rolls, pickles and fresh fruit. Cookies and crackers, fancy cheeses and paté.

When someone dies, people bring food. That's just what they do, and my aunt was no different. But though I knew that all of this food had been provided with love, I still couldn't bring myself to eat anything.

The food just kept coming. Friends, neighbours, more relatives — everyone brought something. And truthfully, I preferred a potato chip encrusted casserole to a bouquet of flowers that would wither and die before my eyes. But still I couldn't force anything down my gullet.

Three days after we'd arrived home from the hospital, someone — I can't remember who — announced that it was dinnertime.

I could have cared less. I went upstairs for a bath, and spent an hour crying salty tears that evaporated in the steam.

But when I went back downstairs, wrapped in my husband's robe, I saw that my father-in-law had opened one of my mother's foil containers. It lay empty on the counter, a wine red residue staining its innards, and the cardboard lid soggy and discarded in the sink.

In a pot on the stove was my mother's boeuf bourguignon. A dish made with stew meat, baby potatoes, onions and red wine, it was far from my favourite thing to eat. In fact, it would probably have languished in the freezer for months, being pulled out for consumption only when there was nothing else left but spaghetti.

But something about the sight of that container on the counter changed things. As I smelled the tang of the meat and the wine, my stomach rumbled, protesting its nearly week long emptiness.

Still, I wasn't sure I could actually force anything in, or that if I did, it would stay down.

I filled a bowl mechanically anyway, and added one of the crusty buns that my aunt had purchased that lay in an open bag beside the stove.

Curling up next to my husband on the sofa, steaming bowl in hand, I took a bite. It was hot, and I could trace the path of the scalding liquid all the way down to my gut. But somehow, some way, that hot boeuf bourguignon began to thaw something inside of me. So I kept eating, lifting spoonful after spoonful to my mouth.

When I took the bowl back to the kitchen and saw that foil container, now empty, I began to cry again. This time, however, the tears were a little bit different, and at that moment I realized why my mother had been so diligent about filling those containers.

Though she hadn't anticipated the exact circumstances, she'd known that somewhere along the way I would need some help, some comfort and some love.

And though I'd initially been amused by her zealous efforts, had been annoyed by the food being heaped upon us by our nearest and dearest, I finally understood.

The food was her way of continuing to care for *her* baby. The food was love, and I wasn't alone.

~Lauren Murray

# Mammie's Meatloaf

*If God had intended us to follow recipes,*
*He wouldn't have given us grandmothers.*
~Linda Henley

My grandmother, Mammie, has lived alone for more than twenty-five years. But you wouldn't know it to look inside her fridge. On any given day, you might find several types of meat, two heads of cabbage, potatoes, carrots, and a few bricks of cheese. Usually, she has a specific meal in mind when she purchases these items.

"Why don't you and Craig come over for dinner?" she'll ask. "I've been making cabbage and a roast."

That's a hard meal to pass up. So if we aren't busy, we indulge.

"What did you do today, Mammie?" I'll call and ask her.

"Well, I washed a few loads of laundry and did some dishes. Oh, and I put on a pot of homemade vegetable soup. You want Craig to come by and pick some up for dinner?"

"Of course, that sounds great!" I say. And then I call Craig and ask him to stop at Mammie's. Sometimes he has already passed her town but there is no such thing as "driving out of the way" when it comes to her cooking.

Mammie cooks for all of us: her sisters, her four children and their spouses, her nine grandchildren and their spouses, and her three great-grandchildren. And though we sometimes joke that her house contains more food than a nuclear fallout shelter, we don't know what we would do without Mammie's meals. In fact, we all have our personal favorites.

Aunt Connie loves Mammie's sweet potatoes. They're peeled, sliced and fried in bacon grease and then topped with butter and sugar. Susie likes Mammie's homemade chicken rice soup. My uncle prefers Mammie's beef roast, seasoned to perfection and tender enough to cut with a fork. My cousins like Mammie's fried chicken and stewed potatoes. And my mom is a big fan of her cabbage and potatoes.

Each of us has a favorite "Mammie" food. And several times a year, she fixes our favorites and invites us over individually. I'm not quite sure how my favorite came to be. I don't remember the first time I ate it but I was probably very young. It's not something that I eat anywhere else; I certainly don't order it at restaurants. As a rule, I don't even eat that much meat.

Mammie's meatloaf is the exception to the rule. It is the most delicious food that has ever entered my mouth. Mammie starts with high-quality ground beef and adds in a mixture of breadcrumbs, onions, and tomato sauce. After it has cooked, she carefully tops it with homemade French fries. Then (this is the best part) she drizzles the fries with a gooey ketchup garnish.

Her meatloaf puts any gourmet meal to shame. Best served when fresh from the oven, the first bite is always soft and tender. The edges, a bit browner than the rest, have a hint of candied sugar. And the French fries, meant to accompany each bite, are just as good when eaten by themselves.

Mammie's meatloaf is consistently delicious—the same cannot always be said about foods from popular restaurant chains and grocery stores. Last July, Mammie called to ask me what I wanted for my birthday. That was an easy enough question to answer.

"I would like a meatloaf! Can I have one?" I begged like a little child.

"I think I can do that," Mammie said.

For my twenty-ninth birthday, my husband, my parents and I gathered around Mammie's table. We ate slice after slice of meatloaf and heaping helpings of cabbage and potatoes. Then, she gave me my own meatloaf to take home. I didn't want to share it with my husband, but I did. It was a fabulous birthday.

This year was the big one. I turned thirty.

"Let's go out for a nice dinner in Virginia Beach," my husband suggested.

"Yeah. This is a big birthday, honey. Don't you want something special?" my mom asked.

I did. I wanted Mammie's meatloaf. That would make it special.

Mammie went shopping for ground beef, potatoes, and a couple of heads of cabbage. And on the night of my birthday, we gathered at my parents' house for our meal. It was a scrumptious dinner.

Maybe if I had her recipe, I could explain it more precisely and its delectableness would be easier to share. But right now I don't have it. And I don't need it. That's because Mammie's meatloaf cannot be replicated. It wouldn't be nearly as good if it were made by anyone else.

I guess that's how most people feel about their favorite foods. The cooks, more so than the ingredients, make the dish special. Mammie's signature meatloaf is the most succulent food in the world. And as long as she feels like fixing it, that's what I want for my birthday.

~Melissa Face

# Magic Tuna Salad

*Friends can be said to "fall in like" with as profound a thud
as romantic partners fall in love.*
~Letty Cottin Pogrebin

"**Y**ou need an artist?"

I glanced up at the editor standing by my desk. "Huh?"

"You needed an artist right? For your February issue?"

I nodded. As the editor of a local children's magazine, I liked to feature interviews with local writers and artisans every month to inspire young readers. Every month, they grew harder and harder to find.

"Call this lady." He slid a scrap of paper across my desk. Adriel McGill. "Her son's an actor—he was in that college cult classic, you know the guy that thumps his throat? Anyway, she's known for her cards and work around town."

I picked up the piece of paper, already reaching for the phone.

"Oh, and call her Squeaky," he called as he returned to his desk. "Otherwise she'll think you're a telemarketer and hang up on you."

Open-mouthed, it took a moment for me to register the quiet voice on the other end of the receiver pressed to my ear. "Yes, is this Squeaky McGill? The artist?"

It was. Which is how one week later I was walking up a long black driveway flanked by thick magnolia trees and colorful rose-bushes. It was muggy and humid, drizzle turning my curls into frizz and plastering my shirt to my back. Ducking under the long arm of a lemon tree, I rang the doorbell, a photographer lingering behind me.

The door creaked open. A tiny woman with a cap of white hair and thick glasses peered up at me, a smile blooming across her face. "Miranda?"

"Mrs. McGill?" I greeted her.

"Call me Squeaky. Come in, come in," she said, ushering us inside as the door swung open. "Have some tea and lemon cookies. Let's chat."

Now normally, when I did interviews, I got straight down to business. Who, what, where, when, why. I had a schedule, a strict rule. In and out in two hours max—there were always more interviews to do, more stories to write.

I stayed at Mrs. McGill's all morning. Time simply crept by, lost to hours of examining her whimsical paintings and listening to her charming tales. Soon, my pen dangled uselessly from my fingers as I sat spellbound, my photographer holding his camera in his lap. We were drawn in by her stories, lost in tales of her past. The tea was gone, the lemon cookies reduced to crumbs.

Finally, I stood and said we had to get back to the office. Taking my hands, she looked up at me. "Will you come back and see me? Come for lunch sometime?"

"I will," I promised, squeezing her withered hands. And two weeks later, I did. I offered to bring something, but she dismissed me with the same laugh as before. "I'll make tuna salad," she said. "No worries."

I took her a loaf of banana bread anyway, which she accepted with the joy of a queen getting her first tiara. And there, as the spring sun shone down on her lush backyard garden, we ate tuna salad and fruit salad with potato chips, chatting for almost three hours.

"I feel like such a pig," I confessed with a laugh, going for my third helping. "I've never had tuna salad before."

"You haven't?" she asked, surprised. "I love tuna salad. It's so healthy, so easy."

"I'd love the recipe," I said, taking another bite.

"Oh, it's easy." She smiled, magic curling across her cheeks. "Just tuna, relish, mayo and celery. A few peas and pickles, a hardboiled egg. It's how my mother made it."

"It's delicious," I said, patting my straining stomach. "I love it."

"Then I'll make it for you when you come again," she said, placing her hand over mine. "You will come again, won't you?"

"Of course." I smiled. "You couldn't keep me away."

And for three years, every month since that first dreary day that we met, I walk up that long driveway under the magnolia and lemon trees. I ring the doorbell and she opens the door, beaming up at me as I hand her another loaf of banana bread.

On the table waits the tuna and fruit salad, with a bowl of potato chips. Sometimes there's a small piece of bread with melted cheddar, sometimes there's pimento cheese or cucumber salad.

Plenty of times I've tried to recreate the dishes I inhale at her home, but it's never the same. There's a magic to the tuna salad, a delicious taste that can't be replicated in my own kitchen. Without Mrs. McGill and her stories, tuna salad isn't the same.

Once a month, I drive across town for not only the best tuna salad I've ever had, but the best conversation with the best person I've ever met.

~Miranda Pike Koerner

# Life, Remodeled

*It takes a long time to grow an old friend.*
~John Leonard

I made the first phone calls in July, attempting to reunite five old friends for dinner. We had been close during our somewhat carefree and unfettered young adulthood. Now in our sixties, we were balancing medical dilemmas and late career issues with grandparenting duties and other long-awaited pleasures. Finding common availability was a challenge. I functioned like a general contractor trying to coordinate the plumber, electrician, carpenter, and painter to arrive in perfect sequence. We finally set a date for the second Saturday in October. It was worth the effort—these are memory-rich relationships. It was also worth the wait—I hadn't spent an entire evening with these folks in over twenty-five years. A lot had changed.

Though I don't see these friends often, I nurture an emotional connection with them. We met in our early twenties, married from the same small pool, and remained close through our children's grade school years. But circumstance pushed us in different directions, and we found fewer and fewer opportunities to be together.

With a date on the calendar at last, eager to begin planning our dinner I leafed through recipes to determine a menu. The meal had to be luscious, healthy, and uncomplicated to prepare and serve. Mike and I did not want to spend most of the evening in aprons, conversing with our guests while juggling whisks and wooden spoons. I polled a trio of girlfriends for ideas.

"Pork roast," recommended one. "Just be really careful not to overcook it," she said.

"Red potatoes," said another, "basted in a blend of lemon juice and rosemary garlic butter every fifteen minutes while they bake, then sprinkled with lemon zest just before they're done. But watch out," she cautioned. "It's easy to forget to add that grated lemon peel while you're visiting with your company."

"A baked root vegetable dish is great this time of year," suggested the third. "And it can be slid into the oven and almost ignored. And oh, hot garlic bread would be perfect."

How big do these people think my oven is?

Finally, I came up with a menu Mike and I could manage and still feel like we'd be part of the party and not a catering team. A salad of romaine lettuce, apple slices, dried cranberries, and Gorgonzola tossed with lime-cumin dressing. A warm loaf of ciabatta. Chicken breasts marinated in seasoned buttermilk and baked in a toasted sesame seed and breadcrumb crust. Orzo cooked in buttery chicken broth. Steamed green beans tossed with olive oil and chopped cashews. And for dessert, pumpkin pie custard topped with a crust of rich buttered crumbs and finished with whipped cream.

Some years back, these friends had spent so much time in my house they could have navigated the main floor blindfolded. But time passed quicker than the shelf life of a cream puff, and suddenly they hadn't been over for decades. So the weekend before our party, Mike and I cleaned from basement to attic in case they asked for a tour of the house's updates or just a hike down memory lane. I wanted to be prepared for whatever the evening would serve us.

Since their last visit the kitchen had been remodeled, and the only feature they'd recognize would be the curve of window seats and the round table they had routinely crowded around in years past. I hoped they'd like the bright whiteness of the room, and feel warmed by the golden oak floor. Room by room, contemporary furniture situated on luminous hardwood replaced what they'd known.

I converted to the Tao of minimalism fifteen years ago, and tossed out the tchotchkes with which they were familiar. Gone were the trappings of raising children. Would they miss the comfort of that "lived in" look?

Outside, a graceful river birch thrived where the old maple lived and died, and we had recently planted a crab apple to shade the front door. The mature arborvitae trees that bookended the house had grown gangly and Mike removed them a few years ago. Recently added dormers perched on the roof might disorient our visitors if the landscaping didn't. I reminded myself to have the front light fixed so our guests could read our address if they were thrown off by the unfamiliar. A lot of the recognizable features of the house were gone, both inside and out, but I anticipated approval by these venerable comrades.

The most significant update my friends would notice was that I had installed a new husband. This would not surprise them, since they'd all met Mike briefly at the occasional wedding, funeral, or chance encounter at the movies. But none of them actually knew him.

They'd soon observe that he was quite different from my former spouse. Two of them went to college with Husband Number One and still join him for a few rounds of golf every summer.

October tenth arrived. Candles were lit and the food almost ready when we opened the front door to our visitors. Roasting chicken seasoned with rosemary and thyme scented the air. The windows were fogged by steam from simmering green beans and pasta. Our guests squeezed into the window seats around the kitchen table just as they used to, while Mike tossed salad at the counter. As I darted between the microwave, refrigerator, and stove, I enjoyed hearing his laughter blend into the happy cacophony of long-familiar voices.

We filled our salad plates and moved into the dining room. The conversation jumped from nostalgia to hilarious nonsense to contemplation, and never lagged. My friends regaled Mike with adventures from the past that cast me in a far more charming light than I remember. We toasted the past and hailed the future.

Near midnight, we pushed ourselves out from the table and rose on stiffened legs. We reveled in a prolonged ritual of fond kisses and lingering hugs mingled with laughter. Our company trooped out and Mike closed the front door.

"I had fun getting to know your buddies," he said. I grinned and gave him a kiss.

"Thanks for being you," I replied, satisfied with the simplicity of the compliment. After we loaded and started the dishwasher we then climbed the stairs, leaving that humming and whirring beast alone in the dark to do its dirty work. I felt half exhilarated, half exhausted.

Once we snuggled into bed, Mike chortled and teased about the fresh rendering he'd seen of me in my younger years. After he dozed off I lay still and happy, reflecting. My friends had seen my current reality. They saw the changes I'd made to my house and to my life over these past few decades. Lots of bricks were shuffled around. Some were removed. I knew they liked my modifications, great and small, and that they still liked me.

I breathed in the same air my husband exhaled. Content, I closed my eyes under the protective roof of this sound home.

~Beverly A. Golberg

# A Taste of the Past

*Animals are my friends... and I don't eat my friends.*
*~George Bernard Shaw*

Occasionally, I yearn to indulge in a "memory meal," biting into one of the nostalgic foods I adored as a child. As a lactose-intolerant Vegetarian-American, some of the most luscious, tasty treats, such as fried pork rinds, Mrs. Smith's Lemon Ice Box pies, and macaroni and cheese casserole are, alas, no longer options. Nibbling my way across an ear of corn is the closest I am ever going to get to gnawing blissfully on a juicy T-bone. Dabbing my spoon into fruit juice-sweetened frozen rice milk is my new ice cream binge.

But old cravings die hard. One day, after a particularly virtuous meal of locally grown organic broccoli, eggplant, onion and tomato, sautéed in organic virgin first cold pressed olive oil, and accented with organic brown rice, I found myself yearning for something toxic, fatty, crisp and crunchy, something that even back in my meat-eating and milk-drinking 1950s childhood people suspected simply couldn't be good for them—bacon.

Bacon came rarely into our household—but when it did, it was an event. I stood in the kitchen, watching my mother lay the lithesome lengths across the iron skillet. I watched the grease accumulate and bubble and I breathed in the pungent woody aroma that soon permeated every room. I was allowed to carefully pat the bacon free of grease. Then I waited eagerly for the four luscious porcine strips that would surround the obligatory egg. I ate the egg first. Then slowly, I took a bite of bacon, letting the crunchy meat lavish my tongue. I ate every morsel of the crisp strip and devoured every bit of the little fatty curl. I always wanted more and I always had to wait months before the next rasher entered our household.

I had not tasted bacon in years, but the moment I mentioned my craving, my partner Ron, who had also given up red meat and pork, began combing the grocery stores for the best "fake bacon." He brought home package after package of protein-textured strips, searching for the brand that could most nearly transport us back to the carefree eating of our childhoods.

But bringing home the bacon was only the first step. Ron then had to learn to cook the product just right, so it could evoke the crisp indulgence of the real thing. Putting the strips between paper towels in the microwave resulted in a desultory piece of vegetable protein that looked and tasted like, well, microwaved vegetable protein. The broiler produced a thin food the texture of cardboard with a smoky overlay. He laid it in a frying pan, without oil, and watched it grow warm but stay limp.

How could he cook that humble soy so it would resemble the heaven of our younger years? The answer came when Ron was sitting in one of his favorite diners, eating a fried fish sandwich and French fries: it was fat. He needed more fat.

The next morning, Ron found a large frying pan and laid the strips out one by one. He turned on a low flame and he added generous dollops of organic butter, our one exception to living dairy-free. Soon, each piece of bacon was surrounded by a bed of bubbling butter. The smell brought me to the kitchen and I watched as he lowered the heat, tenderly turning the bacon so it would brown evenly, cooking each piece until it had achieved the perfect crispness.

Ron laid out bread and piled on the bacon, adding tomatoes and slathering it all with mayonnaise. He presented the sandwich to me as if he were handing me a treasured old episode of the Ed Sullivan show.

I closed my eyes and took a big crunchy bite. The soy actually smelled and tasted like bacon. Ron and I sat next to each other at the table and reverently ate our sandwiches. I thought of my parents, both deceased. My mother was never a morning person, but she rose to the cooking occasion when bacon was on the menu. My father wanted to be a DJ but took a salesman's job so he could provide us with this occasional luxury. Ron and I shared our childhood bacon stories and I realized it didn't matter whether I was eating pork or soy: the memories themselves were just delicious.

~Deborah Shouse

# Battered Love

*I love being married. It's so great to find that one special person you want to annoy for the rest of your life.*

*~Rita Rudner*

"Buy this. Buy this." My husband hollered from the far end of the grocery aisle. In his arms he carried a huge blue bag of something. I couldn't tell what it was from a distance.

Since retiring, filling his day with a variety of activities turned out to be a challenge for Richard. That morning he'd decided we'd spend the day at the local warehouse club. He'd convinced me that I would get in my daily exercise by walking through and browsing the many products in the oversized store.

As Richard approached, I discovered he was carrying a plastic re-sealable ten-pound bag of buttermilk pancake mix.

"What the heck are you going to do with that?" I asked.

"What do you think I'm going to do with it? Make pancakes." He heaved it into the basket, narrowly missing the eggs.

I leaned into the cart to read the label on the back of the bag. "This makes 250 pancakes. Are you crazy?"

"Breakfast for nine cents a day. We're retired, remember?" was his retort. "I have to save us money any way I can."

"But that's enough for a Kiwanis Club all you can eat pancake breakfast. We'll never be able to eat all that," I replied.

Richard's eyes had that glazed over look that meant he wasn't listening to me at all. "That's not a bad idea. Maybe I'll get two bags. You love pancakes, don't you?"

I didn't answer. Actually I preferred a bowl of hot oatmeal for breakfast. I liked to stir in a big glob of creamy peanut butter and then top it off with my favorite, strawberries, kind of like a peanut butter and jelly sandwich. I'm a creature of habit and wasn't in any hurry to change my routine just to save a few pennies.

"It's only 140 calories for two pancakes. I'm saving you money and watching your weight." Richard raced off to the next aisle to see what other bargains he could find.

A few days later I spotted the big blue bag sitting on the kitchen counter. Without being told, I knew Richard's activity for today would involve cooking the cheap, low-calorie pancakes.

I watched him carefully measure out the mix. He slowly poured in the water as he stirred the batter with an oversized wire whisk. Dry pancake mix puffed out of the bowl with each dip of the utensil. Soon white powder coated his face and chest.

The batter sputtered as it hit the hot frying pan. When the pancakes began to bubble, Richard flipped them and they sputtered again. Stacks of golden brown circles began to form on plates sitting on the counter. As soon as one pancake made its way onto the cooling stack, more batter made its way into the pan.

"Do you have to make so many?" I asked.

"If I'm going to charge five dollars a plate, I need to practice." He grinned and winked.

Humming a tune, Richard settled into an easy rhythm of stirring, pouring and flipping. The piles of pancakes grew so tall they leaned to one side. I tried to resist when my mouth began to water as the aroma of breakfast filled the house. Maybe I would like this after all.

A few minutes later I heard the burners on the stove click off. I saw two boxes of Ziploc bags come out of the drawer.

"I need help," Richard called out. "Two pancakes in a small bag. Ten small bags in a big bag."

"Cooking pancakes is awfully messy. Do you really think it's worth it?" I curled up my nose in disgust at the sight of the dirty kitchen.

"You're going to love them, you wait and see," he said as I stuffed pancakes into a sandwich-sized bag. "It's all about the portion control. Only take out of the freezer what you need. Every morning, ready-made pancakes in a minute."

"How long will it take us to eat all these?" I asked.

"When we run out, I'll make some more. I still have half a bag of mix left."

I cringed. "You're enjoying this, aren't you?"

"I should have been a short order cook." He blew me a powdery kiss. "Just wait until you taste my pancakes."

Richard glowed from head to toe, not from the dust or the dots of creamy batter on his shirt, but from the inside out. I should have found the pride he displayed in his accomplishment and the freezer full of pancakes contagious. Except for the fact that I was hooked on my version of breakfast comfort food, not his.

With Richard occupied in the kitchen, the only thing I could think of was oatmeal. Oatmeal with peanut butter. Two minutes in the microwave, one dish to clean up, and a full stomach all morning. It was only a matter of time before pancakes encroached on my morning routine.

A few days later, I noticed that some ready-made pancakes had made their way to the refrigerator to thaw. Twenty pancakes. Breakfast for us both for a week.

"I'm making breakfast this morning," he announced. "Go read the paper."

Still in my nightgown, I curled up on the sofa. I woke up with my heart set on a high fat scoop of peanut butter swirled into my cholesterol-reducing oatmeal, my morning guilty pleasure. In a matter of minutes a warm plate of pancakes topped with syrup, butter and fresh strawberries found its way onto my lap.

Still skeptical I held the plate under my nose, breathing in. The food smelled divine. Then I smeared around the little dabs of butter with my fork, licking the utensil clean. I cut off a tiny piece of pancake and speared it along with a strawberry. Swirling the forkful in a pool of syrup I slowly raised it to my mouth.

I savored the sweetness of the hot golden circles. "Mmmm. This is delicious." The taste surprised me, sweet, creamy, sticky, kind of like my oatmeal only not so lumpy. "I think I could get used to this."

"We have a freezer full. You can have pancakes every day if you want," he replied.

I devoured every last morsel on the plate. "Is there more?" I asked holding my empty plate out for Richard to see. "I think you might have won me over."

Richard's eyes sparkled back at me. He put another pancake on my plate and placed it in the microwave. While it warmed up he reached into the cupboard and pulled out a canister of oatmeal.

"Can I throw this away?" He waved the box in my direction.

"What will I eat when we run out of pancakes?"

"Don't worry. We won't," he answered.

He set down the plate of seconds on the counter in front of me. As I took a bite, I knew we would never run out. Pancakes had made us both happy, satisfied, fulfilled, and indulged. Richard had won me over after all.

~Linda C. Wright

"Now I have to zip back to the warehouse club to pick up the syrup. They wouldn't fit in the car at the same time."

Reprinted by permission of
Marc Tyler Nobleman ©2011

# Love by the Spoonful

*Sharing is loving.*
~Author Unknown

I t was the day after a fabulous Thanksgiving, with almost all of our children, grandchildren and great-grandchildren in attendance. Several of the group lingered for the weekend.

On Friday, those who were interested in a taste of a rancher's life went to the pasture with Frank. Still, there were kids swarming like flies at the house.

I had to feed this tribe. We certainly didn't need nor want any more of the holiday delicacies. Thank God for freezers! I brought out a container with what I figured would be enough beef stew for our lunch. When this was thawed and heated, and the table was completely surrounded by kids and one grandma, we paused to thank God for our meal. I stood to serve bowls from the stove. One dish after another was handed out. When there was only one bowl left to fill—mine—my granddaughter Karen realized the kettle was empty. Immediately she took my dish and served me a big spoonful from her portion. She passed the dish to Kristen, and a scoop was added. By the time my bowl had gone around the table, everyone had a generous serving of beef stew, including me.

We had experienced a moment of family sharing—not just of beef stew, but bushel-sized bowls of love.

~Georgia Aker

# 39

# A Blast from the Past

*Pleasure is the flower that passes; remembrance, the lasting perfume.*
*~Jean de Boufflers*

Recently I went to lunch at a small neighborhood deli that serves a variety of sandwiches on healthy breads. On the counter at the cash register there was an assortment of not-so-healthy homemade cakes sectioned into thick squares, displayed in clear plastic containers with handwritten labels. My mouth watered at the sight of a chunk of carrot cake. I flirted with a chocolate-frosted wedge, but then my heart skipped a beat as I recognized a long-lost love. Memories flooded back from more than thirty years ago and I gave in to that scrumptious chunk of apple walnut cake. I devoured every tasty morsel, even the crumbs sticking to the plastic container.

I sat at a retro wooden table, similar to the one in my friend's old kitchen, to eat my lunch. Every forkful of that apple walnut cake resurrected happy memories of my late friend and our dearly departed mothers. Rose and I were best friends and next-door neighbors for ten years. We had the same warped sense of humor. We shared coffee and sweets, gossip and good news. We cried on one another's shoulders, complained about our spouses and shared child-rearing tips. We parented our parents too—like most women of that generation, we took care of everybody else's needs first.

When we had a little time to ourselves, we would sit in Rose's kitchen as she baked desserts that rivaled those sold at the neighborhood bakery. Her banana cream cake was spectacular and her brownies decadent. But the apple walnut cake, with its cinnamon goodness, had just the right combination of smooth, moist, coffee cake texture, crunchy nuts and fresh fruit. We decided it was a healthy dessert and nibbled on it for days, sliver by sliver, trying to make it last. It was one of our simple indulgences.

Rose and I chauffeured our moms to grocery stores and bingo halls, and we also took them on leisurely Sunday drives. One fall day, they invited us to accompany them on a day trip with the senior citizen group. An old-fashioned picnic with apple picking sounded like something we would enjoy, so we boarded the chartered bus along with our mothers and forty other senior citizens. Rose and I seated our moms up front and then sat across the aisle from one another further back. Bits and pieces of conversations floated our way. We overheard one word repeatedly—nurses. When several ladies stopped to ask what malady our moms suffered from, since obviously they needed their nurses along, we chuckled and explained our relationships.

At the picnic grounds, the seniors lined up to receive their boxed lunches. Rose and I darted to the restroom. As we were heading back, we both gasped at the sight of our moms. We realized that we were too far away to prevent the inevitable from occurring. We sprinted towards them but could only watch as they lifted one leg and then the other over the old-fashioned, wooden picnic bench and placed their open boxes on the table. Simultaneously they sat down. On the same side of the bench! One end of the small picnic table see-sawed up in the air as our moms flopped backwards onto the grassy ground. Their milk splashed them, their apples rolled down the hill and their ham sandwiches ended up in the dirt. By the time we reached our wide-eyed moms, lying flat on their backs with their feet in the air, flustered from the tumble, all we could do was laugh. We regained our composure and helped them up. We apologized for laughing and gave them our boxed lunches.

On the bus ride home, Rose and I couldn't look at each other without giggling. As a diversion, we counted the apples in our bags and we stared out the windows until one of us caught a glimpse of the other in the reflection. We tried to stifle chuckles and snorts, guffaws and snickers. We were a mess. We took our moms home, thanked them for a memorable day and made sure they were okay. Then we laughed all the way to Rose's kitchen. We peeled and chopped our newly picked apples and made another delicious apple walnut cake.

Over the years, there were many times Rose and I sat in her kitchen and shared tidbits of our lives as we devoured delicious home-baked goods. None was ever sweeter than that particular apple walnut coffee cake.

## Apple Walnut Coffee Cake

Beat together:
11/2 cups vegetable oil
2 cups granulated sugar
2 eggs

Sift together:
3 cups flour
1 teaspoon baking soda
2 teaspoons cinnamon (more to taste)
2 teaspoons vanilla

Mix all ingredients
Peel and dice 3 heaping cups apples
Fold in apples
Add 1 cup chopped walnuts

Bake at 350 degrees for 1 hour in greased and floured 9x13 pan.

Cool and dust with powdered sugar.

~Linda O'Connell

# 40

# Food Served with Love Tastes Best

*There is no greater loan than a sympathetic ear.*
~Frank Tyger

"Your mouth looks like chopped liver," the dentist said. "You have three cavities!"

No wonder I had such a toothache. I felt so ashamed. It must have been all those chocolate chip cookies I ate as my dinner. Most days I'd buy a box on my way home from work, along with a paperback mystery—my way of escaping into oblivion. At twenty-three, I was miserable, working at a job I hated, unhappily single while my two best friends were married.

In 1965, "nice girls" lived at home until they married. But the four-bedroom apartment in the Bronx where I lived with my parents was suffocating. It was the sixties, and times were changing. Young singles flocked to Manhattan to work and play.

"Everyone's moving to the city now!" I told my mother.

"So if everyone jumped off the Brooklyn Bridge, would you?" she asked.

I daydreamed about a glamorous life in the city. I'd go to folk concerts, throw wild parties, have fun! But when I actually moved into a studio apartment in Manhattan, my life often felt empty.

To pay the rent, I worked at a state agency, helping men on parole find jobs. Young and inexperienced, I was terrified by those rough guys who'd served time for armed robbery, murder and dealing drugs.

Weekends were daunting. At best there'd be a dinner date, but long stretches of empty time made me ache for someone to love. One evening at a dance, in the arms of a stranger, I feared I'd be alone forever, going to work, and then numbing myself with mystery novels and junk food. I couldn't bear to marry until I was in love, but how long would I have to wait?

When the phone rang, it was often my mother, worrying about me.

"Have you met anyone yet? Are you getting out to socialize? Did you hear that Harriet is engaged to a doctor?" Her barrage of questions made me feel like a total failure.

The worst blues hit on Sunday nights, when I pictured everyone else nesting with their loved ones. That's when I'd pick up the phone and call my Aunt Libby to see if she was home for a visit.

My mother's younger sister, Libby, had never married. Feisty and independent, she was the only woman in my family with a career. As secretary to New York's traffic commissioner, she rode to work in a limousine! Even without a husband or children, she seemed way happier than my mother. Watching her live with zest made me feel less anxious about being single.

On those Sunday nights, I walked down Lexington Avenue, past the florist with lilacs in the window, past the Mom and Pop stationery store, then down the steps to the dingy subway. As the train rumbled along, I daydreamed about seeing Aunt Libby again.

I pressed the bell to her apartment, she buzzed me into the building, and I could hardly wait for the elevator to take me to the fifth floor. There she stood at the end of the hall in the open doorway, beaming at me—a tall, zaftig woman with curly hair, her dark eyes shining with love.

When she enveloped me in a comforting hug, happiness flooded me. I inhaled the lemon scent of her cologne, absorbed her warmth, and knew everything in my life was going to be all right.

Inside the apartment, Libby settled on the loveseat, while I plopped down on the antique oak rocking chair with a blue Chinese rug at its feet. Healthy houseplants in brass pots and oak floors polished to a gleam made the apartment a welcoming home.

After a while, we entered the narrow kitchen where Libby made our tuna supper. It was simple, yet wonderful. Tuna mashed up with plenty of mayonnaise and diced onion. Juicy tomato wedges. Potato salad fixed with mayonnaise, grated carrots and celery. Some slices of soft challah—a braided egg bread with a glossy brown crust that tasted almost as sweet as cake.

As we ate, we talked about everyday things. Libby's friend Dora, who was fighting with her husband. My horrible boss, a skinny man with a beak for a nose, who ordered me to wear suits. My latest boyfriend, or lack of one.

"I don't know what you see in Gino," Libby said. "He's so coarse!"

She meant my Italian boyfriend, a printer with fingernails permanently stained with ink. He spoke like Marlon Brando in *On the Waterfront*. To me, he was tough and sexy, so exotic compared to the nice Jewish men I grew up with. Still, Libby's comment stopped me from considering him as "husband material."

What I remember most is our laughter; Libby laughing so hard tears ran down her cheeks, me laughing until I could hardly breathe. She got hysterical about the time I flushed her ring down the toilet when I was two years old.

"I still owe you a ring," I said.

"You're off the hook." She held out a gold ring she'd found on the street, a piece of good luck proving life was full of wonderful surprises. When she died she left it to me, along with her mother's diamond ring.

Tears of sorrow flooded Libby's eyes when told me how much she missed her mother. Libby was free with her joys and open with her sorrows. Everything between us flowed easily. In Libby's apartment I could be myself without worrying about what I said.

One night, as we sipped tea and nibbled on macaroons, I

confessed I was dropping out of my master's program in English Literature.

"I made such a mistake, wasting a year and all that money. I should finish, but I just don't want to!" I agonized.

"That's why they made erasers," Libby said, brushing away my regrets. What a relief! Libby made me see that mistakes were human. I could change my path and start over.

Just hearing her name still evokes a feeling of home. She's passed on, but her tuna suppers live on in my life, reminding me of her loving spirit. My husband Tom and I fix those suppers here in Portland on Sunday nights, in memory of Libby, and to share a quiet evening of our own.

Together we prepare the tuna. Tom mashes it until it has a flaky texture; I add mayonnaise and salty capers. Like Libby, I arrange tomato wedges along with some new touches: carrot sticks, green olives, sweet pickles, and celery stuffed with cheese.

"I love our Sunday night suppers," Tom said recently. We were snuggled up together on the couch, after a tuna supper, watching a movie.

"Yes, they're so comforting," I said.

When I fix food to share with someone I love, no matter how simple the meal, it feeds my soul. Tuna suppers have become a beloved ritual in our home, and I always feel thankful to Aunt Libby for that tradition, and for the comfort she gave me years ago.

~Barbara Blossom Ashmun

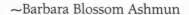

# 41

# A Mouthful of Meatloaf

*Sharing food with another human being is an intimate act*
*that should not be indulged in lightly.*
~M. F. K. Fisher

I often feel guilty when I recall Benjamin Franklin's quote: "One should eat to live, not live to eat." After all, it would seem to make sense to treat food as the fuel of life and nothing more.

Yet I have to admit that my life has been filled with instances where I put food first and was definitely living to eat. And I suspect that if Mr. Franklin, a noted gastronome and Francophile, had been completely honest, there were many occasions when he, too, would have agreed with this sentiment. Personally, I have a longstanding emotional relationship with what I eat.

The emotional value of food hit home fourteen years ago when my wife Cheryl faced a life-threatening crisis. We were novice parents of a one-and-a-half-year-old daughter Sarah and just emerging from the haze that is early child rearing.

Cheryl and I decided to take a midwinter weekend break and head to a lodge in the Laurentian Mountains of Quebec noted for its fine cross-country ski trails and its even finer food. But the break was not the restful getaway we had hoped for.

As we drove through a snowstorm on our way to the resort, Cheryl fell sick. At one point, we stopped and almost called off the trip but Cheryl seemed to recover and we carried on. Once we reached the resort, however, she felt worse and spent most of the weekend feeling nauseous and fatigued.

When we got home, Cheryl's symptoms worsened and she finally saw her doctor. He immediately sent her for tests and a colonoscopy. The shock of that test result was devastating. Cheryl was only thirty-eight but she had colon cancer.

Thanks to the quick and efficient efforts of her doctors and her surgeon, Cheryl's cancer was removed and she would make a full recovery. But once the operation was done and Cheryl's post-operative hospital stay was over, we had to cope with her at-home recovery. Since I had to go back to work, we temporarily hired a nanny to look after Sarah during the day while Cheryl rested in bed.

While I was at work, our helpful nanny not only looked after Sarah, she also cooked meals for us to enjoy. And on weekends, I exercised my dormant cooking skills to help feed the family.

Looking back, what I find notable is that almost all of the meals were basic comfort foods. The nanny prepared such simple and nourishing dishes as pot roast and chicken soup. And without thinking about it, I strayed from my usual limited cuisine and reverted to basic recipes from my childhood.

I started cooking meatloaf and casseroles and macaroni and cheese. Classic comfort foods that hearkened back to my family meals and, as it turned out, Cheryl's family meals, too.

It was as if I wanted to wrap Cheryl, Sarah and myself in the warmth and familiarity of simple meals, meals that would make us feel safe and whole again. The satisfaction of eating those meals was not just the physical satiety they produced but also the emotional warmth they provided.

By preparing comfort foods, I felt like I was comforting Cheryl and myself. We had both been traumatized by her illness and food was the salve that healed our wounds.

It wasn't long before Cheryl regained her strength and we reverted to our regular cuisine. But to this day, every once in a while, I'll make a dish from those post-cancer days. Because sometimes I just need a bit of comfort and a mouthful of meatloaf is often the best medicine.

~David Martin

Chapter
**5**

# Food and Love

## Little Helpers

*Even when freshly washed and relieved of all obvious confections,
children tend to be sticky.*

~Fran Lebowitz

# Along Came a Spider

*It's not easy being a mother. If it were easy, fathers would do it.*
*~From the television show* The Golden Girls

When my daughter Meredith (now twenty-one) started pre-K, it was exciting, frightening, and challenging. Allen and I were busy parents. I had a demanding public relations position that I loved. And now, we had a daughter in Ms. Mimi's Playschool. No problems occurred until the note came home with Meredith.

"The teacher said it's important," Meredith said.

My heart pounded as I read the one sentence note: "It's Meredith's turn to bring nutritious snacks and a beverage for Halloween."

I'd heard that moms rotated providing the snacks. But we'd received a big day, a holiday. Terror struck my heart. In our hectic lives, I had a hard time getting a decent meal on the table. "Mommy, help!" I wanted to scream.

But I was a big girl. I could handle pre-K snacks. So I attacked it like a work project. I scoured my recipe books for ideas. Cookie, candy and cupcake recipes tempted my taste buds.

But would a mother shout at me, "How dare you give my child candy?" Would the parents hunt me down and haunt our house? Worse yet, would our snack leave the students allergic... diabetic... or comatose?

"What about Little Debbie Cakes?" I asked her.

Meredith wrinkled her nose. "Ethan's mom made his snacks."

She described the horse-shaped Rice Krispies Treats with licorice reins and bushy tails.

Great. We don't just send a snack. We have to make them, and they have to pass the creativity test. I could feel the Ghosts of Halloween Past looking over my shoulder to make sure that we passed muster on our first major assignment: pre-K snacks.

And then it hit me. We had to make NUTRITIOUS snacks for Halloween. Wasn't that an oxymoron? Halloween was one day of the year that you could have treats. Would anyone eat greens or grains on Halloween?

"How difficult can it be?" Allen said. "It's just a snack."

By now my blood pressure was elevated. My rational brain whispered with an angelic voice: You can hold a press conference, write a grant, and design a brochure without thinking. You can do this. The red-tailed, forked tongue monster on my shoulder reminded me with a snicker: That doesn't matter here. You have trouble getting Meredith to eat healthy. How are you going to get fifteen students to eat anything nutritious, creative or not?

A new fear sneaked in. What if no one ate them? Would Meredith be ridiculed on the playground? We couldn't afford to slip into a nutritional nightmare.

I explained the dilemma to my mom on the phone.

"Ask Meredith what she likes," Mom advised. "That will tell you what her friends will eat."

So I sat down with Meredith for a serious discussion. After eliminating ice cream, chocolate treats, and anything from McDonald's, we settled on peanut butter, raisins and pretzels. Nothing exotic or creative, but it was a start.

By accident, I found the perfect treat with Meredith's ingredients when I flipped through a magazine. A bewitching eight-legged pretzel spider screamed creative, nutritious, and tasty from the glossy page. Peanut butter between two Ritz crackers held the eight pretzel legs. A dab of PB held the raisin eyes. I couldn't wait to get Meredith's reaction.

She gave it two thumbs up.

On the night before snack day, I planned to fix the pretzel spiders. So I grabbed the raisins, a box of Ritz crackers, and a jar of peanut butter.

Finally, I felt in control until I heard, "Can I make them?"

"No," I wanted to say to Meredith because I still had to make dinner... get her into the bath... and organize her Cinderella princess costume. But then I looked at her expectant face full of excitement and hope.

"Sure," I said. "Wash your hands."

During the preparation of the pretzel spiders, we talked, giggled, and made a memory that future Halloween experiences wouldn't diminish... and still managed to get everything done before bedtime.

The next morning, we arrived early. Meredith straightened her silver crown and smoothed the poufy blue skirt of her Cinderella dress. I took the tray and the bag of juice boxes from the car. The citrusy scent she'd deemed fit for a princess lingered. Her glittery shoes sparkled.

Immediately, costumed classmates leaned over the cellophane-covered tray. A cowboy said, "I want that one!" And then the all-important question surfaced. "Did you make them?"

Meredith beamed and nodded yes.

Ms. Mimi smiled.

Meredith said, "Mom let me put the peanut butter on the crackers... and I stuck on the legs and eyes." The crowd studied the snack. "Wow," a pirate said. "Your mom is so cool to let you make spiders."

"I know," she said, and her dark eyes sparkled.

In that moment, I realized that I'd passed a major test, and it had nothing to do with the nutritious snacks that had dominated my thoughts for weeks. Even then I realized that pretzel spiders would always occupy a special place in my heart. And a nutritious snack could hold its own with bags of candy, chocolate treats, and anything from McDonald's.

~Debra Ayers Brown

# Tough Love
# in the Kitchen

*Children have to be educated, but they have also to be left to
educate themselves.*
~Abbé Dimnet

"I'm staging a cooking strike," I said to my husband when he came through the door from work.

"The kids must be complaining again about all the 'yucky' food you've been cooking." He smiled wryly.

"That's exactly what's happened. Brian asked me to start making smooth 'white' applesauce like they serve at school. Holly wants me to start buying corn that comes in a can. The whole thing blew up for me today at lunch when our junior food critics said the pizza crust was a 'bit too done.' The only thing that's overdone in this house is me!" I lamented.

"Why don't you just tell them you cook to please me and not them?" he asked with a sigh.

"We've used that strategy before and it goes in one ear and out the other," I said. The kids' grousing had created needless mealtime disruptions turning what should be quality family time into a not-so-pleasant dinnertime discourse.

My husband could tell I'd made up my mind to address the problem head on. "You're right; a cooking strike might make them more appreciative of what it takes to prepare meals. So what's the plan and how are we going to implement it?"

Our family was fortunate that I was able to be a full-time stay-at-home mom who loved cooking and baking. We lived on a small farm in Washington State where we raised all our own meat and poultry. Every year we planted a huge vegetable garden, with adjoining blueberry and raspberry patches framed by apple and plum trees. The food was wholesome and plentiful.

My kids, just nine and eleven years old, didn't look at it quite the same way. Their continual fault finding sent a message that what I cooked for them was substandard. The truth was, they didn't know any different, as they'd grown up with nothing other than home cooking and baking made from quality ingredients.

That night, after a thoroughly scrutinized meal of parmesan meatloaf, mashed potatoes and fresh corn and peas from our garden, we told the kids we wanted to have a family discussion in the living room.

"First thing Saturday morning a cooking strike will begin in our house, which means you two are on your own for cooking and preparing all of your own meals," I explained to them.

"Why aren't you going to cook, Mom?" Brian asked.

"You two have been bellyaching about everything I cook for months on end, so it's time to see if you can do a better job for yourselves. You've had more than your share of warnings that I was going to take some action toward ending the complaining and this is it. We'll stock the pantry shelves and the refrigerator with foods you can eat cold, along with some homemade TV dinners for you to just pop into the microwave. Holly, you can manage easy things on the stove like toasted cheese or egg sandwiches and soup.

"The rules are easy: inform either me or Dad if you're going to use the stove; you eat what you cook; and all the dishes need to be cleaned up every time you use the kitchen," I instructed.

"Do you both understand what's going on here and why?" their dad asked.

"I guess so," Holly replied softly. "Dad, how long is the strike going to last?"

"We have to see how things go, but the length of the strike is your mother's call." She and her brother exchanged unsure glances.

The plan was in place and it couldn't have been more perfect!

The mood was light during the first week. The budding chefs weren't taking the strike seriously—it was still a game. I heard a lot of giggling and whispering coming from the kitchen. They teamed up to help each other learn more about using the microwave, and they were good sports about sharing the choice foods.

Grumbling began at the start of week two. I overheard Holly ask Brian if he wanted a fried bologna sandwich, to which he replied, "Oh, not another fried bologna sandwich!"

By the end of the second week there was moaning about having to eat the food they made. They expressed concern about their dwindling supply of provisions, particularly graham crackers and vanilla wafers.

In the first days of week three they started turning on the charm and began enlisting me to cross the picket line to teach them some cooking tips. They were silently hoping at any moment I'd surrender the cause by waving a white apron overhead and prepare a meal that none of us would ever forget. It didn't happen.

By the end of week three it was evident things were starting to fall apart for them. They were getting irritable and some serious bickering had begun. I surmised goodie withdrawal was playing a strong role in their cross dispositions as I hadn't baked their most-loved chocolate brownies or chocolate chip banana bread since the strike began.

Early into the fourth week I decided to test the waters by preparing a meal of grilled pork chops with chunky applesauce, steamed broccoli, garlic mashed potatoes and grilled corn-on-the-cob.

It had been a very long time since we enjoyed a meal so much.

Complaints from Brian and Holly were now replaced by lip smacking and the quiet savoring of a quality meal. Their dad and I hid our faces to cover the glow of parental triumph.

"That was a great supper! Thanks, Mom!" Both children bounced from their chairs when they were excused and dashed toward the sink to scrape, rinse and stack their plates. I even got a big hug from them as they were leaving the kitchen.

The kids understood that generous helpings of love and camaraderie are passed around a family dinner table. It just took some tough love for them to value the time and planning it takes in preparing meals, and to appreciate the challenges involved in pleasing everyone, not just one.

The cooking strike had served its purpose—the complaining came to a halt. The foods and meals I served thereafter received glowing reviews. And when they didn't like something, they were simply silent. They had learned!

~Cynthia Briggs

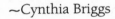

# Unforgettable Cookies

*The mothers of little boys work son-up to son-down.*
*~Author Unknown*

My eleven-year-old athlete, Kyle, slowly walked into the kitchen, scratching like a monkey. "I think I have poison ivy, Mom," he said with his head hanging low. It was miserable enough to be covered from head to toe in pink itchy blisters in mid-July, but what made it even worse was that his traveling basketball team was in their peak of summer activity with one of their largest tournaments just a day away. There wasn't much I could say. His sad face made it obvious that he was already aware that it would be impossible for him to play in the tournament that Saturday.

To some, not being able to play in a recreational basketball tournament might not be a big deal, but for Kyle, basketball is his life. Since he's been coordinated enough to dribble, he's been in love with the sport. He plays nearly year round, participating in school teams, traveling teams and a random tournament here and there.

So, what's a mom to do? My instructions to take an anti-itch oatmeal bath and then follow up with cotton balls and calamine lotion didn't seem to be cutting it. Then I had an idea. "Why don't I make some cookies?" There's nothing like some of Mom's homemade treats when you're having a bad day.

I grabbed my apron and my favorite cookie recipe book and began to hunt for just the right cookie. Nothing really grabbed me. I decided instead to try a new recipe and dedicate it to Kyle's poison ivy.

When the cookies came out of the oven, I put some on one of Kyle's favorite childhood plates. I took them to the living room where he was sprawled watching television and declared, "Kyle's Poison Ivy Cookies," as I presented them to him. "I crossed out the name of the recipe in the cookbook and wrote in 'Kyle's Poison Ivy Cookies' with today's date and a short paragraph about you being covered with poison ivy." His wide grin made me feel great.

Renaming cookie recipes has now become a tradition in our family. Whenever there's a need, we bake some cookies and write our memories in the same cookbook. We have "I'm Bored Cookies," our own rendition of Snickerdoodles, and "Celebrate Winter Break Cookies," a twist on the average sugar cookie. Whatever the occasion, we name a new cookie and we never fail to read through all the old ones too, reliving the memories we've baked up in years past.

~Stephanie Davenport

"My son knows I'll bake him cookies any time he's sick. What he doesn't know is that I know that half of the 'sicknesses' he claims to have are actually the names of STAR WARS characters."

Reprinted by permission of
Marc Tyler Nobleman ©2011

# Mom Knows Best

*A food is not necessarily essential just because your child hates it.*
*~Katharine Whitehorn*

"Mom, are we having hamburgers for lunch?" I walked into the kitchen where my mother stood at the stove stirring something in a skillet.

"Yes, in a way." She added some salt and pepper to the dish.

"What does 'in a way' mean?"

Her answer concerned me. At age six I liked the same old thing: meat and potatoes with an occasional, store-bought, canned green bean thrown in. My mother worked to expand my "Will Eat" list, but I remained vigilant to catch any new food items she might introduce.

"It means I'm trying something new and you'll like it." She drained the grease off the meat, went to the cabinet and pulled out a can of soup: another bad sign.

"Soup? Why would you add soup? I hate soup." I watched as she opened the can and poured the contents into the browned hamburger.

I picked up the empty can and read the label. "Mom, what's chicken gumbo?" The name sounded unusual and dangerous.

She continued to stir the ingredients. "It's a kind of soup they serve in New Orleans. It's French... and you like chicken."

It was true. I loved chicken: fried with mashed potatoes, no gravy.

The exoticness of New Orleans and France appealed to me too.

I had always wanted to visit both places. Maybe chicken gumbo wouldn't be all that bad.

I pointed at the skillet. "What's that white stuff?"

"Rice."

"I hate rice."

"You've never ever had rice, so how can you hate it?"

True, I'd never eaten rice, but that didn't stop me from hating it.

Before I could say another word, Mom added, "Rice is to the Chinese what potatoes are to us. You like potatoes. You'll like rice."

As I thought about that response, my mother added a couple of tablespoons of ketchup to the skillet and stirred.

I loved ketchup. It was the only extra thing I put on hot dogs and hamburgers. Maybe a little would make the dish edible.

"Is it done?"

"Almost. Now go get your father so we can have lunch."

When I returned to the table I found a toasted slice of bread sitting on a plate at my placemat. My mother ladled the meat mixture on top. She said the prayer before we ate. At the "Amen," I scooped up a tiny sample with my fork and stuck it in my mouth, ready to make ugly faces if I hated it, but it tasted great in a new way.

"What's this called?" I asked.

"Hamburger Splatter."

We all laughed. After the first taste, I added it to the list of foods I would eat. Over time Hamburger Splatter became a comfort food for me.

● ● ●

Several years and many helpings later, I asked Mom to make some for lunch when it was just the two of us. I sat at the kitchen table and watched her prepare the dish. After she added the ketchup I put the bread in the toaster because I knew that was the last step before she served the meal. I turned to ask her a question and saw her spoon a couple of tablespoons of yellow mustard into the skillet.

"Mom, you'll ruin it with that mustard. I hate mustard. I won't eat it."

My mother turned to me with a big smile on her face. "I've always made it this way."

Shocked, I said, "I never saw the mustard."

She laughed. "That's because, in the past, I sent you out of the kitchen to do something while I added it and stirred quickly. I knew you'd throw a fit."

These days when I need a little comfort and a bit of home, I make Hamburger Splatter. When the time comes to add the yellow mustard, I laugh. I still hate the stuff, but I scoop two tablespoons into the mixture and think of my mother who knew what to do when the hamburger hit the pan.

# Hamburger Splatter

1 pound lean ground beef
1 10 3/4 oz. can of Chicken Gumbo soup
1/2 cup finely chopped, yellow onion (optional: not in Mom's original recipe, but I like the added flavor)
2 tablespoons cooking oil
1/2 cup prepared yellow mustard
1/2 cup catsup
Salt and Pepper to taste
One slice of toast per serving.

In a non-stick skillet, heat the cooking oil and sauté the (optional) chopped onions until soft. Add the pound of ground beef and brown. Drain the oil and fat off the meat.

Return the meat in the pan to the burner. Pour in the can of chicken gumbo soup and stir. Add the catsup and prepared yellow mustard. (If you have a child or adult who doesn't like mustard, send them out of the kitchen before adding the mustard.) Stir again. Let the mixture simmer for about 10 minutes.

Taste. Add salt and pepper as needed. This is also the time to add additional catsup or mustard if desired.

To serve, place a slice of the toasted bread on a plate and spoon the mixture over it.

Makes about 6 servings.

~Robert Chrisman

# Crazy for Cupcakes

*When you look at a cupcake, you've got to smile.*
*~Anne Byrn*

I t's birthday treat time. My daughter, about to turn six, requests cupcakes for her party. "Yellow cake with lots of white frosting," she pleads.

"Sure!" I agree, thankful she has chosen a simple treat. But my mind is already spinning with ways to make the cupcakes extra special. "Maybe we can add some gummy bears on top," I suggest. "Or even rainbow sprinkles."

Cupcakes have evolved from the plain frosted desserts of my childhood. These days, the little cakes are artistic masterpieces — complete with rose petals, candies, and gooey chocolate centers. Cupcakes have gone gourmet with cupcake bakeries like New York's Magnolia Bakery and L.A.'s Sprinkles Cupcakes drawing rave reviews for their innovative recipes. When Main Street Cupcakes opened in my hometown of Hudson, Ohio, my children were ecstatic.

"I want the one with chocolate chips!"

"Can I have the Oreo cupcake?"

Choosing a red velvet cupcake for myself (red velvet cake smothered in white buttercream frosting), I sat in the bakeshop and marveled at the menu.

"Standard Items" included such flavors as:

- Mimosa (moist champagne and orange cake covered in a champagne and orange buttercream)
- Pomegranate Punch (pomegranate cake made from fresh juices and a tropical punch buttercream)
- Cup of Java (classic chocolate cake mixed with espresso and topped with white buttercream frosting, sprinkled with cinnamon and topped with chocolate covered espresso beans).

There were cupcakes for all seasons, too:

- "The Beverage Collection" featured summer flavors like Pink Lemonade, Margarita, and Mojito.
- "The Fall Collection" offered warm spices like Carrot Cake, Apple Cider, and Banana Nut.
- "The Holiday Collection" came complete with Hot Cocoa, Candy Cane, and Eggnog cupcakes.

As I bit into the rich buttercream frosting piled into a tall peak atop my cake, I understood—the cupcake is comfort food, indulgent yet small enough to justify the caloric intake. Decorate it with candy, cookies and nuts, and a gourmet delicacy is born. Cupcakes are making a comeback. My niece, graduating from high school this year, plans to serve mortar board-shaped cupcakes at her party. The online blog "Hello, Cupcake!" posts recipes and contests for "cupcakers." Even children's author Laura Numeroff is into the act. Her book *If You Give a Cat a Cupcake* tells the tale of a feline who prefers sprinkles to plain frosting.

At $2.50 apiece, gourmet cupcakes are a rare indulgence for my family.

"Maybe we can make our own birthday treats," I suggest to my daughter.

Flipping through *Current Cupcakes for Kids*, I find the perfect idea for my teddy bear loving little girl. "These are teddy bears having a picnic," I explain, pointing out the graham cracker bears sitting under paper parasols atop green-frosted cupcakes. "I think we can make these for your party."

With the help of Betty Crocker, we bake and frost, tinting white icing a light green for "grass." We add colored sprinkles and paper umbrellas before arranging teddy grahams in various poses under the parasols. The result? Cute, somewhat lopsided desserts that are a delight to create and, of course, eat. The sweetest part? Spending a morning with a six-year-old, spreading frosting, love, and cherished memories.

Cupcake bakeries are certainly trendy, fun, and convenient. But in this fast-paced world, it's nice to occasionally remember the pleasures of home baking.

The cupcake is back, filling me with simple sweetness, bite after decadent bite.

~Stefanie Wass

# Dishes Can Wait

*You can learn many things from children.*
*How much patience you have, for instance.*
~Franklin P. Jones

The kitchen is a disaster. There is egg goo on the counter, flour on the floor, forks covered in batter everywhere, and a mountain of dishes that may just take the rest of the afternoon to clean up.

Rewind a little. It's a rainy, cold winter afternoon. The boys are playing in their rooms, so it's the perfect time to do some baking, just enjoying the quiet as I knead bread dough. I have all of the ingredients out on the counter, my bowl and measuring cups lined up ready to go, when there is the sound of shouting, tears, a door slam, followed by one of them calling, "Mom! He hurt me!" and footsteps running up the stairs.

I sigh.

My younger son is standing in front of me in tears. I go to hug him as my older son comes up too, ready to defend his position. All hope of some quiet time has disappeared, but I just don't feel like playing referee today.

"So, who wants to help me bake some bread?" I ask brightly, ignoring their indignant looks at not being able to tell me their tales of woe.

No takers.

"It's fun to bake bread because you get to punch it. Sometimes that can make you feel better when you are in a bad mood."

Still nothing.

"Bread is boring," Tristan finally admits.

"Okay, what would you like to make?" I ask, looking at my afternoon plan sitting on the counter, and wishing I could just get back to it.

"Chocolate!" Sawyer yells, breaking free of my embrace. "Chocolate!"

"Chocolate chip cookies!" Tristan agrees happily.

So we pull out the other ingredients that we need, find the secret recipe from the book in which I write our family favourites, and get to work.

On an afternoon when I was looking forward to doing my own thing, the hardest thing for me to do is to hand over the reins to the boys and let them do the work themselves. But as I watch Sawyer practice breaking eggs and Tristan reading on his own and patiently instructing his brother on how to measure brown sugar — "squish it down real hard!" — and see their excitement as they use the blender to grind oats, I know that there's nothing else I'd rather be doing.

As I said, the kitchen is a complete disaster. But peering through the mess are two happy faces — covered in chocolate, of course, but smiling ear to ear — and the mess, and their previous fight, is forgotten.

As we close the curtains against the damp gloom outside, we curl up together on the sofa, pull the blankets up, and dig into the big plate of cookies, fresh from the oven, baked with love and more than a dash of silliness.

The dishes can wait.

~Esme Mills

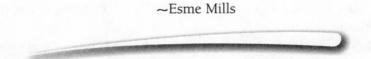

# One-Pot Favorites

*I have not failed. I've just found 10,000 ways that won't work.*
*~Thomas Edison*

I sure didn't buy it for the love of cooking. Meal planning and preparation were things I did more out of duty than pleasure. At the time, our daughters Christine and Mary were about nine and seven. They needed healthy, homemade meals, while I wanted them fast and easy. I was also in the throes of a mild addiction to televised home shopping.

So when I saw a "one-pot" cookbook offered on TV, I grabbed the phone and ordered one. The book had recipes for seemingly luscious meals with creative names that I was sure my family would love.

Three days later, the cookbook arrived. My supportive and consistently hungry husband, Frank, was enthusiastic that I give the recipes a try. Since his own father often worked the second shift, most of Frank's childhood meals came in the form of TV dinners.

"Mom, what's for dinner? I'm starving!" Christine, my older daughter, was right at my heels, practically climbing into the pot.

"Give me some space, here. I'm trying to cook this new recipe from that cookbook I bought on TV. Call your dad and sister, will you? It's almost ready."

"But what is it? And how can you buy a book from TV, anyway? There's no one to pay."

I caught the edge of disapproval in my daughter's questions. The girls weren't overly fond of my television shopping habit, especially when it interrupted their favorite cartoons.

"Since you're not calling them, I will. Come and get it!"

In waddled Mary, clutching "Bearie" to her chest.

"No stuffed animals at the table," I admonished. "Everybody wash their hands?"

"Yes," three voices responded.

"Good." Nearly preening with delight, I set a steaming casserole on the table. Three pairs of eyes stared at it.

"What have we here?" my husband asked. I noted his smile looked forced.

"A one pot favorite," I quipped, poking a soup ladle into its mushy center. "It's a layered macaroni casserole. Everything's in here. There's pasta and hamburger, vegetables and seasoning—all in one pot!

"But I don't like my food touching!" Mary squealed.

"Me either, Mom. You know that," Christine complained.

"When I was a kid, I didn't like my food to touch either, but it doesn't matter," Frank said.

I smiled, thinking of those compartmentalized TV dinners.

"It doesn't matter because it all goes to the same place, anyway," he continued.

"Ew, Daddy. Gross."

After spooning out portions onto everyone's plates, we began to eat. It might not have been the most appetizing-looking dish, but it tasted fine, though the elbows were a little overdone.

"There are so many good recipes," I enthused, my fork in mid-air.

"What kind, Mommy? Could you let us know before you try any more?" Mary asked, intent at the task at hand. She had succeeded in separating her peas, carrots, and elbows into tiny piles on her plate.

"How does Continental-style country ham and noodle casserole sound? You girls like ham."

"Ham's okay, but not continental country stuff," Christine said.

Ignoring them, I dipped in the ladle for another serving.

Later that night, taking out a bag of trash, I spotted something red and shiny in the garbage can. I plucked it out and charged angrily into the girls' bedroom, not caring if they were asleep.

"What's the meaning of this? I found my new cookbook in the garbage! You never throw a book away, especially not one of mine."

Under the covers, Mary's little voice squeaked. "We don't like one-pot favorites, Mommy."

Christine piped up. "You can keep the book. Just don't make anything from it. We like it when you use lots of pots."

"We're sorry," came the chorus.

I couldn't be mad, not when they looked nearly angelic lying there. Bending over to kiss them good night, their hair smelled of grass and spring air.

Now both girls are grown and on their own, strapped for time, just like me all those years ago. I often ask them what they're eating, hoping they're not living on cereal and pizza.

Christine's go-to dish is stir-fry, using chicken, vegetables and rice. Mary simmers vegetables and sauce, and then adds them to boiled pasta. How ironic—both dishes are made in one pot.

~Judy DeCarlo

"We 'misplaced' Mom's cookbook after her latest disaster, but I don't know what we were thinking. The alternative—her cooking without it—is much worse."

Reprinted by permission of
Marc Tyler Nobleman ©2011

# Worm Food

*Any man can be a father.*
*It takes someone special to be a dad.*
*~Author Unknown*

After an annual checkup for our very stubborn young daughter, the doctor told us he was concerned about her lack of weight gain. We told him the truth—that our daughter simply did not like to eat. No amount of coaxing, rewards, or punishment seemed to work. She nibbled at "kid" food, picked at "adult" food, and never ate for more than a moment or two at a time.

"What does she like?" the doctor asked.

"Butterfly crackers," my wife replied, startled by the doctor's concerned tone.

The doctor raised an eyebrow.

"They're shaped like butterflies," my wife explained. "She likes to eat the wings off them."

"If that's what it takes," the doctor suggested, "then be creative. But you've got to get her to eat."

My wife fought tears on the way home. She was a good mother; she did everything she was supposed to. But she couldn't fight our daughter's strong-willed resistance to food. I didn't know which I hated more—seeing my daughter underweight or seeing my wife berate herself. I resolved to solve both problems.

A secret my wife never knew about me was that, as a child, I was just as stubborn as our daughter when it came to eating. I refused to eat certain foods. I wanted to eat others all the time. Not only that, but I was allergic to a handful of foods, and to keep me away from them, my own father had to make up dozens of stories. Some prevented me from eating harmful foods. Others encouraged me to eat beneficial ones. Some of the stories were gruesome, involving the number of worms contained in ketchup. Others were funny, heart-wrenching, or appealing. Remembering them gave me an idea.

Dining on chicken and mashed potatoes one night, I watched our daughter stare at her plate with her chin in her fists.

"Please eat," my wife begged.

Our daughter answered only with a sigh. She looked at the food like its very presence would make her cry.

"I'll get the butterfly crackers," my wife conceded.

"Wait," I said. I took a straw from the cabinet. It was neon pink, and I flashed it around like a magic wand. I didn't say a word, and my silence only intrigued our daughter. I used the "wand" to tap the saltshaker, the pepper shaker, the plate of chicken, and finally my daughter's milk.

I took a sip from her glass. "Mmmmm," I hummed, halting the dance of my magic wand. "Now it tastes like rainbows!" Her eyes bulged as she took the cup from my hand and gulped.

"Doesn't it taste like rainbows?" I asked, winking at my wife.

She answered with a nod. Then she looked down at her plate to see what other wonders might happen.

"Now let me show you about worm food. It's a family secret, so you can't tell anyone."

Her face grew serious.

I stuck the straw into her potatoes and handed it to her. "Try it," I said.

But she wouldn't take it. I flattened the straw, expelling a line of mashed potatoes in a swirly pattern that looked just like a worm. "See?" I said. "Worm food!" I stuck the straw again into the mashed potatoes. This time, she took it. She slurped the potatoes and handed me the empty straw. I filled it again.

And again.

She was eating!

She learned to fill the straw herself, and she ate and ate and ate. It didn't stop with "worm food." For dessert we had "banana men," all three of us—bananas stuck upright in a dish with faces cut out and replaced with raisin eyes, chocolate chip noses, and licorice mouths.

She ate.

Over the next few days, we perfected our creativity. We made popcorn with butter dyed green or blue or red. We dyed cream of wheat pink and told her it came from fairies. I spelled out names and shapes with pancakes, rolled cold cuts into finger-sized rolls, and cut cheese slices with cookie cutters.

She ate.

At our follow-up visit to the doctor, he asked how we were able to bring her weight up to normal. "After all," he said, "your daughter seems very stubborn—strong-willed. How did you do it?"

My wife looked at me proudly as I answered. "It wasn't that hard," I said. "I have a little experience with stubbornness myself. All it takes is a little love. And besides," I said, "I had a little help from the worms."

~Scott Pelela

Chapter
**6**

# Food and Love

## In Memory of...

*We acquire the strength we have overcome.*

*~Ralph Waldo Emerson*

# Getting to Know Jennifer

*Tell me what you eat and I will tell what you are.*
~Jean Anthelme Brillat-Savarin

The dark blue vinyl notebook on the kitchen bookshelf looks ordinary enough. Glancing through the three-ring binder, I note the neatly printed white tabs labeling the categories—appetizers, vegetables, seafood, poultry, meats, desserts, miscellaneous. They are written in Jennifer's neat printing, in blue ballpoint pen; this book speaks of an organized mind. The opening pale yellow page is splattered with a splotch of oil, so it appears to be well used. Some of the recipes, like the ever-popular Caramelized Brie, have been photocopied from newspaper clippings, while others, like Mozzarella Crostini, have been typed out on white paper. The calorie counts and serving sizes are dutifully noted at the bottom of each. So, I can conclude that Jennifer was a woman who liked cheese and counted calories. These facts seem to be contradictory.

There are handwritten notes, in Jennifer's big loopy script, noting the origin (*Miami Herald*, Mom, Mrs. Guilford, Kathy) of each recipe. So Jennifer was apparently a woman who cared about the origin of things. Pockets on the sides of the binder are stuffed with a variety of assorted recipes, in no particular order. These, I assume, were not the tried and true recipes in the main section, but recipes to be experimented with at a later date. Some were torn out of magazines (Grilled

Lamb Chops from *Bon Appetit*), some handwritten on legal pad paper (Pasta Rustica) and some neatly cut off of packages (Indonesian Shrimp and Rice). Other recipes are from restaurants (Jalapeno Corn Bread) or grocery stores (Black Bean Chili) and some have handwritten notes attached.

"Jennifer, here is the recipe for the pound cake that I promised you. Also, one of my favorites—Banana Supreme. It's easy to make and delicious if you like bananas and nuts." Did Jennifer like bananas and nuts? I wonder. And there are Creole recipes (Red Beans and Rice), which I know she collected because her husband loved Creole food.

I know this because her husband is now my husband. Jennifer died at thirty-nine of lung cancer, leaving behind three young daughters and a grieving husband named Zeke.

When I first started dating Zeke, there were pictures of Jennifer—a striking brunette with chiseled features and heavy bangs—around his house, as well as her books and the ceramic cats she collected. According to Zeke, she loved reading, cats and, more than anything else, her daughters. A tax attorney who chose to stay at home after her second daughter was born, Jennifer truly loved being a mom. She was also smart, getting a perfect score on her SATs, something I could never hope to do in a million years.

But Zeke sold his house, I sold mine and we bought a new house that would be "ours." The books and ceramic cats have been packed away, so what I am left with are these recipes in this blue vinyl binder; this everyday item that links me to my stepdaughters' mother and to my husband's deceased wife. I am reluctant to throw away any of the recipes she collected. What if it was a family favorite?

So I ask my husband if he remembers eating Pacific Rim Glazed Flank Steak or Greek Pizza. He does not. "What about Mahogany Beef Stew or Horseradish Mashed Potatoes?" I inquire. He shrugs with an apologetic look.

"Did Jennifer have any specialties she liked to cook?" I ask him as we walk around the block of our new house.

"She did make a good tuna curry," he offers. I remember the

discussion of the curried tuna before. It was a recipe that Zeke first loved and then came to dread, as it made repeat appearances on a weekly basis. I look at the recipe: chopped onion, green pepper, butter, sour cream, curry powder and canned tuna, mixed together, baked and served over rice. I cannot in my wildest dreams imagine making this dish. Nor the one on the other side of the same sheet for African Chow Mein made with ground beef and rice. Yet, here's a recipe for Chili Cheese Soufflé that sounds interesting, and another for Mexican Chicken Strata that I have actually made many times. I wrote next to my recipe, clipped from the paper, "Everybody liked" in pencil. Of course, that was a different marriage, different husband, different life, and now with three little girls raised on pizza, pasta and chicken fingers, all bets are off with any recipe involving sourdough bread, black beans, and green chilies.

Looking at this collection of recipes, I feel an inexplicable sadness for the brief life of a woman I never even met. There's one for Bear Biscuits, complete with illustrations, on how to turn refrigerator biscuits, raisins and maraschino cherries into a smiling bear face.

I wonder if Jennifer ever got the chance to make these with her daughters. They were only four, five and eight when she died. Mamma G's Meatloaf was a recipe passed down from Zeke's mother. I imagine Jennifer as a young bride mixing together the pork, beef and veal with sage, parsley and eggs to make her husband's favorite dinner in the hope it would please him. I have made the same meatloaf (as a not-so-young bride) with the same hope in mind.

And here's a collection of recipes printed off the Internet from The Barefoot Contessa, which promise "scrumptious party platters sure to sate even the most grinch-hearted guest" for the holidays. The five pages are stapled together and include recipes for Sun Dried Tomato Dip and Grilled Lemon Chicken with Satay Sauce. I look at the date it was printed—11/30/00. This was a year after she was diagnosed with cancer, two years before she died. "So," I think, "she was still planning on having dinner parties and entertaining." In the face of chemo and cancer, I admire her optimism and zest for life. She gathered these recipes because she planned to live, love and cook, despite the unlikely odds.

"Her Poppy Seed Torte was good too," Zeke adds, while we walk. I know this recipe as well. Zeke and I have attempted to make it together on two occasions. Each time we have gotten stuck at the same place and have had to call Jennifer's mother in California for clarification. Each time she has laughingly obliged and talked us through the recipe. I have made a note of it for whenever the third attempt may be.

So, I will make the Bear Biscuits with Jennifer's girls, who are now mine, I will make Mamma G's meatloaf to serve my family when they are in need of comfort and I will try out the Grilled Lemon Chicken with Satay Sauce in hopes that it will sate a Grinch-hearted guest. I will carry on the legacy and cook the foods that Jennifer cannot, because this is what we do. We carry on in the face of uncertainty, we put one foot in front of the other even when it doesn't feel possible and we plan dinner parties for the future because it gives us hope and happiness. And then we eat.

~Gina Lee Guilford

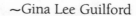

# Chicken and Dumplings

*Food, like a loving touch or a glimpse of divine power,*
*has that ability to comfort.*
~Norman Kolpas

When I came home from school on a crisp fall day, I knew that if the aroma of chicken and dumplings filled the air, little stood between culinary heaven and me. Even through adulthood, the mere thought of Mom fixing my favorite comfort food set my taste buds to salivating. So when I called her as I was on my way over to visit and she said we'd be having chicken and dumplings for dinner, I could hardly wait to get there.

Mom was finally settled into her new apartment. All the boxes were unpacked and new custom made drapes, an extravagance she still couldn't believe she owned, hung on the windows. Dad had been gone just over a year and she was moving on as best she could.

When I arrived, Mom was walking down the hallway on her way to the mailbox. I noticed she was a bit out of breath, but Mom's emphysema had been a part of our lives for so many years her labored breathing didn't faze me much.

"There you are!" she said, as I came through the lobby door. "I can hardly wait to get started."

"Get started? You mean supper isn't ready yet?"

"No. You're making supper tonight."

"Me? You said we were having chicken and dumplings."

"We are, and you're making it!"

"But Mom. I don't have a clue."

"Well it's high time you learned, darlin'."

I accompanied her to the mailbox and then we turned around and headed back to her apartment. As we walked down the hall I noticed her labored breathing yet again. As soon as we arrived, she plopped down in a kitchen chair panting just a bit and declared with a slight giggle, "It's official Annie, I'm... old."

"You've been saying that for the last ten years, Mom."

"Yes I know," she said. "But this time I said it's official." I looked over and caught her winking at me and we laughed.

Together we chopped the carrots, onion and celery, then added them along with a few bay leaves to the pot of chicken already simmering in a rich broth.

"What's next, Mom?"

"Oh now we just wait about an hour and then the fun starts!"

While we waited Mom and I shared a pot of tea and gabbed, catching up on family news and reminiscing about the past. She seemed so content and happy with her new surroundings, but I couldn't ignore the weary look in her eyes. My mom, always neat as a pin, looked run down and unkempt as she sat across from me. I thought getting used to her new life must have been taking its toll on her, but she'd fall into a comfortable routine soon enough.

When we'd finished our tea, Mom eyed the clock. She peeked into the stew pot and declared, with the confidence of a master chef, "It's time!"

In my opinion, Mom's dumplings belonged in the dumpling hall of fame. Her dumplings started out as drop biscuit dough. Then by the time they bobbed to the surface of the bubbling stew, some kind of "mom magic" transformed them into perfect puffy little tender pillows swimming in oodles of scrumptious chicken gravy.

Mom was right. I couldn't live another day of my life without learning how to do this. I watched intently as she thickened the broth with a bit of cornstarch mixed with cold water.

"Now pay attention here Annie. This isn't hard. The important thing is to mind the pot. If you undercook them you might as well play ping-pong with them. And if you overcook them, well there's really no way to explain a sin that grave." So I paid strict attention.

First, she whisked together the flour, baking powder, cream of tartar and a pinch each of salt and dried rosemary. Then she added melted butter and milk until the flower mixture was just moistened. The batter looked lumpy to me but Mom assured me that over-mixing only put you on the fast track to failure.

"Lumps in the batter spell success."

"If you say so, Mom. You're the expert."

Now that the batter was ready, Mom plucked two serving spoons from the dish rack and lifted a slightly heaping spoonful of dough out of the bowl. Then she used the other spoon to gently slide the dollop of dough into the bubbling gravy.

"Now you try it, Annie."

I scooped a spoonful of dough and hovered over the pot preparing to launch it, with Mom watching my every move.

"Gently Annie! Gently! You're not shooting pool you know. If that gravy splashes up on you, you won't soon forget it."

So I set about the task with a little more ease and a little less firing power until the dough bowl was empty.

Mom set the kitchen timer for fifteen minutes. Then just as we finished setting the table and tossing the salad, the kitchen timer chimed. With Mom by my side I lifted the heavy cast iron lid off the Dutch oven and peeked inside. There they were, those puffy little pillow masterpieces bobbing to and fro in a sea of piping hot chicken and gravy.

"Look at that, Annie. You're a pro already."

"Well, I can't take all the credit." I said. "I had a good teacher."

Mom looked at me with her soulful brown eyes and I noticed they were brimming with tears.

"Annie, that's the nicest thing you ever said to me."

"Wow, Mom! I've never come up with anything better than that in forty-four years?"

She wiped the tears from her cheeks with a laugh and admonished me. "Don't make fun of me. I'm your mother."

We dined in style that evening with lit candles and the new Glen Miller Orchestra CD I'd just surprised her with playing in the background.

As I was leaving the next day, Mom mentioned she'd scheduled a doctor's appointment for some time in the coming week. She said she didn't know if there was a remedy for getting old but though it might be a good idea to see if the doctor had anything on hand. I smiled and kissed her goodbye.

Three days after my cooking lesson Mom was diagnosed with lung cancer and lived only ninety-nine days from the date we found out.

Though she never let on, I know in my heart Mom planned that cooking lesson because she suspected her days were numbered. She wanted me to have a lasting memory that would forever bring a smile to my heart. I learned many lessons about grace and dignity as I walked the path of those last ninety-nine days with her. But then again, I had a good teacher.

# Chicken and Dumplings

Stew Ingredients:
2 1/2 pounds chicken thighs or legs without skin
5 cups chicken broth
3 bay leaves
1/2 teaspoon dried basil
1/4 teaspoon dried thyme
3 carrots, cut into 2-inch pieces
2 celery ribs, sliced
1 medium onion, cut into eighths
1 (10 oz.) package frozen peas
2 tablespoons of cornstarch
1/2 cup of cold water

Dumpling Ingredients:
2 cups all-purpose flour

1 tablespoon baking powder
1/2 teaspoon cream of tartar
1/4 teaspoon salt
1/2 cup butter
2/3 cup milk
1/2 teaspoon dried rosemary

Place chicken, broth and bay leaves in a 5-qt. Dutch oven. Cover and simmer over medium heat for 1 to 1-1/2 hours or until chicken is tender.

Remove chicken from broth; allow chicken to cool enough to be able to handle.

Remove chicken from the bones and cut into chunks. Then return it to the broth.

Add next eight ingredients. Cover and cook over medium heat for 15-20 minutes or until vegetables are tender.

Meanwhile, combine flour, baking powder, cream of tartar and salt in a bowl. Cut in butter until mixture resembles coarse crumbs. Stir in milk, dried rosemary, and parsley.

Thoroughly mix cornstarch with cold water and add it to the pot. Bring it to a boil until stew thickens just a bit (about 2 minutes) then turn heat back to simmer.

Drop dough by rounded tablespoonfuls into simmering stew. They will sink to the bottom. Cook covered for 15 minutes. As the dumplings cook they rise to the top. To make sure the dumplings are fully cooked, a toothpick inserted to the center should come out clean.

~Annmarie B. Tait

# Soup's Good

*When someone you love becomes a memory, the memory becomes a treasure.*
*~Author Unknown*

I cut the roots and leaf stems off six leeks and wash them well. I slice the white and light green parts of the stalks. Their onion-like scent permeates the kitchen. Soon onions will join them and carry their fragrance throughout the house.

I don't remember when I first made my version of potato leek soup based on a recipe from *Joy of Cooking*, but once I did, it became the most popular dish in our family's Easter tradition. "Did you make the soup?" was the first question everyone asked when they arrived to celebrate the holiday. I didn't dare stop making it.

I peel and slice a couple of large white onions. Tears sting my eyes. Chopping onions is a good way to grieve without being obvious. I add chunks of butter to a large stainless steel stockpot and turn on the burner. Returning to the cutting board, I continue chopping. The pile of vegetables grows. When I finish, I toss everything in with the sizzling butter.

No one loved my soup more than my husband's older brother Jo-Jo. The creamy flavor satisfied even the taste buds of this heavy smoker. He was always first in line when we served the soup and back for seconds soon after.

I wash and peel potatoes. After rinsing them again, I pat them dry with a paper towel. I stop and stir the butter-leek-onion sauté between slicing potatoes. The kitchen smells even better than before.

Even after Jo-Jo had surgery for throat cancer and ate via a feeding tube, he enjoyed the soup. He thinned it a bit to pump it into his stomach. "Soup's good," he told me, his eyes as bright as his smile. We talked about the books we were reading and favorite authors as I put the final touches on the holiday meal.

I add the potatoes to the pot and pour enough chicken stock in to cover everything. The soup needs to simmer until the potatoes are tender. I've dirtied several spatulas and dripped stock across the stove. The counters are covered with discarded damp towels, onion skins and potato peels. I am not a neat cook, but neatness doesn't count. Flavor does.

Jo-Jo and his wife invited the whole family for Thanksgiving. "He's not doing well," my husband Paul said.

"Let's make the soup and take it," I suggested.

A hint of a smile crossed Paul's face. "He'll like that."

We arrived at their home, carrying a large container and a chafing-dish. "We brought the soup," I said.

An echo went up around the dining room. "She made the soup." Jo-Jo hurried away from the football game playing on the TV and smiled. I handed him a small glass bowl filled with soup specially thinned for him that I'd kept warm.

A batch at a time, I puree the soup in my food processor. The blades whirl, transforming the potatoes and vegetables into a velvety concoction that I return to a clean stockpot. I season with white pepper and salt and then add the final touch right before serving, a pint of light cream.

Thanksgiving was the last time Jo-Jo enjoyed my soup. He passed in early December of that year.

I only make the soup for special occasions. Every time I prepare it, I pause and shed a few tears. I think fondly of Jo-Jo, remembering how much he loved it. I imagine he's watching my ritual with approval and telling me, "Soup's good."

When I call the family to dinner, I wonder if they hear Jo-Jo too, because before long, someone always shouts, "Soup's good."

~Elaine Togneri

# Whenever You Need Me

*Although it's difficult today to see beyond the sorrow,*
*May looking back in memory help comfort you tomorrow.*
~Author Unknown

When the phone rang at 6:45 that morning, moments after my husband left for work, I assumed it was him calling. I never expected to hear my sister-in-law's frantic voice telling me that my mother-in-law was dead—died in her sleep, an embolism most likely. My sister-in-law was a nurse and had words like "embolism" in her vocabulary; all I had was "dead." A combination of shock, grief, and dread washed over me.

Shock: I just talked to Mom the day before and offered to bring the kids for a sleepover. I knew she missed seeing them every day since I stopped working, which had resulted in her losing her job as their daycare provider. She had been elated when I called and had spent the rest of the day at the grocery store stocking up on sugary treats.

She was looking forward to seeing the kids; she couldn't be dead.

Grief: Once I stopped working, my mother-in-law and I finally had time to build our own special relationship. It was during those two years that we started doing things together, just me, her, and the kids. She had started teaching me to cook her Hungarian family recipes—the trade secrets to happiness and love. Mom was known for her cooking. For several decades, she alone prepared thousands of meals in their quaint family restaurant, each meal served with the same love she put into feeding her own family. Even after closing the restaurant to retire, she still spent her days in the kitchen. Cooking was what she loved to do because food gathered her family around her.

There was still so much I wanted to learn about her, questions to ask, stories to share, recipes for her to teach me; she couldn't be dead.

Dread: Picking up the phone, I tried to figure out how to tell my husband his mother had died. They were close and this was a moment I had pretended we would never have to face. Yet, here it was, without warning or illness to prepare us. I dialed his cell and it went to voicemail. He had a twenty-mile drive to work and was probably just arriving. I dialed the main office line and told them to have him call home.

"Come home now! It's your mom," I told him when he called moments later. I worried about him being too grief-stricken to drive safely and didn't say the rest until he walked through the door. By then, I didn't need to—he knew without being told. All that was left to discuss were the questions: How? Why now? What next?

"What next?" was the hardest question. We weren't prepared for this. Our first thought was taking care of Dad, who hadn't spent a day apart from his wife in fifty years, and who always said if she went he would go right afterward. Not "wanted to go," but "would go." Together, we rushed to the home that his parents and his sister shared, guessing that was the logical way to face the next step. Somewhere between the blur of hugging, consoling, the coroner's arrival, and going to the funeral home, we all decided my sister-in-law would focus on taking care of Dad, while my husband and I would host the wake at our house. Mom was the glue for not only the family but also for a network of Hungarian friends, not to mention loyal restaurant patrons who had grown to adore her over the years. We expected all of them to attend.

The next day flew by in a fog of things to take care of, people to contact, phone calls to return. People were coming from hundreds of miles to say goodbye. The outpouring of love was phenomenal. Yet, through it all, I was terrified of hosting the wake. I am a planner by nature, so hosting was not causing my distress. It was this event, an event to honor a person who meant so much to so many, and I wanted it to be perfect for her.

The morning of Mom's funeral, I woke before sunrise with a vice-like pressure on my chest, panicked that I was missing something. I wanted more than anything to make one of her recipes for the wake, something she would have made. I could only think of one thing, an appetizer-style cracker spread that she had made for every party and holiday since I'd met her. Along with heartier, complicated dishes — goulash, cabbage rolls, stuffed peppers — that took hours to make, she always brought this thick, creamy dip as a starter. No one asked if she was making it — we expected it.

I knew I needed to make this seemingly simple appetizer for the wake. The problem was, I couldn't even pronounce its vowel-laden Hungarian name, let alone guess how to make it. Whenever I had asked her to teach me this particular recipe, she always said, "Don't worry, darling. I'm happy to make it whenever you need it."

The sun was coming up. The house was quiet but my mind was reeling. I went to the kitchen and opened my cookbook cabinet, desperate for something, anything resembling a Hungarian dish I could prepare. Reaching for my standby cookbook, my eye caught the spine of an unfamiliar one. A thin paperback with yellowed pages and no pictures. I opened it and saw her handwriting inscribing the book to me with her love. It was dated one year earlier and I suddenly remembered the night she gave it to me: a gift after one of her many delicious meals that simply celebrated family togetherness. A thin sheet of notepaper stuck out between pages marking a traditional Hungarian pastry. Here she had written a note reminding me this was my husband's favorite Christmas treat.

My mind flashed to the evening she presented the book to me. The exchange was followed by a warm hug and a mutual understanding of the love being handed across generations. I proudly put the book in my collection, but as time passed and weeks blurred into months, I had forgotten about it until this moment. Tears welled in my eyes as I read and reread her inscription, her writing so fresh and alive.

As I began to turn the pages, I saw them all. Recipe after recipe of familiar Hungarian dishes. Then my eyes saw it. Somehow I read the name I couldn't pronounce — kőrőzőtt. The recipe I most wanted to make was right there.

I pulled ingredients from the fridge and seasonings from the cabinet. I usually follow recipes to the exact measure, doubting my own ability to blend flavors. However, as I began mixing the ingredients, an unfamiliar instinct took hold. I omitted, added, and changed quantities without hesitation. When my husband came downstairs, I nervously asked him to try it, knowing he was the ultimate critic. He tasted it, and with fresh tears in his eyes said, "It's perfect — exactly like Mom's."

And I knew she kept her promise — when I needed it, she made it.

## Kőrőzőtt

1 pkg (8 oz.) cream cheese, softened
1/2 cup butter, softened
3-4 tablespoons sour cream
3-4 tablespoons green onions, finely chopped, include greens
    for color
1 tablespoon yellow mustard
2-3 teaspoons Hungarian paprika (use high-quality, imported
    paprika for best results)
1-2 teaspoon ground caraway seed
1/2 teaspoon salt

Blend ingredients in a mixing bowl until smooth.

Spoon into a serving dish and shape.

Garnish with a dusting of paprika and sprig of parsley, if desired.

Chill and serve with crackers (Ritz-style crackers are preferable).

This is the base recipe. All ingredients can be adjusted to taste.

~Andrea Lehner

# Bread of Life

*Here is bread, which strengthens man's heart,*
*and therefore is called the staff of Life.*
~Matthew Henry

The hot, yeasty aroma of fresh baked bread floated out of the kitchen, wafted across the living room, entered the hall and lingered in the remotest corner of the house. The fragrance carried with it memories of times long ago when Frances herself had stood in the kitchen preparing meals for her growing family.

Today my friend Frances wasn't serving in the kitchen. She lay in a small bedroom at the end of the hall. Her frail body, all skin and bones, hardly made a dent in the soft mattress.

I had arrived at eight o'clock that morning, right on schedule, to care for my friend during the day while her husband Newell headed off to work. Both Newell and Frances knew that a deadly form of leukemia was attacking her body and that she was slowly losing the battle. With each passing week, her flesh became more translucent. Her wisps of hair thinned. Her strength diminished. The only thing that seemed to grow was the pile of blankets keeping her warm.

Our friendship had begun several months earlier when my church bulletin had announced that Newell needed help in caring for his wife. Newell continued to take the night shift, waking throughout the wee hours to care for his wife's needs, but other people, like myself, volunteered to cover the day shifts. Though I was a newlywed and had no nursing experience, I was willing to learn whatever was necessary for her care. Frances and I grew close over the ensuing months.

She slept much of the time. I would read my book quietly by her bed during those moments. When she woke, we would look at picture albums and talk about better times when she was raising her family. She shared her wisdom on being a wife and mother. Sometimes I sang old hymns to her. The tunes brought back other memories, and she mouthed the familiar words as I sang. When needed, I helped her transfer from the bed to her chamber pot. I used those brief moments to pull the sheets smooth and rearrange the blankets.

Around noon I would fix a light lunch for the two of us. Newell often had leftovers in the fridge, casseroles that other church friends had brought so he wouldn't have to cook. Other times I prepared a tasty soup that would supply warmth and nutrition at the same time. As the weeks went by, however, Frances ate less and less. She picked at a few crumbs, nibbled at a sandwich. Her disinterest in food made it hard for her to keep up her strength.

For this reason, today I had brought a grocery bag full of baking supplies. Taking off my cap, shaking the snowflakes from my coat and stamping my boots on the welcome mat, I called a greeting to Frances. Picking up my grocery bag, I made my way down the hall to her bedroom.

"Look what I brought," I said, settling the bag on the edge of her bed.

I took out flour, sugar, salt, oil and yeast. At the bottom of the sack were bread pans, a mixing bowl, measuring cups, wooden spoons and teaspoons. Frances's eyes brightened as she realized what I was doing. There by her bed, I poured warm water into the large bowl and dissolved the yeast. Just as my mother used to do with me when I first learned to cook, I encouraged Frances to dump in a cup of flour. I found an egg in the fridge and added it to the dough. I stirred, mixed, kneaded. Frances slept while the dough rose.

By lunchtime, the bread was in the oven. The crusty aroma of fresh hot bread wafted from the kitchen, all the way back to the bedroom. When the loaves came out of the oven and were cooling on the rack, I was ready to serve lunch. I asked Frances, "Would you like to sample a piece of the bread?"

When she nodded, I cut a thick hot slice and slathered it with fresh butter. To my surprise, she gobbled it down, a drop of melted butter sliding down her chin.

With the eagerness of a baby bird, she asked for more.

I cut a second large slice and coated it with butter. Again it disappeared down her throat.

"Would you like another piece?" I asked. "With jam this time?"

When she nodded, I smiled. This baby bird had rediscovered her appetite.

From that day on, I made bread often when I was caring for Frances. Without her being aware, I started slipping in extra ingredients. More eggs. Wheat germ. Powdered milk. Oatmeal. Each thick slice packed a meal's worth of nutrition into her fragile body.

Yes, Frances' body eventually weakened. The leukemia never loosened its grip. But in those final months, my love for Frances grew stronger even as her body grew weaker. And as I baked bread, read scripture and sang hymns to her, she in return taught me how to live, how to love and, at the end, how to die.

~Emily Parke Chase

# Tomato Soup
# from Heaven

*Only the pure in heart can make a good soup.*
*~Ludwig van Beethoven*

I heard the soft creek of our front door. From my upstairs bedroom, the sound was distant but distinct. I'd been in bed for over a month with herniated disks in my back, and I was lonely. I knew a visitor when I heard one.

"Baby Girl?" My grandfather's voice traveled up the stairwell. Same kind tone, same name he'd called me all my life, though I was now past the girlish stage. I was thirty-something and pregnant with my third son.

"Papo, come on up," I called. I tried to roll to my side, but even that was painful and difficult.

It seemed ages before Papo ducked his head through the doorframe. He pulled his hat from his head and held it in his worn hands. "How are you today, darlin'?"

"Same, same, same, Papo. Ready to do something different," I said.

"Are you hungry?" he asked.

"What did you bring?" I couldn't help but smile. And I was betting he had brought his homemade tomato soup. I could just imagine it, in a blue-handled Kemp's ice cream bucket, with the lid pressed on for secure travel. It was about thirty miles from my grandparents' door to my bedside.

"Why, I'll be," he said. "What makes you ask that?" Papo's grin now matched my own.

"Is there soup in the kitchen?" I asked.

"I'll bring some up," Papo said. He walked into the bedroom and bent, slowly, to kiss the top of my head. Then he disappeared. Out the door. Down the stairs. Into the kitchen to ladle some soup.

Papo's tomato soup had been a comfort food stitch in the fabric of my life. He was a gardener long before my grandmother's health failed and he became the cook. The tomatoes for his soup came plump and fresh from dark Mississippi River Valley soil. The weather could be too dry, too wet. The blight would hit and even sturdy tomato plants would spot and spoil, yet somehow Papo's plants would yield juicy tomatoes. He'd peel, cut, and cook the tomatoes and seal them in clear, shiny Mason jars. When we were sick or sad, in need of a hug or just plain hungry, the jars would be extracted, one by one, from the shelf in his basement. Then he'd pour them into his heavy, old stockpot. He'd add creamy cold milk, garlic, seasonings, a spot of butter and pinches of parsley and soda. The result would be thick and delicious, fresh and smooth, a slight red that filled the bowls and tummies with something warm and wonderful.

Papo usually served his soup with crisp, salty crackers, and he didn't skimp. He didn't let me down that afternoon, either. A few minutes later, Papo once again climbed the stairs, this time even more slowly than the first. I could see a steaming bowl balanced on a tray, crackers piled high on the side. I caught the garlicky aroma before he hit the bedroom, and my mouth watered.

"Papo," I said, "it was so kind of you to bring me this soup. It smells amazing." I tried to prop myself up enough to support the tray on my lap. The shooting pain was softened by Papo's response.

"Oh, darlin'. I wish I could do more," he said. His hands shook slightly as he placed the tray over my legs.

I reached out to embrace my grandfather. He once again leaned in, careful not to upset my lunch. "Can you stay?" I asked.

"Your grandmother's in the car," he said. "She just can't make it up the stairs today. But she said she loves you. And we'll be back, soon."

I could only imagine what he must've gone through, getting my poor, sweet grandmother to the car. Her legs had just about given out and traveling was a real sacrifice.

"I love you," I said.

"I love you, too, Baby Girl," Papo said. Then he squeezed my hands and once again left the way he came. I sat alone, on my bed, and slowly sipped spoonfuls of soup. When the bottom of the bowl peeked through, I tipped it forward to scoop every last drop. Funny as it sounds, the flavor was more than tomatoes and garlic and cream. To me, hurting and alone, the soup tasted like love.

A few months later, after a healthy delivery and a healed back, Papo called me to his kitchen. He wanted to teach me to make the soup. He'd instruct and I'd work under his watchful eye. Then I'd go home and try to make it for my family. The soup would scorch. The soda would turn the kettle to a pink, frothy mess. I'd get too much garlic and we'd pant for water like thirsty dogs. I just couldn't get it right. But my Papo was a patient man, and we kept trying, until one day I got it. I didn't understand it at the time, but those moments stooped over the stockpot were in preparation.

A few years later, I no longer have the blessing of learning in Papo's kitchen. And "How 'bout some soup, Baby Girl?" no longer travels up the stairwell, through the kitchen, from Papo's heart to mine. But those words echo in my memory, and they bring precious peace. When one of my five boys is hurting, sad, or just needs some extra loving, I pull the copper-bottom stockpot from the pantry shelf. I reach for tomatoes that I learned to "put up" for all seasons. I stir the ingredients together and get the recipe just right. And I remember my grandfather, dear sweet Papo, full of encouragement and love.

Then I sit at the table with my son and enjoy tomato soup from heaven.

## Papo's Tomato Soup

2 tablespoons butter
2 tablespoons flour

4 cups milk
1 quart home canned tomatoes (use crushed if using canned
    tomatoes purchased from store)
1/4 teaspoon baking soda
garlic powder, salt, pepper

Warm milk, in saucepan, over low/med heat. Add butter, stirring constantly. Sprinkle in flour.

Add baking soda to tomatoes.

While continuing to stir, add tomatoes to milk mixture (will froth a bit).

Season to taste with garlic powder, salt, pepper. Stir until creamy.

(Very important to work with low/med heat. Don't boil… soup will curdle.)

~Shawnelle Eliasen

Chicken Soup
for the Soul

# My Father's Famous
# Tuna Melt

*Sometimes the poorest man leaves his children the richest inheritance.*
~Ruth E. Renkel

I can still remember the smell of hot tuna fresh out of the oven. I could be all the way up in my bedroom on the third floor of our old Victorian-style house and the odor would snake its way around corners, up three flights of stairs and to my bed where it would hover over me, jolting me from a sound sleep. I would be nauseated, on the verge of retching, covering my face with my pillow, but I just couldn't escape the fact that my father was making one of his famous, much-beloved tuna melts. Fresh white albacore with just the right amount of mayo, topped with an expertly browned piece of melted cheddar on a slice of toasted seeded rye. It was simple, but according to experts, it was perfection.

My father was as proud of his culinary creation as he was of his son winning a Little League trophy. His tuna melt was legendary. Friends and neighbors found any excuse to drop by on the off chance he would offer to make them one. And of course, he would rarely disappoint their eager palates. Everyone loved my father's tuna melt. That is, everyone but me.

The truth is, I never tried one. Not even a bite. I was just a kid and my taste buds demanded the simpler things in life — pizza, burgers, hot dogs. They were not sophisticated or daring enough to take a chance on hot fish covered in cheese.

My father pleaded with me through the years to give it a try. "Trust me," he would say, "you'll love it. Have I ever let you down before?" Truth is, he hadn't. His love guided me through my childhood, making sure I never had to worry about a thing. He taught me how to throw a baseball, patiently walked me through homework and spent countless hours teaching me about the world. Like many boys, I idolized my father. To me, his word was gospel.

But when it came to tuna melts, I would not budge. It pained me to disappoint this man who gave me everything, when all he was asking of me was to take a bite and share in his joy.

One day, when I was fifteen, after years of prodding and pleading, I finally agreed to give it a try. For him. I stood by his side in the kitchen as the ceremony began. He approached his ingredients like a surgeon approaching a patient in the operating room. He slowly pulled a long serrated knife from its wood block, expertly cutting a perfect slice through the warm loaf of rye. His control of the blade was masterful as he stabbed it into the waiting stick of butter and in one fluid motion slathered a generous amount all over the steaming bread. He opened the tuna can so fast you would have thought it was never sealed. He mixed the tuna and a perfectly rounded tablespoon of mayonnaise in a large bowl that gave him enough room to work his magic. His hands moved with lightning speed and precision as he put dollops of tuna onto the waiting bread. There was intense concentration in his eyes as he placed a slice of aged New York cheddar perfectly centered over his masterpiece. As a finishing touch, he sprinkled a dusting of paprika over the top. Sweat formed on his brow as he scooped up the entire creation and centered it in the pre-heated oven.

As the cheese began to bubble and brown, the corners bonding with the bread below, I could feel my father's excitement build at the thought of finally sharing the creation he loved with his only son. But as the bread began to toast and the cheese began to melt, the smell of the tuna as it began to heat up filled me with dread. I knew, at that moment, that I would never be able to do it.

I blamed it on a stomachache, running out of the room before he even had a chance to remove it from the oven. And before I was able to see the look of disappointment on his face. That was the last tuna melt he ever made before he got sick.

As the cancer took its toll on his body, my father lost his appetite. As great as his will was, he could no longer do many of the things he loved: playing catch in the backyard, helping me with school-work, cooking. And he lost his ability to go through the painstaking steps necessary to create his tuna melt. Anything less than perfection would not be accepted. And surely the smell of hot tuna would not sit very well with him anymore.

What pained him more than not being able to eat his beloved tuna melts was not being able to make them for others and share in their joy and pleasure. Now neighbors and friends stopped by for a different reason.

My father had lost a lot of weight along with his appetite and could no longer leave his bed. I spent many nights lying next to him as he attempted to cram in all of life's lessons in the few weeks he had left. It was a long goodbye that went too quickly.

One night, as I sat by his side, he jolted up in bed with an energy I hadn't seen in months, uttering five simple words, "Make me a tuna melt."

Trying to be a dutiful son, I put aside my apprehension and ran to the kitchen. I felt unworthy as I stepped onto his stage. Laying the ingredients on the counter, I did my best to honor his ritualistic performance. I cut the bread. Slathered the butter. Mixed the tuna. Carefully placed the cheese. Sprinkled the paprika. I put it in the oven and watched it come to life. It was not the masterpiece my father spent years perfecting, but in my own way, I feel like I did him proud. As the bread toasted and the cheese melted, the smell of the heated tuna did not bother me as much.

I couldn't wait to see the look on his face as he took a bite of my first tuna melt. But as I brought it to him, though he tried to hide it, I could see him wince from the smell. He just couldn't do it. Dejected, I placed the plate on his night table and took a seat by his bedside. "Thank you," he said. Even through his nausea, he was beaming with pride. And for the first time, the smell of the melted cheese, toasted bread and even the warm tuna made my mouth water. I picked up the tuna melt, and took a bite. A smile crept over his face. He was right. It was delicious. He had never let me down.

My father died a few days later. He was way too young and so was I. But I still remember everything he taught me and try to live a life that would make him proud. To this day, I make my father's famous tuna melt once a week just the way he used to make it. And I don't even mind the smell anymore.

~David Chalfin

# The Tea Party

*Strange how a teapot can represent at the same time the comforts of solitude and the pleasures of company.*
*~Author Unknown*

My induction into the world of tea began with a gift from my mother—a beautiful cobalt blue tea set she had purchased on a trip to Japan. The tea set came in a satin-lined white leather box. The cups, saucers, and teapot were delicately hand-painted in their rich cobalt blue color with a gold crane and a thin gold line around each rim. I was never quite sure why she purchased the set because the extent of her ownership was transporting it back to the United States, going through customs with it, and then storing it on a shelf in her closet. It had never been used.

Her trip to Japan was one that would have excited most people, but my mother was newly widowed and her enthusiasm for life had vanished with the death of my father. She was in her mid-forties at the time, and, though she never said it aloud, it was evident that she felt cheated. She made reservations for the trip, alone, with much apprehension. "Dad left you enough money to travel. Go somewhere, Mom. Meet some new people. Do something nice for yourself. Have some fun. Do something exciting." She did not want to go, but she did. With the death of my dad, the life in my mom slowly seeped out of her. Traveling alone in a foreign country made her life even more overwhelming. The most enthusiasm she could muster was over the cobalt blue tea set she had purchased. "It's so beautiful," I said.

"I thought so, too," she said. "It reminded me of when you were a little girl and used to have tea parties. Remember?"

I really did not remember, but I nodded my head anyway. I remembered playing with my cousin's toy pickup truck and his fire engine, but I did not remember tea parties.

"It'll be yours someday," my mother said. "You can have it now if you want."

"Mom, you should enjoy it now. It's so pretty. Put it out somewhere so it can be seen. Make tea! Put it in your breakfront. Show it off!"

Instead, the tea set sat in its box on a shelf in her closet for twenty-five years.

Eventually, I moved with my family across the country. My mother visited often when my children were young, less often as they grew to have their own lives and schedules. On one of her many trips, she brought the cobalt blue tea set.

"It matches your home so much better than it does mine," she said. She was right. "I want you to have it."

While my mother was there, I left the set out, in its box, with the lid open. I wasn't sure where to put it, and with five cats and two sons, I wanted to keep it where it wouldn't be broken. I showed it to everyone who came into my home. Eventually, when my mom left, I closed the case and put it in my cabinet to keep it safe. I was truly afraid to use it. But I loved it nonetheless. I had always been particularly fond of cobalt blue china and knew it was hard to find, especially pieces that lovely. I also knew how difficult the trip to Japan had been for my mother, and though I never told her this, I am not sure I would have attempted that trip by myself had I been in a similar situation.

Maybe it's part of being an adult, but I wanted to show my mom how much I appreciated the gift that she had transported from Japan to her home and then, many years later, to mine. I purchased several types of tea and a special pot for brewing the tea. My plan was to make a delicious tea and to serve it to my mom when she visited the next time. We would have a tea party I really remembered instead of pretending to remember the ones from my childhood. I was sure my mother would enjoy the effort and appreciate the sentiment.

Not being a tea drinker, this required much self-education and experimentation. Before receiving the cobalt blue tea set, I thought "tea" was a teabag dunked in boiled water with a lot of sugar and honey in it, sitting on my night table when I was sick. Tea was a weak watery drink served to all patrons at the local Chinese restaurants. Tea was not my beverage of choice.

I experimented with many flavored teas. Though I had been accused of being addicted to diet soda and coffee before this, I suddenly preferred tea to all other drinks. The variety of flavors made it an adventure. There were so many choices. Yet, each time I brewed a pot of tea, I could not bring myself to pour the tea into the cobalt blue cups. I was saving their inauguration for my mother's next visit.

Unfortunately, that never happened. My mother grew too sick to travel and eventually succumbed to heart disease.

I took the tea set down several times after her death and stared at it. Everyone mourns in different ways. I stared at the beautiful tea set and cried. What was it about the tea set? Was it the memory of a tea party my mother had that I could not remember? Was it the effort I put behind my master plan that I could never fulfill? Perhaps it was the one tie my mother wanted to have with me — one that she felt was missing in her life as I grew up and away from her. With my children growing up and moving away, I was beginning to feel this emptiness as well, a generation later, and I knew somehow the tea set was our bond, even if neither of us could put it into words.

On the day she would have been eighty years old, I brewed a pot of strawberry-kiwi tea, the tea I felt would most likely be served at a little girl's tea party — sweet and delicious. I poured the tea into two of the beautiful cobalt cups. I slowly sipped mine, and then I slowly sipped from the cup I had poured for my mom. I rinsed both cups, dried them, and put them back into the satin-lined box.

~Felice Prager

# One Hungarian Summer

*Let food be thy medicine, and let thy medicine be food.*
*~Hippocrates*

"I don't want to go," I said, the tears starting to fall again.

"You have no choice," my father replied. "I'll be working long hours all summer and I might even have to do night shifts. You're too young to be left alone. I'm sorry, but there's no alternative. The ticket's booked and you're going."

"No, I'm not," I shouted. "I'm nearly fourteen and I can look after myself."

I rushed upstairs to my room and threw myself on the bed. However, I knew that I wouldn't win this argument. Mom had just died of cancer and Dad had decided to send me to Hungary to spend the summer vacation with her sister. Mom and I had visited her last year, and I had gotten along well with my aunt, but I now was confused and lonely. I missed Mom and I didn't want to go to Hungary on my own.

Three days later, I stood in the departure lounge at London Heathrow airport. I was still thinking of a way to get out of the trip, but deep inside I knew that I had to go. After just a few hours, the plane landed in Budapest. My aunt, Gizi Neni, which is Hungarian for Aunt Gizi, came towards me and gave me a hug. She looked as if she had been crying. I realized that although they hadn't lived in the same country for many years, she had also loved my mother and now missed her.

When we got to her house, Gizi Neni tried to persuade me to eat something, but I wasn't able to face food. I burst into tears, which made her start crying. Her daughter-in-law was visiting, and she too began to cry. She had also been close to my mother. We were three women of different ages, but we were united in grief for a woman who had touched us all deeply. Eventually I went to bed without eating, and I cried myself to sleep.

I woke up late the following morning, having had a restless night. I looked in the mirror and my eyes were puffy from crying. I wanted to hide, but then the wonderful smell of baking wafted into the room. Suddenly, I felt very hungry. I crept into the kitchen, feeling shy and unsure of myself. The room smelt even more extraordinary when I went in. There were plates of cakes and pastries on all the surfaces, and Gizi Neni was busy preparing more. I could hardly believe what I was seeing. My mother loved to cook as well, but I had never seen anything like this before.

"Here, take," Gizi Neni said.

"Thank you," I replied. "It all looks delicious."

Gizi Neni didn't speak much English, and I didn't speak any Hungarian, but it didn't seem to matter. I smiled at her and looked around. This was an amazing breakfast, much better than cereal and toast! I headed straight for a cherry pastry. It was still warm and it was delicious. I could feel my appetite returning. I took another pastry, believing that this was my breakfast. However, while I was eating, Gizi Neni had taken some eggs from the fridge and was scrambling them. Fresh bread appeared, with hunks of cheese and slices of ham. By the time I had finished the meal, I felt completely filled up.

Not surprisingly, my aunt loved to eat. When she was a young woman, she had been extremely slim, but after she married, her love of cooking emerged. She started to eat much more and became very large. Although she was a lawyer and led a busy life, she would still cook with fresh ingredients every day. She always made sure that everybody in the house enjoyed their food and was well fed.

The long, hot days of summer slipped by. Contrary to my expectations, I happily settled into life in Hungary. Friends were often invited to the house, and the days would revolve around meals and entertaining. On the weekends, my aunt would think nothing of serving seven courses for dinner. Gizi Neni made delicious soups and goulashes. Soured cream was poured over her stews, and paprika was used liberally in many of her savory dishes. I developed a taste for paprika that summer and still use it a lot in my cooking today. Gizi Neni's cakes and pastries were always wonderful. As I loved desserts, I had to be careful to pace myself at her marathon dinners so that I would have room for them. One outstanding memory I have involves an enormous plate of doughnuts. Gizi Neni brought them to the table after we had finished dinner one evening. I was already full by this time, but I found room to try one. My aunt had one, then another, and then another. She stopped when she had eaten a total of fourteen!

Since the weather was hot that summer, we would sometimes have barbecues. I remember a friend of my cousin's bringing a deer to cook outside one evening. I can still recall the smells wafting around the garden and into the street. Even though I have been a vegetarian for many years and wouldn't be tempted by these smells anymore, the memories of those barbecues conjure up visions of sultry summer days that I spent with people who cared about me. Eating outdoors was a unique experience as well. Although they are popular now, barbecues weren't common in England when I was a child.

The summer ended all too quickly and I had to go back to school in England. As much as I hadn't wanted to go to Hungary, I now didn't want to return home. My aunt had helped me through the initial difficult stages after Mom died, and I wanted to stay longer with her. However, I was lucky enough to spend every summer after that with Gizi Neni until I was in my early twenties. Although she has been dead for many years now, whenever I think about my aunt, I remember the doughnuts, the pastries, the goulash, and all the other delicious food that she carefully prepared. She gave me so much love and comfort at a time when I needed it, and I will never forget the larger-than-life lady who loved her food and loved me as well.

~Irena Nieslony

# The Magic Waffle Iron

*A grandmother is a little bit parent, a little bit teacher,*
*and a little bit best friend.*
*~Author Unknown*

I don't believe in fairies. And I don't believe in magic. And I don't believe in miracles.

I believe in the waffle iron.

I didn't cry when my grandmother died. I tried, but I just couldn't get the tears out. It was like something silvery and quick slid shut behind my eyes and blocked out all the light — numbed my ability to feel.

It wasn't that I didn't love my grandma. Everybody she ever met loved her. She had this uncanny ability to look right through you, as though you had turned translucent under the yellow light in her kitchen and she could see your thin, blue veins and nerve endings and bones, and she loved all of it. She loved everything that made you into yourself. And you felt so hollow and light and clean in her eyes. Like you were okay. Like you were free.

And she made waffles. She had this big, black, cast-iron waffle press that weighed about as much as a toddler, and when anyone was having a bad day, or going through a hard time, or just needed to talk, she'd invite them over. And when they got to her house, she'd hand them her big wooden spoon and have them mix the waffle batter. I have the suspicion that if she had more contacts in the political world, there would have been at least two wars quickly resolved by her free, waffle-oriented therapy sessions.

So, a few months after she died, I set off for her memorial service, still tear-free. At that point, I was beginning to feel as though I was cast in some kind of ice, or stuck behind a tinted glass wall—able to observe and jot things down in my notebook, but completely removed. I knew how to make all the motions—to tilt my head and furrow my eyebrows and gently touch someone's arm when they told me how wonderful my grandmother was, to smile sadly and shake my head when their eyes glistened with a pure, shiny film.

And I hated everyone who could cry so easily, feel so quickly and thoroughly. I felt like crying was an indulgence that everyone except me could have.

The waffles came up in almost every conversation I had. People said that talking to my grandmother over waffles had saved their jobs, marriages, children. They said things would seem scary and impossible, and my grandmother would make it all better with breakfast food. People also told me that I reminded them of her, and all I could think was, *I don't even freaking like waffles.*

But, oddly enough, about halfway through the memorial, I noticed that someone had set up her big, black, cast-iron waffle press on one of the tables, with a big stack of waffles next to it. I picked one up and looked at it for a while, turning it over in my hands and tracing my fingers on the grooves pressed into its face.

And then I was crying. Tears were running down my face and my neck and bleeding into my shirt and sinking into the waffle.

And I thought, *Oh my God. She can make it all better with waffles. She really can.*

~Robin O'Steen, age 16

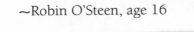

# Food and Love

## A Bite of Fun

*Give a man a fish and he has food for a day;
teach him how to fish and you can get rid of him for the entire weekend.*

*~Zenna Schaffer*

# Pickled Egg Surprise

*Pride goeth before destruction, and an haughty spirit before a fall.*
*~Proverbs 16:18*

My mother-in-law was my biggest competition when it came to cooking. Her homemade cornbread was the perfect combination of crumble and crust—mine was mostly crumble. Her baked ham embellished with pineapples and a can of Coca-Cola was succulent and sweet. Mine was bland and boring. She had that special thing that made food delectable.

My husband and I had only been married a short time when I decided to tackle his favorite snack... pickled eggs. Although I hated the rotten smell, I wanted him to be proud of me. (And I secretly wanted to show my mother-in-law that she wasn't the only one who could make them!)

Armed with a dozen eggs and a special solution, I set them on the kitchen counter.

Later that evening, my husband walked in the door and his eyes grew as big as half dollars. "You made me pickled eggs!" he shouted. "You are the best! I will let them get good and pickled for the big game this Sunday!" He was extremely happy... and so was I. Take that, Mother-in-law!

Soon it was game day and my husband was in the kitchen preparing his snacks. I heard his fork clank against the side of the jar. Then all of a sudden he asked, "Honey, didn't you peel the eggs?"

"Peel them?" I asked bewildered. "Why would I peel them?"

"You know... after you boiled them."

Boil them? At that very moment I cringed. I wanted to sink between the couch cushions and hide forever.

"Sweetheart, you did boil the eggs didn't you?"

With a red face and a broken spirit, I remained silent. Then he came and wrapped both arms around me — laughing of course — and said, "I love you!"

~Jeannie Dotson

# Badger Meatloaf

*Man is the only animal that can remain on friendly terms*
*with the victims he intends to eat until he eats them.*
~Samuel Butler

The freezer paper bore one scribbled line: Badger Meatloaf. I can't say it surprised me to find that in my own refrigerator but I was intrigued. It was a remnant from my brother-in-law's pet-sitting visit and not the worst thing I could have found from his bachelor's stay. Still, it was a little different than dried up pizza crusts or a quart of soured milk.

I'm a country girl who married an outdoorsman, so I have a skewed view of what's unusual. I have also discovered some things about truly fine dining over the years and have learned to savor the gifts from our own environs. For instance, I've watched my husband trim up a fresh batch of dandelion and wilt it into submission with hot bacon dressing from his grandmother's recipe. Thanks to my grandmother, I'm an expert at soaking the wild morel mushrooms in a pan of saltwater until all the little bugs come out and the mushrooms can be sautéed in real butter.

As far as I'm concerned, the finest cut of Angus beef can't touch a fresh venison tenderloin cozied up to a baked potato. I have dined on grilled trout from our local creek — rainbow, palomino and the brookies. I long ago learned how to wrap wild turkey and pheasant with bacon and slow roast them, to five-star family reviews. I've eaten rabbit casserole and rolled out dough for squirrel potpie. I also once used a package of Shake 'n Bake to cook up a rattlesnake plucked fresh from the garden. (It tastes just like chicken and goes well with a nice Bordeaux.) Elk, caribou, moose, frog legs, and turtle soup have all been on our menu. But badger meatloaf? That was new.

I remember unwrapping that brown chunk of leftovers with an open mind, but by the time I ran across it at the back of the fridge, it had definitely failed the sniff check, even by bachelor standards. As I tossed it into the trash, I also remember asking my husband if badgers were even native to Pennsylvania. He was watching football at the time so I doubt he really focused on my random inquiry.

The badger meatloaf was easily forgotten; it hadn't been odd enough in my world to have even become a story. Our fridge regained its former personality and the weeks went by until we all gathered for dinner with my father-in-law. Unlike us, he lived in a residential development and shared backyard boundaries with three other families. Conversations drifted to twenty years of neighborhood memories as it often did and he joined his two grown sons in regaling me with stories of the marvelous homemade dinners and fresh-baked breads frequently delivered by their friends next door, Don and Ellen.

Surrounded by my husband and the in-laws who loved me, I was instantly catapulted to family legend that night. The moment has survived more than three decades of story telling. It was really my own fault for letting out the audible "Aha!" and recounting the tale of the meatloaf discovery with no thought to how it might haunt me. The light came on for me during story hour around that kitchen table and, of course, I still bear the brunt. The mystery meat I had tossed had been a gift—from Don and Ellen Badger.

~Mitchell Kyd

"It's a family recipe. Whose family? That I don't know."

# Happiness Is
# a Full Freezer

*It pays to plan ahead. It wasn't raining when Noah built the ark.*
~Author Unknown

"Mom, what's for dinner?" my ten-year-old son, Jordan, asks me. It's seven a.m. and the child is shoving in the Apple Jacks like he hasn't eaten in weeks.

I sigh. The what's-for-dinner conundrum. It's the question I most dread being asked. (Well, besides the whole where-do-babies-come-from thing. But that's a whole other thing.) Yet each of my five children—yes, five!—asks me at least three times a day what fantastic fare he or she will be dining on that evening.

Often, the question is posed before I even manage to get out of my jammies.

This bugs me and they know it, but it doesn't seem to stop them from asking. Once, I asked Jordan why he did this. "Why, oh why, do you need to know what you'll be eating for dinner twelve hours from now?"

"I like to know what to get hungry for," he said with a smile. "It makes the food taste better when I get to think about it all day."

I thought about his answer. It made sense in an odd sort of way. And really, I was doing the same thing—spending inordinate amounts of time thinking about dinner. But I was worried about the cooking aspect of the process. (I've got the eating part down pat.)

All day long, the what's-for-dinner deal plagued my thoughts. "What am I going to make?" The question hung over me like a proverbial dark cloud. It was time to find a little silver lining.

I'd heard about this thing called "once-a-month cooking." Cooking only once a month? That sounded like heaven on earth. So my friend Google and I checked it out.

I waded through what felt like a million hits. I printed dozens of recipes and joined a really great online cooking group. The general consensus among the group was that if I wanted to start doing once a month cooking, I needed to start small.

Start small? Not me. I never do anything halfway.

I set aside an entire Saturday for my first marathon cooking session. I bought every boneless, skinless chicken breast within a fifty-mile radius and a whole cow's worth of hamburger. I purchased canned vegetables, fresh veggies, and some frozen ones too. I got tomato paste, tomato sauce, and even tomato puree. I bought so much food that I had to ask Jordan to grab a second cart. To which he said, "Ooh, I can hardly wait to have dinner tonight!"

I took everything home and started sorting the food. I got out the brand-new recipes I printed off the Internet and started compiling casseroles. I quadrupled all the recipes, figuring I could make four casseroles nearly as quickly as I could make one. All afternoon, I was like the Tasmanian Devil in my kitchen. Finally, my freezer was full of a month's worth of casseroles.

Inevitably, one of my kids meandered into the kitchen and asked the inevitable question. "So, Mom, what's for dinner?"

I grinned because for the first time in my life, the question didn't irk me. I already knew the answer. I retrieved one of my fabulous new casseroles from the freezer and put it in the oven. "Dinner will be ready in thirty minutes," I said, patting myself on the back.

I was still singing my own praises as my family took their first bites of my very first once-a-month cooking creation. "Wow, this is... not my favorite," my husband said slowly. And my kids were not nearly as tactful. "Mom, this is nasty," one said. Another child actually spit the food back onto her plate.

They didn't like my casserole. And I had three more in the freezer just like it.

After I finished crying, I got back online and discovered some important advice I'd ignored the first time around. It said, "Don't double, triple, and certainly don't quadruple any recipe that you haven't tried before. It doesn't make any sense to have dinners in the freezer that nobody will actually eat."

Now they tell me.

I revisited the "start small" advice and realized it had a lot of merit. The ladies in the online cooking group advised me to consider making meal starters, rather than whole meals for the freezer. "Catch a good sale on ground beef," they said. "Buy a ton, brown it all, and then freeze it after it's cooked. Then when you want to use it, thaw it and turn it into tacos, sloppy joes, or use it in a casserole."

I cringed at the thought of another casserole, but the taco idea sounded great. A few nights later, I put it to the test. I thawed the meat in the microwave, added the seasoning and warmed the tortillas, and had tacos on the table in less than ten minutes.

It was so easy and stress-free.

And best of all, nobody spit their dinner back onto their plate.

My new online friends told me I could do the same thing with chicken. I put some boneless, skinless breasts in my crock pot with a bit of chicken broth. I let it cook all day and then that night, I shredded the chicken with two forks. I froze the pieces in small containers, ready to be thawed and turned into chicken salad, quesadillas, or barbecue chicken pizza.

Or even—gasp—a casserole.

Another part of the "start small" philosophy is to double familiar recipes. If you love your lasagna recipe, make two pans or even three. Eat one for dinner that night and toss the extra one in the freezer for another time. It will come in handy, but remember, only do this with a recipe you've tried before. (Trust me on this one. Remember those casseroles I made? They're in my freezer, where they've been for a year and a half now.)

But I've come a long way with this once-a-month cooking thing.

Now, when one of my kids asks me what's for dinner, I don't panic. I know that my freezer is full of foods that make dinnertime easier, more organized and far less stressful.

Once-a-month cooking has helped me become a much happier mama.

And by the way, if you happen to know anyone who's holding a potluck dinner, I've got some casseroles in my freezer I'd like to unload.

~Diane Stark

# Cereal Killer

*There is no sincerer love than the love of food.*
~George Bernard Shaw

My friend Dominique and I are innkeepers at Channel Road Inn. Working at a bed and breakfast hotel is fun! We take reservations, help guests with their dinner plans and we bake homemade cookies, breakfast cakes and goodies from scratch every day for our guests.

Dominique and I have been friends for a while now. We've shared secrets, lots of laughs and even a few tears, but lately something has come between us... it's her granola recipe. She won't tell me (or anyone!) how it's made.

Dominique's granola is the best thing I've ever tasted. Sure I love the homemade banana bread and blueberry cakes we bake at the Inn. Our scones, egg soufflés and French toast are amazing and our homemade chocolate chip cookies are to die for but nothing—NOTHING!—can top Dominique's granola.

When you ask Dominique what's in the granola she pretends to tell you. "Oh, it's simple—just your basic granola but I add in some fruit and I sweeten it with coconut and honey," she says (while not looking you in the eye). But she must be leaving something out of her description because I have never tasted granola (or anything) that tastes as good as this. I cannot even hear, much less talk, when I'm eating this granola. The whole world stops moving and all I can hear is the crunching of the granola in my mouth. I can't hear the phones or the doorbell ring and even when people talk to me, I can see their lips moving but their voices sound like they are in slow motion. In that sense, Dominique's granola is an occupational hazard for me, so I try to eat it only after my shift has ended.

I am known to get overly exuberant about certain things, so I took a sample of Dominique's granola to one of my girlfriends at Curves so she could tell me if she found it as amazing as I do. By the time I drove home, there was already an e-mail from my girlfriend saying, "Wow, you were not kidding! That stuff is addictive! Yum, yum, yum! I'm thinking Dominique should start small and go to farmers' markets, fairs, etc... and just sell locally... word will spread!"

And word has spread! Though Dominique has not had time to go to farmers' markets or fairs yet, we do have guests e-mailing and calling to ask for the recipe for Dominique's homemade granola. Over the past twenty-three years all of the innkeepers at Channel Road Inn have been open and generous with our recipes. We freely and willingly give them to our guests and we'll even let them watch us bake the cakes or prepare the egg soufflés and French toast so they can replicate them at home. Dominique's granola is the only recipe they cannot have. Their response is always the same. They laugh and say, "I always knew you innkeepers had a few tricks up your sleeves," and then they add, "No problem. But can I buy some of that granola? Could you mail it to me? I keep thinking about it."

I like these phone calls and e-mails because they reassure me that I have not lost my mind. This granola is that good! I think about it every day and always hope Dominique has had a chance to make it when I come into work. I've even been known to call down to the Inn on my days off just to see if, by chance, Domi has made any granola. I scour the freezer at the Inn looking for leftovers and hidden stashes, but I rarely find any because the guests eat it by the heaping spoon-fuls. On the days Dominique's granola gets served, our homemade cakes are barely touched. People are nuts for this stuff.

My girlfriend from Curves asks me on a weekly basis how she can get more of Dominique's granola. Though she has an apartment nearby, she's considering booking a room at Channel Road Inn just so she can come to breakfast and eat granola. It's that bad — this granola is ruining the lives of everyone who eats it. We all become addicts and start devoting our lives to finding out how and when we can get more granola.

And all the while, Dominique sits in the kitchen feigning surprise that everyone is rabidly searching for more granola. She's like the Master of the Universe — the one who holds the key to our happiness. When she knows I'm having a hard week, she definitely makes granola. One time she even went out and bought coconut herself because the Inn was out of it and she knew I wanted and needed (yes, actually needed) her homemade granola that day.

We have a repeat guest at Channel Road Inn who has stayed at the Inn several times a year for the past ten years. She's crazy about Dominique's granola too! Like me, she has begged for the recipe and then finally settled for just eating a bowl of granola once she realized that Dominique's vague description of "fruit, coconut and honey" is just a dodge. We all adore this guest — from her Missouri drawl to her darling grandchildren and impeccable manners, she is the most charming woman in the world.

Under normal circumstances, there's nothing I would deny this guest, but when she checked in last week and immediately asked if "Dominique had made any granola" I had to think fast. The technical answer was, "No, Domi has not had time to make granola today." But the underlying truth, the one that troubled my heart was, "Domi has not had time to make granola today... but she did give me a small bag of it last week. I have it hidden in the back of the freezer with my name on it and I have been rationing it out to myself half a cup at a time."

I stared at our loyal guest, wondering if I should share my secret stash with her. I love this guest... but I also love Dominique's granola. I adore this guest... but I also adore Dominique's granola. I should have shared my granola with this guest... but I didn't. I tried to ease my conscience by offering her a cup of tea and a slice of hot vanilla streusel cake, fresh out of the oven. She politely said, "No thank you" and as I watched her walk down the hall to her room, I felt slightly bad—but not as bad as I would have felt had I given her the last of my granola.

Dominique shows her love for Channel Road Inn's guests—and employees—through her baking. She works on her recipes for weeks to perfect them and is truly delighted when the guests "ooh and ah" over her creations. She is generous with most of her recipes, except for one. And that's okay, because this granola is so good, I'm betting one day it will be available in stores, and then our charming guest from Missouri, my girlfriend from Curves, and I can all eat Domi's granola to our heart's content!

~Rebecca Hill

# The Scam

64

*It's important to our friends to believe that we are unreservedly frank with them, and important to the friendship that we are not.*
~Mignon McLaughlin, The Neurotic's Notebook

The dinner party was set for Saturday night. I was busy all week preparing the menu, shopping, cleaning, and cooking. There would only be four of us at this dinner but you'd have thought that I was preparing for royalty. The reason? Our very good friends were coming to dinner and we wanted everything to be perfect. What better way to show people you love them than with the food on your table?

We do love our friends very much, but they have one habit that drives us crazy. They think they are coffee connoisseurs and they don't hesitate to inform you of that fact. Over and over and over again. They talk about this new bean and that new growing area, coffee cups versus mugs, black versus cream and sugar, various brands of coffee makers, etc., etc., etc. You get the idea. And we tolerate it. But just because you tolerate your friends' behavior doesn't mean you can't try to fool them. My husband Frank and I were planning to pull off the scam of the century.

Our friends arrived on time and we had some wine and appetizers out on the patio. Then it was time to move inside for dinner. The table looked beautiful and, if I do say so myself, the food didn't taste bad either. We finished dinner and soon it was time for coffee and dessert. I excused myself from the table to go into the kitchen and make the coffee.

Now it began. Frank knew what he had to do. He had to keep our friends occupied so that they wouldn't come into the kitchen. If they did, the whole thing would be ruined. And he did a great job; I could hear lots of talking and laughing going on in the dining room.

I was nervous. Would our scam work? Frank and I can be pretty devious when we work together, but our friends were coffee experts and Frank and I were not. We liked good coffee and drank it every day but, according to our friends, we just didn't really understand all of the finer points and techniques that go into making a really good cup of coffee. They always offered to bring and make the coffee when they came to our house for a meal. I could have been insulted by their offer, but instead I decided to put their taste buds to the test.

I made lots of noise while preparing the coffee. I hoped that our friends would think that all the noise meant better coffee. I turned on the coffee bean grinder that I had bought especially for this scam. Boy, does it make a lot of noise! Of course, they wouldn't be able to tell that I had put rice in the grinder rather than coffee beans. The noise level would be the same. Then I put a fresh coffee filter in the coffeemaker, added the filtered water, and very, very carefully counted out the number of scoops of coffee I needed for twelve cups. Twelve cups of instant coffee, that is! From a jar. No beans to be seen.

Now you have to understand that as far as our friends were concerned, to drink instant coffee is a terrible, horrible sin. They would never, ever do it. It would be like talking back to your mother, or worse! They would rather drink nothing than drink instant. They said it tasted terrible. They said they always knew when they were served instant coffee. No one could fool them. And they were always talking about this bean or that bean from this country or that country. Frank and I were sick of it. Tonight, we would test their knowledge. Their special coffee this evening would be made from "instant" beans!

Time to serve. I took a deep breath and entered the dining room carrying the china cups and saucers, and a silver coffee urn on a silver tray. Presentation is everything. They didn't take cream, sweetener or sugar. Nothing would hide the flavor of the beans. I set the tray down on the table and poured coffee for everyone in grand style. They sniffed, they swirled, they sipped, and then they sighed. Yummy, they said. Absolutely delicious. Could they have a second cup? And then maybe just a little more?

Of course.

They complimented me over and over again and said that finally I had learned how to make really good coffee. They said it was obvious that the beans I had chosen had made all the difference. I thanked them and tried not to look at Frank. They asked which beans I used. I told them that it was a secret blend of various beans that a friend had suggested and I wasn't able to divulge the exact combination.

After they left, Frank and I had another cup of my fabulous "secret blend" coffee and just laughed and laughed. Both Frank and I had done our parts and we had pulled off the scam of the century. Our coffee connoisseur friends never guessed that they were drinking instant coffee. And we never, ever told them—it remains our little secret. To this day they still talk about the delicious coffee that I made for them a few years ago. When I get up enough nerve, I am thinking of trying the experiment again, but this time I think I will make... instant decaf!

~Barbara LoMonaco

# 65

# Baby Wants Steak

*The only time to eat diet food is while you're waiting for the steak to cook.*
*~Julia Child*

The craving was intense, undeniable, and unyielding. There was no doubt about it: Baby wanted steak. "What do you feel like for dinner?" my husband Scott had asked as he opened the fridge. Rubbing my five-and-a-half-months pregnant belly, I stood on my tiptoes and peered around Scott's arm to take a look.

There wasn't much to work with. Granted, Scott is a certified chef, but not even MacGyver and Rachael Ray could join forces to make do with a half-full carton of almond milk, a sack of black seed-less grapes, a few sticks of unsalted butter, and a pack of "meatless" hot dogs. A trip to the market was definitely in order, and for Scott that was anything but a chore.

And I was about to place the proverbial cherry on top.

"I want—no, need—a steak," I replied, albeit bashfully, raising a hand to my mouth to ensure that I wasn't salivating at the mere thought of a succulent piece of red meat.

Scott turned around so fast that I thought for a second he might have suffered whiplash. His expression seemed to say, "Finally! Please tell me you're serious!"

Much to his delight, I repeated, "I. Want. Steak."

You see, for nearly five years I had been a vegetarian, and while my eating habits made me feel amazing, being married to a granola-munching wife was, quite understandably, a less than ideal living situation for a meat-loving chef. Being the dutiful husband he is, however, he has whipped up a myriad of delectable meat-free creations during the course of our four years of marriage—vegetable lasagna, homemade French fries with a hint of sea salt, and ratatouille, to name a few. I was most appreciative—this was coming from a man who would much prefer to make chicken cordon bleu for two, after all.

But now that I was pregnant, my vegetarianism was on hiatus. Roasted chicken, turkey with gravy, and the occasional cheeseburger were back on the menu.

At last, Scott was in his glory. Especially tonight.

"I'm making Steak Oscar," Scott announced.

"Steak what?"

"You'll like it," he said. "You'll see."

Forty-five minutes later, Scott returned from the market, threw on his chef coat, and went to work. Motivated by equal parts curiosity and hunger, I held court at the island in our kitchen as Scott organized his mise en place: an assortment of pots and pans, a whisk, a pair of stainless steel tongs, and his knife kit. (No measuring cups were in sight. "Chefs don't need them, we go by appearance and taste," Scott always says.) And then there were the raw ingredients: three eight-ounce beef tenderloin steaks, a bunch of fresh asparagus spears and lemons, and a container of lump crabmeat.

"You're in the way," Scott quipped. "Call Mom and invite her over for dinner, then have a seat in the living room. Put your feet up."

He didn't have to tell me twice.

Nearly an hour later, there was no need for Scott to beckon my mother and me to the table; the mouthwatering aroma wafting through the house had already done the trick. We settled in at the table and what Scott placed before us nearly knocked us out of our chairs. In the center of my stark white plate sat a pyramid comprised of—from the bottom—a cloud of garlic-mashed potatoes, a perfectly cut round piece of steak, a hearty scoop of crabmeat, crisscrossed asparagus spears, and a stream of hollandaise sauce (sans raw egg, of course).

When Scott joined us at the table with his plate, I said grace and paused before I dug in. I had to remind myself to eat slowly and actually taste this masterpiece because it would have been all too easy to inhale it in three bites. What ensued for the next few minutes was a series of "Oooohs" and "Mmmmms" followed by bouts of chewing in silence. My craving had been sated.

With our plates clean and our stomachs pleasantly packed, we eased back from the table and exchanged looks of glee.

"Have you had enough?" Scott asked.

"Yes," my mom answered. "I'm stuffed."

"Me too," Scott added.

Then all eyes fell on me.

"Tangerines," I said. "Baby wants citrus."

And back to the market Scott went.

~Courtney Conover

**66**

# Valley of the Dammed

*Marriage is an alliance entered into by a man who can't sleep with the window shut, and a woman who can't sleep with the window open.*
*~George Bernard Shaw*

Mashed potatoes nearly ended my engagement. Every Sunday my fiancé's family would gather at "the farm" for dinner after church. His grandparents had lived there for years, doling out segments of land to their children who lived an easy shout away. The grandchildren lingered but were becoming independent: dating, preparing to marry, and starting careers.

This was a bit of a change for me since mine was a city family. I'd lived in seven cities by the time I was in eighth grade. I saw my grandparents on rare special occasions. The only thing constant was change. Not only were we nomadic, we also dined. And when we dined, we dined out. By high school I could use chopsticks, loved hummus, and knew which wines complemented which entrées.

My fiancé's family ate. Lots. Sustenance over style. Food to keep you going from morning milking to moonlight harvest. On Sunday they would sit down to chickens that had been clucking just yesterday, or a roast with a name—"No, this wasn't Betsy, it was Mildred. She's tastier." The accompanying beverage was always milk, butter was consumed by the stick, and cream came in pitchers instead of little flavored cups. "Low fat" was the grease at the bottom of the jar.

The dinner of deadly mashed potatoes began like any other. The meal was laid out in the minuscule farmhouse kitchen and the ten of

248   A Bite of Fun : Valley of the Dammed

us perched on mismatched chairs, the piano bench, and tall counter stools. Before us, an immense roast beast dominated the table, surrounded by side dishes covered by sauces that obscured any nutrients buried beneath.

Joining hands and bowing in prayer, we acknowledged the goodness of the giver, then served ourselves. I tried to stick to my city-folk diet of lean meat and steamed organic vegetables. Organic we could do. The garden outside the kitchen window was resplendent with flowers, fruit, and vegetables. I usually helped myself to beans and broccoli and then surreptitiously dabbed the butter and cheese sauce off with my napkin. I am, however, only human. The heavenly aroma of hand-mashed potatoes dripping with butter, while not worth selling my soul over, was worth a few extra miles on the treadmill so that my wedding dress would still fit.

"Honey," I asked my fiancé, "may I have a bite of your potatoes?"

"Sure." He slid his plate toward me.

I froze with my fork suspended above his plate as I admired the topography. It was a food-scaped replica of the rocky west. Layers of meat rose and fell in marbled hills, green sprigs of asparagus peeked from a cheesy field, and next to them was the crowning achievement, a massive lake flowing with dark gravy waves hemmed in by white potato hills.

If I had wanted to merely taste the buttery banks, disaster would have been averted. But what are mashed potatoes without gravy? Not thinking, I snatched a bite from the bank, broke the levy, and mixed the two together. It was the perfect meld and I chewed, eyes closed, until the velvety goodness slid down my throat, warming my stomach and my soul like no steamed veggie ever could.

When I opened my eyes, my fiancé was looking at me like I had just slaughtered the Grand Championship rooster.

"What have you done?" There was horror in his voice.

"What?" I hadn't done anything. Right?

"Look!" He gestured to his dinner where the broken dam was flooding his plate with muddy goodness. The northern half of the lake drained across his deteriorating landscape.

"So?" It's food. It all goes to the same place last I checked.

"You ruined my lake." He could barely speak as he watched the floodwaters head toward the green asparagus peaks.

Oh, the humanity!

"I'm sorry." My eyes brimmed with tears.

We finished the meal in silence and I was sure my fiancé would ask for his ring back as soon as we were alone. He had been too good to be true from the beginning. In heavy silence we walked the fields after dinner. One bean field, two cow pies, and ten cockleburs later, I could stand it no longer.

"Are you going to break up with me over mashed potatoes?"

He considered, for much too long, before answering. "No. Not this time. But from now on, don't mess with the lake."

Yes, mashed potatoes nearly ended my engagement. But I've since learned that a farm-raised man who will fight for a gravy-filled lake will fight even more heroically for his marriage and his family.

~Becky Tidberg

# The Great Family Cook-Off

*Life is uncertain. Eat dessert first.*
*~Ernestine Ulmer*

"Do you think they see us?" I whispered as I peeked over some sweet-smelling cantaloupes. My almost-grown daughter, Sarah and I hid in the produce section of our local grocery store.

"No. They're too busy inspecting chicken breasts. I thought you said we only had fifteen dollars to spend. What if they go over?"

"They forfeit, and we win!" We high fived each other.

Thus began The Great Family Cook-Off.

We drew names. Fate paired the men against the women. Though I lacked the killer competitiveness prevalent in other family members, and the only prize was "bragging rights," I could literally taste victory.

The rules were simple. Each team would create a dish from a fifteen-dollar budget and any extra ingredients on hand in our kitchen. We traveled home from the store in our family van, tight-lipped about our purchases, joking about our upcoming victories.

Our opponents secured their position near the refrigerator. Sarah and I set up adjacent to the pantry. After much consultation, Sarah and I opted for chicken quesadillas since we had all the ingredients. It was colorful so it would plate well, and who doesn't like quesadillas? Plus, we had an extra culinary surprise up our salsa-spotted sleeves.

My husband is a master in the kitchen. While I tend to "throw" together various items from the fridge, Tom crafts his entrées. He carefully chooses and inspects for visual appeal and freshness. After his meticulous choices, he begins to create. A pinch of this is added to a smidgeon of that. He tastes and stirs. When he is satisfied, he plates the food. Tom can serve buttered toast that makes you gasp with delight.

My daughter described our cooking differences to a friend like this: "Mom makes four things at once from whatever is in the fridge, and I usually like one of them. My dad concentrates on one item, and it's fabulous."

Even with my seeming handicap, I persevered. The reputation of womanhood throughout history hinged on the outcome of our contest.

Our male counterparts cut, sliced, and diced. The aroma of sun-dried tomatoes and garlic permeated the kitchen. I almost panicked.

"Micah, get sweet onions out of the fridge," Tom instructed our son.

I started to sweat.

We sautéed and simmered. Both sides sneaked sideways glances at each other.

It was time. The men served sautéed lemon chicken with capers, cilantro and sun-dried tomatoes. They plated the food on a large white serving dish with two sprigs of asparagus shooting off from a cut lemon placed strategically in the center. Paprika adorned the edges, composing a perfect balance of colors, complete with a heavenly aroma.

We spread the quesadillas artistically around an Italian ceramic platter painted with whimsical flowers. We added a sweet corn and tomato relish over each piece of chicken. Colorful peppers and sliced limes dotted the dish. A bowl containing sour cream, salsa, and two small yellow peppers that surrounded a lone peapod sat in the center of our creation.

Time for the taste test. We adjourned to our dining room, placed cloth napkins on our laps, and asked the Lord for a blessing—as I silently petitioned Him for a victory.

Both were tasty, almost dead even. Tom and Micah's masterpiece was pretty and moist, but lacked Tom's usual panache. Ours was attractive, and yummy, but your run-of-the-mill quesadilla. Still, we hadn't decided.

After we finished the main course, Sarah and I pulled out our secret weapon. Dessert.

We had enough money in our budget to purchase store-bought cookie dough. We spread rocky-road ice cream between the warm cookies for an amazing culinary delight.

Time for the vote. Tom mumbled something about cheating and declined. Sarah and I registered our vote for all women everywhere. Micah remained silent.

"So what do you think, Micah?" Sarah asked.

There was a long pause and then Micah looked up, hands covered in chocolate and vanilla ice cream. "I don't know. All I can think about right now is this cookie."

Yes, victory is sweet.

The best fifteen dollars we ever spent.

~Pauline Hylton

# Vitello alla Toonsie

*A woman's heart is a deep ocean of secrets.*
~Gloria Stuart

I f you can't keep a secret just turn to another story. If my husband finds out about this, I'm in serious trouble.

You see, Prospero's favorite meal is Italian-style veal cutlets. It's really a very simple dish of thinly sliced veal dipped in an egg wash seasoned with salt, pepper, garlic powder, pecorino cheese and then coated with Italian seasoned breadcrumbs. That's the key—Italian breadcrumbs. Don't pull out your plain American crumbs, or, Heaven forbid, corn flakes. And this certainly isn't the time for panko crumbs. Save the Japanese fusion for another meal. No, classic Vitello Milanese, as they call it in Italy, is breaded veal cutlets fried until golden in a pool of olive oil and served with lemon wedges. Simple.

Of course, in this country we like to take this dish and cover it with tomato sauce and mozzarella cheese for veal parmesan, but I prefer more traditional sides when I'm making it at home. In cool weather I sauté broccoli rabe in olive oil with garlic chips and hot red pepper flakes. There's nothing better on a cold day than topping your veal cutlet with a steaming ladle of thick escarole and white bean soup and eating it by the fire.

During the summer months I have the bounty of my garden from which to select. I like to pick an assortment of peppers and sauté them in olive oil and a splash of white balsamic vinegar with cloves of garlic, which soften and can be spread on bread. A salad of arugula, tomatoes, basil and red onion dressed with olive oil and balsamic vinegar makes a cool, refreshing topping for veal on a warm summer evening. Of course all of these dishes are served with crusty Italian bread and a lovely Italian red wine.

I always have to be sure to make extra because nothing is more delicious than a sandwich of veal and one of the toppings on hearty Italian bread. It's the only sandwich Prospero will take to work and he always calls me afterward to profess his undying love, which still tickles me to no end.

The problem is that veal is becoming pricey, although my sainted mother, Terry, would disagree.

"Veal cutlet is very economical," she would insist, "There's no bone, no fat, no waste. You eat the entire cutlet."

Well, she had a point there, but veal has been selling for $19.99 a pound lately, forcing me to stock up when I see it on sale, thereby breaking another one of my mother's golden rules.

"Always buy veal fresh from an Italian butcher!" my mother would command.

And for many years I did just that, but even in northern New Jersey, that bastion of Italian-Americans, Italian butchers are becoming tough to find. So I buy my veal when I find it on sale, freeze it—the horror!—and defrost it when I need it.

That's what created the problem.

The veal was sitting on the counter in its supermarket plastic wrapping, happily defrosting until it was time to cook. I was outside with Toonsie, our black long-haired cat, who was terrorizing a chipmunk on the patio. I picked her up and put her in the house while I gathered my things to come in. When I walked into the house I heard, ka-plump!

"Toonsie, what are you doing?" I called.

Usually that sound means that she's somewhere she doesn't belong, but Toonsie was sitting innocently on the kitchen floor. Everything was fine until I began to prepare dinner. My veal, my precious veal, was partly ripped from the package and the ends were nibbled!

What was I going to do? I had already told Prospero to get his mouth set for veal cutlets. My veal cutlets. Homemade. With sautéed peppers.

Sometimes you gotta do what you gotta do. I cut off the portion of the veal that was sticking out of the wrapper and served the rest for dinner. And if you tell Prospero what I did I swear I'll hunt you down. If he had an inkling that he ate Toonsie's leftovers for his supper, he'd hit the roof.

I had to tell this story because I could no longer bear the burden of keeping this a secret. Never before have I kept something from my husband. We've had thirty-one years of honesty until a little kitty cat with the appetite of a Bengal tiger decided to indulge in a snack.

I can't help feeling that if I had only listened to my mother and bought fresh veal from a real Italian butcher it would have been sitting safely in the refrigerator instead of on the counter, and this whole mess wouldn't have happened.

~Lynn Maddalena Menna

"The cat got into the fish I was defrosting for tonight, so to teach her a lesson, WE'RE going to eat HER food."

Reprinted by permission of
Marc Tyler Nobleman ©2011

# The Slacker Seder

*Tradition is a guide and not a jailer.*
~W. Somerset Maugham

Since I was born, every spring, the family piled into the car and we drove up I-95 with the rest of the Jews who had left the motherland of New Jersey. Every car on the Turnpike was stuffed with antsy children, tired parents, and boxes of matzoh, schlepped up from Washington, D.C. as if we'd somehow be unable to find suitable matzoh once we crossed into the Garden State.

We went to New Jersey because my great-aunt hosted the entire family for the first seder. Four sisters gave birth to many children who gave birth to many more children, therefore, her house was so packed that the seder table traveled through two rooms, down a hallway, and in some years, even had satellite island tables shunted off to the sides in order to accommodate all of my aunts, uncles, and cousins.

This is what I did for twenty years, even after I left home to go to college. Being part of the tradition was important to me; it was the comfort of ritual, the reconnection with family. The few times that my great-aunt couldn't host, another person in the family opened up their house and we still had the same meal, read from the same hagaddah (the book used during the seder), and laughed over the same inside family jokes.

Until my senior year of college.

Through a strange glitch in timing, Pesach didn't align with spring break. I went to college in the Midwest, making it difficult to swing by New Jersey for the yearly seder. My mother told me that I was just going to have to skip it this year; everyone would understand.

*They* might understand, but what was *I* supposed to do? Sit in my apartment and think about all of them enjoying themselves together while I was stuck in snowy, lake-frozen Wisconsin? Many of my East Coast friends were in the same position. We were all stuck in the Midwest, cut off from the Jewish motherland of New Jersey, with only the tiny Hillel on Langdon Street to keep us company.

Someone suggested that we go to the Hillel for the first night and hold our own seder the second night. It made sense—I often held dinner parties at my apartment and what was a seder if not a large, complicated, flour-free dinner party? My friend, Ari, was the son of a rabbi and he could lead the service. We invited all of our Jewish friends who remained in town, a pathetically small handful of people, and then started adding in their non-Jewish significant others. Once we already had a critical mass of Catholics, it seemed silly not to keep adding to the guest list. Curious Episcopalians and never-been-to-a-seder-before Methodists and college-variety atheists were all included. Very few people knew each other before they stepped into my living room; their only connection was through Ari or me. And none of us knew the random cute boy I met at the first seder the night before, who I threw into the mix because there were already too many people to fit comfortably in my tiny apartment anyway.

The day of our seder, Ari came over with an egg. He told me that we needed to roast it for the seder plate. Having never held our own seder before, and egg roasting not being a skill mastered by the average college student, we shrugged our shoulders and stuck an egg into the preheated oven. It promptly exploded, filling the apartment with the stench of burnt shell.

This facilitated the first of many phone calls back to our parents that afternoon. How did one make charoset, the apple and nut mixture served during the seder? And what sort of wine did one serve with matzoh ball soup? And how does one clean an egg explosion out of a very hot oven?

Several hours later, the guests arrived and dutifully sat on the floor, Ari's Xeroxed seder booklet in their laps. The Catholics fumbled over the transliterated Hebrew, the Jews reminisced about the seders they were missing back home, and everyone politely refrained from mentioning the stench of burnt egg in the air.

The meal was equally eclectic—vegetarian matzoh ball soup and various salads and a plate of French fries and a potato kugel courtesy of a falling-apart cookbook I found in the Hillel library. There were more drinks than there was food. Someone inexplicably contributed an enormous Tupperware filled with baked apples for the meal. Upon reflection, there did not seem to be a main dish or any protein whatsoever. No one made dessert because we weren't creative enough to come up with an alternative to our usual cakes or cookies.

It was nothing like my family's seder. It was chaotic and wine-soaked and contained one thousand percent more curse words and college-related gossip. Yet there is nothing like being in a room with people who have nowhere else to go and yet find themselves exactly where they want to be. It may not have resembled the traditional seders of my childhood. The seder plate may have been made from paper and decorated with Magic Marker drawings of parsley and horseradish. We may have left the shank bone still encased in Styrofoam and plastic wrap since no one wanted to touch it. We may have had more salad dressing options than protein in the meal. But I still cherish the pictures I took that night as well as all the people who joined in keeping me company when it was too far for me to travel home.

~Melissa Ford

# Walter's Secret Ingredient

*There ain't no such thing as wrong food.*
~Sean Stewart, Perfect Circle

My phone rang again for what seemed like the hundredth time this morning. I picked it up in the midst of doing my monthly report to my boss, all the while juggling various deadlines for "rush" requests from a variety of clients in different departments in my company. A pretty typical day at work for me; such is the life of a corporate reference librarian.

The phone continued to ring. Frazzled, I picked it up, expecting to get yet another "rush" request to work on before lunch. I was relieved to hear a familiar voice. Instead of "I need this information by two o'clock this afternoon," I heard my husband Walter say, "Don't worry about dinner. I'll take care of everything. It will be ready when you get home."

Walter is no stranger to the kitchen. He can cook, and he helps out whenever he can, especially on those days when he takes a vacation day while I go off to work. I don't mind so much. The way I figure it, someone has to support this family! And, it's kind of nice to know that, when I get home, dinner will already be started, the table will be set, and we can look forward to a pleasant time together, breaking bread and catching up on the day's events. And then I wake up from my fantasy.

If Walter is cooking dinner, three things are likely to occur:

1. The entrée will be hamburgers, rare on the inside, charred to perfection on the outside.

2. No vegetables will be served.

3. The kitchen will be smoke-filled due to the fact that Walter likes to grill, and always abides by the same rule: Cook on high no matter what.

Holding the above three truths to be self-evident, I knew what was in the cards for me later that day.

Arriving home after yet another "stress-free" day at work, I opened the door to the family room, only to find Jeffrey balancing his metal baseball bat on end, in the palm of his hand, running between the TV set and an almost brand-new table lamp. That got the ol' blood a-pumpin', and prepared me for what I was about to face upstairs in the kitchen. To my credit, I didn't let this dissuade me. I forged ahead.

Slowly climbing the six stairs to the kitchen, I was almost overcome by the smoke billowing through the kitchen door. I couldn't see anything except the vague outline of the kitchen table. The sizzling and spattering noises emanating from the corner of the kitchen where I knew the stove to be almost drowned out the friendly voice, saying, "Hi, Donna. Dinner's almost ready."

I stared at the smoky fog that enveloped my kitchen, and there, miraculously finding his way to the top of the steps, stood Walter, smiling proudly, spatula in one hand, a plate with the charred remains of dinner piled high in the other.

"Come on up. Everything's ready."

I took one last breath of air before I ventured up the steps. I would need that reserve oxygen until I could get upstairs and turn on the exhaust fan while Walter opened a window or two. Within minutes of having done that, the kitchen began to take on its familiar appearance.

I made a quick salad, and we all sat down to eat, with the ever-present ketchup bottle taking its customary place as the centerpiece of our dinner table. Walter looked at me, expectantly. "Well? How is it? How does it taste?"

I bit through the crunchy exterior, and chewed on the soft-textured, bright pink inside. "Delicious!" I exclaimed, knowing it had the added advantage—I didn't have to cook it.

While Walter's cooking style may be considered unconventional by some, his recipe for burgers is ordinary for the most part: ground beef, a pinch of onion salt and garlic powder, sometimes adding a splash of Worcestershire sauce. But he always adds his secret ingredient: a large dollop of love.

~Donna Lowich

# Food and Love

## The Taste of Tradition

*Cultures grow on the vine of tradition.*

~Jonah Goldberg

# Family Connection

*Tradition does not mean that the living are dead,*
*it means that the dead are living.*
~Harold Macmillan

As I was looking through old recipes, I found a piece of family history. It was my mother's recipe for the caramelized sweet rolls that she'd traditionally made for Jewish holidays. She had written it in pencil over thirty-five years ago. Although it was faded, I could still read parts. No one made schnecken like Mama did. Nobody ever tried more than once.

My mother was immersed in Jewish culture, but she never seemed to know the origin of her customs. That really used to bother me. Why do something if you don't know why you're doing it? When I was growing up, we kept kosher, which included not eating shellfish.

"Why can't we eat lobster?" I asked Mama when I was a kid. She didn't know, so I found out. I self-righteously told her, "According to Jewish law, scavengers are forbidden." To me, it was pointless to keep kosher if she didn't know why she was doing it. But my mother knew why. She just had her own reasons.

At age thirteen, I stood in front of the congregation one Friday night for my Bas Mitzvah. For months, I had rehearsed the Hebrew prayer I was to sing. I learned it phonetically from a recording, so I had no idea what I would be singing to hundreds of people.

"What's the point?" I said to Mama, as she listened, in rapture, to me singing my Bas Mitzvah song. "I don't even know what I'm saying!" It was always hard for her to answer my rebellious questions. She answered, "Because that is what we do."

That response always aggravated me, but it also gave me the impetus to find my own answers about Jewish practices. I'd arrogantly announce the results of my research to my mother. And it amazed me that she wasn't enthralled.

Every Passover, we put a glass of wine outside the door for the angel Elijah—sort of like putting out cookies for Santa. Once, I put adhesive tape at the level of the wine. In the morning, I showed Mama that the wine was at the very same level as it had been the night before. "Elijah is a myth," I declared victoriously. But in spite of my proof, she kept putting the glass out every year for the angel.

"Why Mama?"

"Because that is what we do."

Every Friday, at sunset, she lit two candles and said, in Hebrew, the Sabbath prayer. In the darkness, her hair covered in delicate lace, she'd move her hands in a slow sweeping motion around the trailing smoke of flames so that it wafted around her. She never knew that this beautiful gesture symbolized the welcoming of the Sabbath. With closed eyes, she'd recite the blessing, not knowing what it meant. But that didn't matter to her. What mattered was that our family was together as she kept alive this ancient tradition. She was fulfilling a sacred vow to teach us by her example. She was our matriarch—the officiator of the ceremony. And she welcomed her powerful mission.

Did it matter what the Hebrew meant? Of course not. Now I understand it was all about family. "That is what we do," meant, "That is what we do to provide a continuous thread of connection linking families past, families present and families yet to be."

My parents are both gone. On the anniversary of Mama's death, I decided to recreate her schnecken. They were good, but nowhere near as delicious as hers were. I realized that didn't matter. In a surprising moment, my heart was touched by a profound connection with my mother I hadn't felt for decades. It was such an odd sensation — almost like she was there. And you know what? I bet she was.

I vowed to re-establish the tradition of making Mama's schnecken once a year for my birthday and I will ask my family to do the same on the date of my birth after I am gone. Perhaps their children will pass it on. Even though Mama's penciled recipe will continue to fade with time, from this day forth, it will be truly everlasting.

Generations from now, someone may ask, "Why do we make these every year on this date?" No one will know. But that won't matter. What will matter to me, as it did to Mama, is the continuation of connection that the schnecken will provide — between families past, present and families yet to be.

And therefore, I pray my successors will fully grasp the rich significance behind Mama's answer, "Because that is what we do."

~Saralee Perel

# The Last Tamale

*Unable are the loved to die. For love is immortality.*
*~Emily Dickinson*

During the holidays there were always wonderful treats to snack on, but my favorite of all foods was my grandmother's tamales. Every year my grandmother would start early and shop in the specialty Mexican food store in the old downtown area. My grandmother had very little money. She was a widow who was too old to work. But she was also a giver. She always wanted to take care of others. It filled her with such pride and joy when she could help someone else out. During the Christmas season, Granny would work tirelessly around the clock making those tamales. After the presents were opened and our bellies were full, she would send us home with a batch of tamales to enjoy later.

Two years ago, my grandmother became very ill. We knew our time with her was short—we just didn't know how short. Her wish was to make it through one more Christmas. Not only did she get her wish, but she also lived one more year past what the doctors had predicted. Early in December the next year, she was weak and fragile. Yet, she went to her favorite Mexican specialty shop and purchased the ingredients for her homemade tamales. She worked hard for over a week to make a large batch of tamales. She finished up and froze them as always. Then on December twenty-third, my dear sweet grandmother went to heaven in her sleep. I flew in for the funeral. We all talked and reminisced about her and about how much she will be missed. But my grandmother had one more wish that came true. She left us all with her special batch of Christmas tamales. And in a strange way it was like she was still with us. Although it was bitter-sweet—eating the tamales without her—we knew she was smiling from up above as we enjoyed her special gift to us.

~Celeste M. Barnard

# 73

# A Tradition Continued

*Giving your son a skill is better than giving him one thousand pieces of gold.*
*~Chinese Proverb*

I t's often said that you don't know what you've got until it's gone, and on November 6, 2010 that became my reality. At 5:38 a.m. I awoke to a telephone call that my lovely mother, Joan Coscia, passed away after a brief battle with cancer. Family life was changed forever.

We all have unique relationships with our mothers. My relationship with my mother was about food, recipes, and television chefs. We were always talking food and adding a pinch of this or a tablespoon of that to give our recipes a new and improved flavor.

We gravitated towards the culinary expertise of Mary Ann Esposito and Lidia Bastianich: the queens of Italian cooking, in our humble opinion. Mom was an Irish girl but when she married my Italian dad in 1956 she became an honorary Italian and embraced Italian cooking. Without a Food Network channel she had to rely on her in-laws, her own instincts, and the trial and error approach.

Truth be told, Mom was an incredible cook, though she would never admit it. I could never understand why. There was always a self-deprecating quip whenever I offered a compliment. Maybe it was modesty. Maybe it was because she wasn't a born-Italian so she felt like an outsider and feared being judged by the real Italians. But through the years Italians and non-Italians gathered around the dinner table and feasted on her delicious meals.

In the days following the funeral I reached for the index card box Mom kept on the top left shelf of the cabinet above the kitchen counter. Inside were her recipes neatly typed on three-by-five index cards. As I held each card, a flood of memories came rushing back. I remembered sneaking into the refrigerator late at night to steal a slice of peppermint or chocolate cream pie, to nibble on a stuffed Cubanelle pepper, or to savor one of Mom's beloved potato croquettes.

Not all the recipes were in the box. Some, like the stuffed peppers and potato croquettes, were part of Mom's being, her soul, and never needed their own index cards. Once I asked about the potato croquettes and she told me how she made them — well, not exactly. She listed the ingredients without the amounts, except for the potatoes, of which there were a dozen.

Those potato croquettes were truly heavenly. Being so time-consuming to make, they became a special family holiday tradition, and not a year went by without the potato croquettes sitting center table on a white porcelain platter. With Mom now gone I decided to make them myself. It was my way of easing the huge void that her death created.

In order to prepare, I wanted a "mom" atmosphere in my kitchen. The first thing I did after I peeled the dozen potatoes and put them in a pot of boiling water was to put on some of Mom's favorite music: Neil Diamond.

While sautéing the onions in olive oil I remembered the time we all went to see Neil Diamond in concert. Our tickets were up in the rafters, the nosebleed section, and to see Neil we needed to use binoculars or watch the huge video screens that book-ended the gigantic stage. Just the look on Mom's face when Diamond crooned "Sweet Caroline" or "Song Sung Blue" was worth it. By the end of the concert she was like a teenager, cheering and applauding.

The next step in the recipe was to mash the potatoes and add the parsley, sautéed onions, parmesan cheese, butter, and salt and pepper. This was going to take some effort with my mashing tool, so I poured myself a glass of wine, white zinfandel to be exact, to prepare for the task.

Whenever I visited Mom we would open a bottle of white wine and we'd sit around the kitchen table catching up. Eventually we'd add cheese and crackers to help soak up the wine, and then whatever else we found in the refrigerator. After a while the conversation would veer from the latest on the grandchildren to what we wanted for dinner. Food. Recipes. Our special connection.

After more wine and more mashing the mixture was ready for the next step: the dipping and the sautéing. I carefully rolled the mashed mixture into oval balls, dipped them in beaten eggs, rolled them in Italian style breadcrumbs, and gently placed them in the heated olive oil. I did this for forty-eight croquettes.

As the first one was finished I couldn't resist the temptation and took a bite, igniting my senses with years of potato croquette reminiscences. It was delicious, but not quite as good as Mom's. It was missing a little something that only Mom could give it: her touch, her love. But there they were — the first batch of potato croquettes I ever made. I served them on a white porcelain platter for the perfect presentation.

In my heart I know that with the potato croquettes Mom lives on, and every holiday they will be part of my holiday menu. A labor of love. A fond remembrance. A tradition continued.

## Joan Coscia's Potato Croquettes

12 potatoes
2-3 tablespoons olive oil
2-3 onions chopped
Pinch of salt
Pinch of black pepper
4-6 tablespoons butter
Chopped fresh parsley
1/2 cup grated parmesan cheese
8 eggs beaten
Breadcrumbs
Oil for sautéing

Peel potatoes. Boil them as if making mashed potatoes. Drain the potatoes.

Sauté chopped onion in olive oil.

Mash the potatoes and add onion, salt, pepper, butter, parsley, and grated cheese.

Form into croquettes.

Dip each croquette in the egg batter and then roll in the breadcrumbs.

Sauté the breaded croquettes in the oil until golden. Drain on paper towel.

Makes about 4 dozen croquettes.

~Michael Coscia

# 74

# A Daughter's Toast to a Father's Bagel

*Old as she was, she still missed her daddy sometimes.*
~Gloria Naylor

"Four sesame, two poppy in a plastic bag if I could?" I say to the nice man with a pierced ear behind the bagel counter. Bagels have seasoned my nutritional and emotional world since I can remember. My father's butter and bacon bagel sandwiches dripped a salty sweetness on Sunday mornings. The richness matched his warm love that started from his sloppy blue leather slippers and spread to the top of his peppery gray hair. He enjoyed making me these breakfast sandwiches as much as I enjoyed eating them. We could only eat one kind of bagel: New York City's H&H. He'd pick up half a dozen every few days. Never more — you can't eat a bagel that's not fresh. We weren't big on cream cheese, unless it was cream cheese and olive sandwiches on Jewish rye. But H&H bagels only needed butter, spread when the bagel was still hot so my father's fingers jumped a little as he called, "Bagel's done!"

When I was sixteen years old, my parents got divorced and my dad moved out. I stopped eating butter and bacon bagel sandwiches — among other things. Bagels, however, remained. My father continued to bring home the bagels to a different house and eventually a different wife. The bagels were always there when I visited; he'd toast them just right. I only ate one half and always plain. I'd seen a friend dip her bagel in tea. I tried it, thinking of Oreos in milk, donuts dipped in coffee. But I only needed to do it once; a soggy wet bagel was not part of my heritage.

Once a week, when I was at college, a large padded manila envelope arrived, stuffed with bagels — poppy and sesame seeds sprinkling their way into our dorm room. I shared more than I ate, but the smell made me feel at home. At age nineteen, I bicycled 4,200 miles across the country. The ten mail stops along the way brought ten bagel packages. From Independence, Missouri to Reedsport, Oregon, my father never missed a bagel delivery.

When I transferred from upstate New York to a Colorado college, not only did the bagels have to travel farther, but I was in a town that hadn't heard of bagels. A breakfast round with a hole in the center was a "donut" in Boulder, Colorado. Now the bagels arrived by Fed Ex to keep their freshness. When I fell in love and moved in with the man who is now my husband of twenty-five years, he'd smile when the Fed Ex truck arrived. "The bagel truck is here!" he'd call out with the same excitement as kids when the ice cream truck shows up. He loved to spread cream cheese on his bagel and add a slice of ham. When I got pregnant with the first of our three children, I reintroduced butter to my bagel... and lots of it.

Next came the question of religion and how we were to raise our children. Since my husband was a Catholic and I was a Jew, the situation demanded a compromise. We agreed we'd raise the children with meditating, eating bagels, and celebrating both Hanukkah and Christmas. My son's first solid food was tiny pieces I broke off my morning bagel. As a toddler, I took him to the first bagel shop that opened. He was verbal enough to say, "Papa Mike bagel better." I had to agree. With the birth of my second son came the opening of Moe's Broadway Bagel in our area, and my kids had finally found the magic.

It was a Friday evening in winter when I had to tell my father the truth. "Dad I think... I think we found a good bagel out here." We were both quiet and I knew I needed to say more.

"Dad, I really don't think you need to keep sending them." I hesitated and added, "Or maybe, just not as frequently."

My father quietly answered, "Oh."

Like breaking the Sabbath bread, our bagel bond was broken that Friday evening. I knew I had to be the adult and reassure my eighty-year-old father that it didn't mean I didn't love him. We both laughed at how silly it felt that we were making such a big deal about bagels. But we also knew that years of feelings were spread thick atop those sesame and poppy seed bagels.

My children now connect with me through bagels. A "mommy" bagel is one that is slightly toasted and spread with butter, never margarine. As each has entered adolescence, there have been shouts of, "Isn't there something DIFFERENT for breakfast than bagels?" My older son now attends college in Florida. No bagel deliveries are necessary. But when he flew in for the holidays late one night, I did make him a "mommy" bagel, toasted just right. I can only hope he tastes the sweet warmth I felt as my father's daughter.

~Priscilla Dann-Courtney

"No, it's not a poster, and yes, they are still hot."

# 75

# Goodbye, Old Friend

*The happiest memories are of moments that ended when they should have.*
~*Robert Brault,* www.robertbrault.com

"Julian! Carol! How are you?" It's Sunday night. I'm about eight years old and my family is out to dinner at Armando's, an Italian restaurant in my Connecticut hometown. Some couple is greeting my parents. Maybe it's the Sterns, or the Cassels, or the Friedmans, or the Millers. It doesn't matter. The point is, whenever we go to Armando's, we know half the people there—either friends or patients of Dad's. We even refer to Armando's as The Temple, since we always find every other Jewish family eating there too.

When I think of eating out as a child, it was always Armando's. It was a place where families were made welcome. I could fight with my brother, accidentally spill my soda, drop spaghetti, and no one minded. The waitresses would swoop down, laughing, and clean up whatever. The waitresses always greeted my parents by name and knew the order without asking: sole française for Dad, eggplant parmagiana for Mom, spaghetti and meatballs for the four kids. If we really wanted to splurge, garlic bread all around. It was where I was first introduced to fancy-shmancy blue cheese salad dressing, which, to this day, seems the height of sophistication to me. It was where we celebrated birthdays and anniversaries. It was while eating there that I first told my parents that I had met the man who would become my husband.

My dad liked to eat early and in a hurry. No lingering over drinks.

No alcoholic drinks, period. Dessert? "We have just as good at home," he would say. Sometimes he could get the six of us in and out of there in twenty minutes, often getting us home in time for the six o'clock news. Armando's was the only place where he could pull off this routine comfortably and without feeling embarrassed. When it was suggested that maybe we could try another place, he always sighed and said, "Why, when we can get what we want at Armando's?"

Armando's heyday came and went, of course. Soon the smart set moved elsewhere; only we remained amidst the faded glory. But the food still was great—an unparalleled vodka sauce—and the waitresses remained friendly. When my son, Levi, came along, we started taking the next generation. They didn't care that he spilled water, got more dinner on the floor than in his mouth, and occasionally vomited. He would demand his "cumbers, please" (for a while, cucumbers were his only sustenance) and they appeared, stacked on a plate, skins painstakingly shaved off.

There are circles to life, however. My dad passed away. After that, I couldn't muster the nerve to go back to Armando's. I couldn't face that initial warm welcome from the waitresses, their inevitable question, "And where's Dr. Levine this evening?" I couldn't bear telling them they'd served their last twenty-minute sole française. I wanted so much to go back, but before I got up the fortitude, it was too late. One day, I drove by to see that, after fifty years, Armando's had finally thrown in the oven mitt. It was coming down. I didn't even get enough warning to go for a last meal.

They say that grief comes at odd times. It's not really the funeral or holidays that get you. Those you expect, can plan for. But grief catches you off guard while you're waiting on line at the supermarket and a certain song comes on the Muzak. It's in the smell of a long-forgotten sweater, or a hauntingly familiar expression on the face of your own child. These bring the deep ache of loss. For me, it was sitting in my car outside of what was left of Armando's, gripping the steering wheel while peering out the windshield. There, it hit me that we could never again be the family we once were. And I realized how desperately I missed being my father's daughter.

But as I said, there are circles in life. A few weeks later, my husband and I took our son to try out a new Chinese restaurant in town. We walked in to a large place, packed with families we knew. We felt at home, knowing immediately that Levi could talk loudly, hop around and spill his drink and it would be okay. The waiters fussed good-naturedly over him, bringing his Sprite with a cherry, pineapple and a tiny paper umbrella that his toy Batman eventually held. Then Levi dipped into sushi and crunchy Chinese noodles with an awakening I once felt at that blue cheese dressing. "This is just the way Armando's used to be," I said, feeling simultaneously a stab and release of recognition. I knew we'd be back.

Armando's leaves, a new place arrives. Life goes on. Maybe forty years from now, Levi, paunchy, tired, will sit in the parking lot of this Chinese restaurant, gripping his steering wheel. While peering out the windshield, he will remember back, so long ago, when he was full of energy and adventure, when Mom and Dad were invincible, and when he was part of a family that was part of a community. And I hope he'll think to himself, as I did in Armando's lot, "This was the place and time when I was aware, for the first time, of unconditional love and of the kindness of strangers."

~Beth Levine

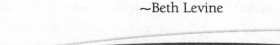

"Can you make something off this menu? It's from the restaurant that was here before."

# Tabbouleh Memories

*Dad, your guiding hand on my shoulder will remain with me forever.*
*~Author Unknown*

When my father died after a long battle with heart disease, I was suddenly struck with what I can only describe as near panic. All the usual realizations sunk in: I would never see my father again, hear his voice, listen to his corny jokes or buy him a Christmas present. But what really hit me hard, what caused the sudden panic was the thought that I would never again taste his tabbouleh salad.

I knew, even in the midst of my grief, that worrying about salad was a little silly. But for my family, food had always meant much more than simple nourishment. Food was a sign of love, a care-taking act of selfless devotion. My father had grown up at the elbow of his Lebanese grandmother who had come to this country when she was a teenager. Her family had come from a small mountain village to make a better life, and with them they brought family recipes and a desire to share love through these special foods.

My father had learned to make dishes like tabbouleh, a salad with bulgur wheat, tomato, onion and parsley, and kibbeh made of beef, bulgur, pine nuts and seasonings. They also made stuffed grape leaves, meat pies and hummus. At every holiday and special event these same foods found their way to our dinner table, and the generations of love that went into making, serving and passing them down found their way into our hearts.

I'll admit I didn't always appreciate my father's cooking. As a teen I complained more than once about my father's need to add lemon and garlic to every dish he made. I would get upset with him when he insisted on making "special" hamburgers with spices and herbs when all I wanted was what my friends were eating. And though I knew that having a father who cared enough to make these foods for us was unique, I let the opportunity to learn pass me by.

When I realized the opportunity was gone forever, that tabbouleh salad loomed large, representing everything that my father had been to me. And because I had never learned how to make the traditional recipes, those flavors and that part of my relationship with my father were forever lost.

Or so I thought.

Luckily for me, my younger brother, Brian, had been paying attention. I didn't know that Dad had shown Brian how to make many of the family dishes, and several months after our father died, Brian surprised me for my birthday with a bowl of tabbouleh. I couldn't believe the flavors and the textures. They were spot on. Brian's gift of love remains one of the most emotionally thoughtful I have ever received.

In fact, the tabbouleh inspired me, and I asked Brian if he would teach me to make a few of our father's dishes. Between him and my Irish mother—who had been my father's chief taste tester over the years—we muddled through. Brian took me to the public market and we bought fresh produce and ingredients to make tabbouleh, kibbeh and hummus. Brian, a chef by trade, spent the afternoon cooking, and when he was done I had a house full of the smells, textures and flavors of my youth.

Over the next few weeks, I worked with Brian to write down recipes that had only been passed down orally before that. My mother came over and helped me get flavors just right and filled in the gaps in my memory with stories about my dad, the foods he made and even notes on which he liked best or those even he didn't care to eat. As we worked, I rediscovered a love for the foods that as a kid I sometimes shunned. I even ventured to make a few dishes myself.

Soon I was chopping and soaking and combining, calling Brian for the proper mixture of spices. As I tried out different foods, my mother suggested we take a few field trips to local Mediterranean restaurants. I sampled stuffed grape leaves, hummus, and several versions of tabbouleh, and I found myself constantly comparing the flavors to what I had grown up with.

Along the way I discovered my father had attempted to write down a few recipes, too. Brian produced Dad's typewritten recipe for baklava, a dessert made with layers of phyllo dough, nuts, honey and spices. The dish is time consuming to make, but if it is done well, the results can be astonishing.

Brian and I set about making the dessert, and my kitchen soon rang with our laughter at the various handwritten notations Dad had made in the margins. Our father's sense of humor shone through with notes like, "Do not cheat. Paint every sheet," referring to the need to brush each thin sheet of dough with butter. And, "You may give this recipe to whomever you choose. Although it is a family secret." Now every time I make baklava for Christmas or a special occasion, I smile and laugh, remembering the best parts of my father who even left us jokes in his recipes.

Through this culinary journey, I realized that a simple salad like tabbouleh had reestablished a connection with my past. It helped me gain a better appreciation for my father and his heritage and inspired me to document our family's recipes. Now I can pass down to my own children the food of my childhood and the spirit of love in which it was given.

Sure, my boys have shown little interest in sharing my Lebanese food, save for the awesome pita breads and baklava, but perhaps one day they will give it a second chance, as I did. Maybe they will even teach their own children how to make tabbouleh or will wonder if a restaurant's baklava is as good as Mom always made it. Whatever the future holds, I know it is richer for the food, the love and the memories I hold.

# Kibbeh

2 lbs. top round beef, ground twice (ask your butcher to do
    this for you)
11/2 cups fine bulgur wheat
1 large onion grated
salt and pepper to taste
1/2 cup cold water
1/4 cup of pine nuts
3 baby (or 1/2 to 1 regular) sweet red peppers, diced small
1/4 teaspoon red pepper flakes
1/4 cup olive oil
2 tablespoons butter
pinch of cinnamon

Preheat oven to 350 degrees.

Soak bulgur in a bowl of water to soften (about 15-20 min).
When soft, drain and squeeze out excess water. Set aside.

In a medium sauté pan, cook two tablespoons of butter, a
pinch of cinnamon, red pepper flakes, sweet peppers and
pine nuts on medium heat until pine nuts are slightly brown.
Remove from heat and let cool.

In a large bowl combine pine nut mixture, softened bulgur,
beef, and salt and pepper. Mix with your hands. When completely mixed, add the water and continue mixing until no
longer runny.

Press mixture in a well-greased 9 x 13 pan and bake for about
20 minutes, or until cooked through.

Cut diagonally to create diamond-shaped pieces, drizzle with
olive oil and serve.

# Taboulleh

1 1/2 cups of fine grain bulgur wheat
2 roma tomatoes, diced small
1 cucumber, diced small (optional)
1 bunch parsley, stems trimmed and chopped fine
1 bunch scallions-whites and greens, ends trimmed and sliced
    thin
juice of 2 lemons
3 tablespoons of olive oil
salt and pepper to taste

Soak bulgur in cold water for about 15-20 minutes, using enough water to cover bulgur by four inches.

Drain water and refill, soaking for an additional 15-20 minutes.

Drain and squeeze excess water from bulgur.

Combine all ingredients and toss gently. Season to taste. Serve chilled.

~Lisa Tiffin

# Cottage Clambake

*Rejoice with your family in the beautiful land of life!*
*~Albert Einstein*

What a crisp, colorful autumn afternoon. Crimson-tipped maples paint the rural landscape as we drive to my aunt's shady lakeside cottage. Overhead, a flock of geese fly in "V" formation, seemingly pointing to the Ohio/Pennsylvania border, past miles of roadside pumpkin stands and endless fields of late season sweet corn. Finally, my husband turns down a familiar gravel road. I spot the lake, glistening in the warm October sun.

"We're here!" I rustle my girls from the back seat.

"Hurry and say hello to everyone."

The small white cottage reminds me of a dollhouse—the good kind of cozy, where friends and family happily gather, spilling into the yard when the quarters get a bit tight. I smile as I walk past the well-manicured lawn, bedecked for fall with orange and yellow mums peeking from cast iron buckets. As always, dried cornstalks climb the back porch rails. I spy a row of perfectly orange pumpkins, gifts from my uncle's garden. Every year he sends a pumpkin home with each child, just in time for Halloween.

Hopping from the car, the girls crunch through the leaves, hoping to sample appetizers on the back porch table. In an instant, their cheeks are stuffed with crab dip, Amish Swiss cheese, and trail bologna. Family seems to be everywhere. Cousins, aunts, and uncles trickle from the cottage, sharing hugs and gossip in the wooded yard.

Gathered in groups, my chatty Scotch-Irish clan prepares for our autumn tradition: an outdoor clambake, held annually the first Sunday in October. Husks fly off golden sweet corn ears as we all pitch in, removing silky threads from more than forty cobs. Great aunts, unaware that they could be sitting down, scurry about setting tables, slicing juicy red tomatoes, and taking surreptitious sips of homemade berry wine.

The men hover as they always do — around the fire pit. I chuckle at this primitive scene: men tending the fire and women preparing vegetables. Salty steam, heavy with clam and roast chicken flavors, teases my taste buds. What could be better? Somehow, I can't imagine being anywhere else on this idyllic autumn afternoon.

Sitting around card tables in the yard, we say a quiet prayer of thanksgiving. Then, at long last, it's time to dig in. Tearing open the mesh bag of steamers, I generously swirl each clam in drawn butter. What a gloriously gritty delicacy. Heaven seems near as a lobster tail is placed on my plate, followed by sweet potatoes and steaming clam broth. My daughters, content with an ear of sweet corn each, amazingly don't care for seafood.

"I can help you out there," my husband teases, reaching for their leftover lobster. We laugh with cousins and swap family news before gorging on a final, overindulgent treat — homemade cheesecake and raspberry pie.

As the sun sets, we pour second cups of coffee, warm mugs that prolong our time together, if only for a few precious minutes.

"Don't forget to take a pumpkin home," my aunt says.

"Did you get a candle off the mantel?"

Our girls pick their future jack-o-lanterns as I select my party favor — a homemade cranberry scented votive. In the year ahead, it will fill my house with the love, light and warmth of family.

"Thanks again for the clams, the pumpkin, the candle..."

The following morning, I struggle to compose a thank-you e-mail. How can I adequately show my appreciation? Finding next year's calendar, I flip ahead to October, making sure to highlight the first Sunday in bright orange marker.

Perhaps the best sort of thank you involves simply being present for cherished traditions. Next year, and hopefully for many years to come, I will be there, feasting with family at our cottage clambake.

~Stefanie Wass

# Memory Meals

*What is patriotism but the love of the food one ate as a child?*
~Lin Yutang

"Mom, thanks for making barbecued meatballs and rice before I left," said Betsy with misty eyes. She hugged me goodbye while her dad finished loading the car with packed boxes. My daughter was moving from our home in Florida to her apartment in Washington, D.C. to begin her new job. "I'm really going to miss your cooking," she added.

Betsy's comment about home-cooked meals gave me an idea. I decided to make special gifts for my three grown children, who were in various stages of leaving home for college and careers.

After Betsy waved goodbye, I drove to the store and bought three yellow recipe boxes and decorated index cards. For several days I copied family recipes from my food- splattered cards, including Betsy's meatballs, the traditional bunny cake Lori requested each Easter, Steven's special lasagna, and the family's favorite, fresh apple cake.

I included precious recipes I had gathered from country neighbors when our family spent summers on our farm in Missouri, knowing they would rekindle fond memories. I chose Cousin Donna's recipe for the beets she pickled, after she harvested them from her picture-perfect garden. I copied Lestie's tangy freezer slaw ingredients she had scrawled on a used envelope years ago. I made note that Pat's instructions for making her outstanding homemade rolls included driving thirty miles for fresh yeast.

When the handwritten cards stood alphabetized in their boxes, I closed the lids and set them aside until I would be with my children again. When the time came, I presented each one with the recipes and enjoyed their wide grins and shrieks of delight as they thumbed through the cards.

"I remember making this bread in my second grade class," remarked Steven.

"Oh, this is the best macaroni and cheese ever!" recalled Lori.

"Look! Here's one for the homemade ice cream we churned on the farm each summer!" squealed Betsy.

Over the years the boxes of recipes continued to be popular resources in their kitchens, reminders of the food and love they were served during their childhoods. Now, with children of their own, they explained the stories behind the recipes to my nine grandchildren, and inspired them to become young cooks.

One day, a video arrived on my computer. I watched my animated, eleven-year-old granddaughter, Amy, as she pretended to be Julia Child and demonstrated how to make an omelet. When she finished, she held it up to the camera and imitated the famous, "Bon appetite!"

I think it's time to give Amy her own small box filled with handwritten family recipes.

~Miriam Hill

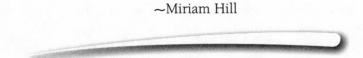

# Homemade Love

*The family is a haven in a heartless world.*
*~Attributed to Christopher Lasch*

Valentine's Day is usually spent with the one you love. Not me. Mine is spent with the four people I love. It wasn't always that way, but six years ago a new tradition was started.

It started when my husband and I got a sitter for our three kids and went to our favorite Italian restaurant. The smell of warm bread and dipping oil wafted out as we approached the restaurant. I had barely eaten that day just to leave room for all the yummy food I was about to consume. Would I have chicken parmesan? No, chicken marsala. I couldn't make up my mind.

We waited for a table, along with twenty other people. I knew it was Valentine's Day, but was this everyone's favorite restaurant? To make matters worse, the people who were seated took their time. They savored every bite and then ordered more. They sipped their wine, lingered over the meal and then ordered dessert.

Two and a half hours later, we were seated. The food had lost its appeal. It was no longer dinnertime, it was bedtime. Nothing was worth that long a wait, but we knew every other place would be the same. In an attempt to save the evening, I put on a smile and worked through my lasagna. Never again would I subject myself to that kind of torture.

The following year, John asked, "Where are we were going for dinner?"

"Nowhere!" I said. His look was quizzical. "It's a surprise. Just be home by six."

While John was at work and the kids were at school, I got busy with the preparations. I warmed some cream and added a split vanilla bean, the essence floated on an invisible cloud. After whipping some egg yolks and sugar to a light yellow color, the cream was added and melted dark chocolate was folded in. Then the crème brûlée was put into the refrigerator to set.

I began setting the table. It was better than any restaurant I had been to. The red tablecloth was sprinkled with pink rose petals, then layers of white toile were added. Votives were scattered around the settings of my best china. I placed a box of chocolates and a hand-written card on each plate. All my table needed now was a good meal and my family to enjoy it.

I preheated the oven and began to stuff a large chicken. I used onion, a quartered lemon, a whole head of garlic, thyme and salt and pepper. Then, under the skin, I rubbed a butter mixture with shallot, thyme, salt, pepper and lemon zest.

As the chicken cooked and the skin turned a golden brown, I began to boil potatoes. Once they were cooked and drained, I whipped in some warm cream and lots of butter, creating a mound of fluffiness.

The meal was coming together. I roasted some asparagus, warmed some rolls and made a rich gravy out of the pan drippings from the chicken. This was the kind of meal to be talked about for years to come.

The kids came home full of questions. "Aren't you going out to dinner?" my daughter Caitlin asked.

"Do we get to drink out of those wine glasses?" my six-year-old son asked. My fourteen-year-old son didn't say much but I caught him looking over his book, gazing at the table.

"When is Dad going to be home?" Caitlin asked impatiently.

"Don't worry, Dad won't miss the fun. Now go play while I finish our dinner." She couldn't pull herself away and she remained under my feet while I placed the food on platters.

John walked in the door as the last tray of food was placed on the table. He handed me a bouquet of roses that I placed in the center of the table. Perfect, I thought, as I looked at the glowing faces around the table.

It was a meal we would never forget, especially when I torched a layer of sugar on top of the crème brûlée. No one wanted to be the first to get up. I had never seen the kids so mesmerized or well behaved. There were no elbows on the table and the napkins were placed on their laps.

In the years to come, the kids would start talking about dinner weeks before Valentine's Day arrived. I always surprised them and tried to top the year before.

Now my oldest is twenty, and he still makes sure he is here for Valentine's. Instead of having four loved ones to spend it with, I now set the table for six, seven, even eight people. The kids bring their dates, because no one wants to miss out on the festivities.

Maybe one day I will be lucky enough to share this tradition with my grandchildren. I smile as I look across the table at my husband. This is what Valentine's Day is about—showing your family how much they are loved.

~Helen Zanone

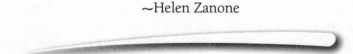

"For years we alternated between food that was red
and food that was heart-shaped, but starting this year
we will be switching to food that tastes good."

# Tasting My Past

*Mothers and daughters are closest when daughters become mothers.*
*~Author Unknown*

First, I must prepare. At the farmer's market, I select what seem to me the best tomatoes—red and plump and promising. Next, I look over the peppers, choosing eight sweet red ones and a dozen hot red ones. Their shiny skins feel smooth to the touch. Finally, I buy onions, their flavor wrapped loosely in thin brown skin. Eight of them will join the tomatoes and peppers, vinegar, and seasonings as ingredients in my chili sauce.

Before we moved to our smaller, urban property, I grew what I needed myself. It felt right then, standing in my garden, pushing aside foliage and finding the perfect vegetables for this project. Now I buy from farmers who picked their crops hours before.

I remember my mother strolling among the selections at the market and choosing carefully. Like her, I continue to seek the best.

I keep her recipe in a special place. When I take it out, it feels like I greet an old friend. It has been a kind of companion all my life.

At home, I remove the huge silver-colored canner from its basement shelf. Next, I assemble pint jars. Some still wear their gleaming metal bands that will hold the lids. Although I packed them away carefully, I scrub them to ensure their cleanliness.

During more than forty years of marriage, I have assembled countless boxes of jars and lids as I canned our garden's vegetables and fruit. Most important, I have that family recipe, given to me to continue the tradition. I must carry out this duty.

The chili sauce I make connects me, with love, to Mother and to others in my family, long gone. I hear them ask my mother, "Where is your chili sauce? I'd prefer that on my hamburger." My father smothered his breakfast eggs with it.

Whenever I prepare to follow the recipe, I remember helping Mother. She did not actually need my assistance, but she must have realized I needed the practice to make the sauce myself some day.

I begin as she did, soaking the tomatoes in hot water to make their skins come off easier. As the red orbs bob in the sink, I hear Mother say, "Go out to the garden and find one more good-sized tomato."

She was always well prepared. The day before she planned to cook her chili sauce, she peeled the tomatoes. That day, the one prior to the actual canning, my father and I anticipated the flavorful result of Mother's efforts. It seems as if it were just yesterday that my mother's inviting chili sauce aroma filled every room of the house, tantalizing and teasing.

When I prepare the onions and the peppers, I grind them in my cast-iron grinder. As I grab the wooden handle and crank it, I see my mother turning into a white-haired woman who continued making chili sauce until the year before she died. Working this way puts me in touch with she who went before me.

Just after I started my chili sauce cooking this day, my youngest child called from her California home. "I am making chili sauce," I told her.

"Oh, wow. I wish I could smell it," she said and reminisced about coming home from school as a young child and smelling the chili sauce from the sidewalk on the corner. "The house smelled so wonderful for a few days," she said. I remembered that was true all during my childhood as well.

Today is not simply the day I fill waiting jars with the taste of summer we will savor all year long; it is the stirring of love and warm memories. My grandmother and her mother before her canned every fall. As a child, I explored their basement food pantries lined with home-canned fruit, tomatoes, and pickles. I knew at some family dinner during the coming winter, I would taste some of those put-away treasures.

Perhaps, my mother's recipe came from one of them. I do not know. Someone perfected that recipe and gave it to the next in line. And we continue to follow it, handing it down in an endless circle of labor and care for our families just as the earth continues to yield its bounty.

I imagine my own daughters may someday follow the same directions I do. My older daughter inherited her grandmother's dark blue canning pan. Perhaps, someday a daughter of one of my daughters will decide to engage in the family tradition. Then, her today will merge with all those yesterdays and her family will taste the past.

And when she stirs the simmering concoction, I hope she thinks of me with love.

## Chili Sauce

30 ripe tomatoes
8 medium onions
6 green sweet peppers (Mother preferred a rich red color so
    she used all red sweet peppers)
12 red hot peppers
1 quart cider vinegar
3 tablespoons salt
4 cups sugar
1 teaspoon allspice
1 teaspoon ginger
1 teaspoon cinnamon

Scald tomatoes in boiling water to loosen skins. Peel and cut into quarters.

Chop fine or coarsely grind onions. Put vinegar and onions in large non-aluminum pan with tomatoes. Bring to a boil, then simmer, uncovered, for 20 minutes.

Seed and chop fine (or coarsely grind) peppers. Add peppers and all other ingredients to pan. Simmer until it is a little thicker than ketchup, four hours or more.

Clean jars thoroughly. (Recipe yields from 6 to 10 pints.) Put jars and lids in hot water. Carefully drain and then fill hot jars with warm chili sauce. (If jars aren't heated enough from the hot water, they will break.) Clean off any drips from jar rim. Place warm lid on jar top and screw on ring to hold lid in place.

Place warm jars in rack in canning pan. Lower jars into water so they are completely covered. Bring to a boil. Boil for 25 minutes. Lift rack. Refrigerate any jars that do not seal.

Use the sauce on fried eggs, hamburgers, hot dogs and sausages. Mix with soy sauce for a marinade for fish or with mayonnaise for salad dressing. Use in any recipes calling for a sweet or spicy sauce. I like to add it to a white sauce to use in a casserole with noodles and clam.

~Sandy McPherson Carrubba

81

# Chicken Soup for the Soul

# A Recipe for a Family

*At the end of the day, a loving family should find everything forgivable.*
*~Mark V. Olsen and Will Sheffer, Big Love*

I always felt like the black sheep of Patrick's family. I wanted to "fit in," but no matter how hard I tried, I was the square peg trying to fit in the round hole. I accompanied Patrick to every birthday party and holiday celebration at his family home — a three-hour drive down winding backcountry roads. But I always left feeling empty, like I missed the mark at another social gathering. I desperately wanted to be accepted into his tight-knit family.

Pat's mom was a quiet woman who rarely shared her feelings. Instead of respecting this, I tried to peel away at her emotional layers, hoping she would embrace me. Pat's dad was the opposite, singing in the kitchen as he sprinkled spices in his spaghetti sauce, seasoning it with a little bit of everything he could get his hands on. He handed me a glass and his stories flowed as easily as the wine. Every tale described how his parents emigrated from Italy, and how they struggled to feed their hungry children. Most stories were built around food.

Every visit to Pat's family ended the same way, with his brothers and sisters huddled around the cozy dinner table filled with endless pans of lasagna, spaghetti laden with meatballs and eggplant parmesan. Pat's dad made the best salad dressing in the world. It was a recipe he created and although I tried to replicate it, I could never get it to taste as good as his. Pat would try my version, look upward, and say, "This is good." He would nod his head approvingly, take a few more bites and smile. "It just takes practice," he would say. "You're getting there."

"I don't understand how mixing ketchup with brown sugar and vinegar can taste so good," I said.

"There are two secrets to this recipe," Pat's dad said quietly. "The spices are very important," he paused, looked over the rim of his glasses, and continued, "tossing it wildly, mixing everything up, is essential."

Pat's dad filled plastic containers with leftovers and sent us on our way. He would wave goodbye as he stood on his porch. He did this no matter how many harsh words were spoken throughout the day or how many tears were shed. Above all else, he wanted peace in the family. The way he chose to achieve this was through food. We always came together to share food and talk about the recipes. We could set aside our ill feelings and escape in a world of pasta.

I started many of the family fights by speaking my mind while we were playing a game or having a conversation. No matter how much I told myself to keep quiet, I simply couldn't do it. One argument transpired as we played the game Scruples.

"How dare you accuse me of being a thief!" he snarled. His crimson face wore a mean expression, something I wasn't used to seeing.

"It's only a game," I said, trying to lure him back to the couch.

"I don't want to play anymore," he said walking into the kitchen.

I looked at Pat and felt dismayed as he whispered, "Nice going."

"Oh, great!" I snapped, smacking the sofa cushion between us. "You're angry with me too?"

"How could you be so insensitive to my father?" he jeered.

"It's a game!" I yelled. "Why can't anyone in this family play a game without a fight ensuing?"

"Are you accusing my family of being argumentative?" his sister shrieked, picking up the board game.

"Let's have a glass of wine," my father-in-law said, carrying a handful of glasses by the stems. He set them down on the coffee table and filled the glasses halfway with a luscious burgundy red from the Finger Lakes region of New York State. "This is an exceptionally mellow grape harvested two years ago in Hammonsport," he said, swirling the wine as he held his glass high and said, "Salute."

And with that, the family brawl ended on a happy note.

The family dynamic changed when Pat's parents passed away and one sibling moved out of state. The family home was sold and household items divided. His sister took the casserole dishes; a brother took the pie plates and loaf pans. Pat took the pasta pot.

The family remained vibrant through food. Every Christmas, Pat made a pan of ziti exactly the way his dad used to do it. The family would take turns celebrating Christmas at each other's houses. Pat always brought the pasta. Thankfully, the only thing that was missing was the arguments.

This past Christmas was challenging because there wasn't extra money to spend on gifts for each other. Some family members had lost their jobs, others had their salaries lowered, and we all were trying to pay for college educations.

"Let's exchange Mom and Dad's recipes instead of presents," Pat said excitedly. "It doesn't cost anything and it will be the best gift!"

I nodded my head, knowing he was right. "I'll write to everyone and get them all on board," I said.

Pat and I enjoyed sorting through our recipe box, reading handwritten recipes that were passed down from his parents. We compiled a special file and presented it to his family at our holiday celebration. We all chose our own ways to commemorate the family meals that we all had shared over the years. Pat's sister compiled her recipes in a booklet with this note included:

"Our family has gathered for over fifty years for birthdays, holidays, weddings, graduations, funerals, or just for the heck of it. The centerpiece of all of these celebrations was to come together for a meal, to share our lives, our memories, our love. Over the years we enjoyed many classic dishes like Dad's spaghetti and Mom's apple pie. While there were many successful feasts, there were a few failures too, like Dad's canned eggplant. It looked like a science experiment that had gone bad. Food was a big part of our gatherings and no one could cook like them. If you went away hungry, it was your own fault! May God bless and continue to allow us to gather for years to come, just as Mom and Dad would want us to do, to create more memories and to help us to appreciate and love each other. We are their legacy."

By the time I finished reading her note I had tears in my eyes as I realized I always had been a part of this tight-knit family. Each family member was like my father-in-law's Italian dressing recipe; a lot of different ingredients that came together to make something exceptional. The secret to it tasting so wonderful was the spice and mixing it up. Those two magical elements made our family uniquely special and I'm reminded of it each time I use their recipes.

~Barbara Canale

# 82

# What Mothers Are For

*Being a full-time mother is one of the highest salaried jobs in my field,
since the payment is pure love.*
~Mildred B. Vermont

September 1987.

The phone rings. It's my daughter Jill, calling from Indiana University, where she has just started her freshman year.

"Mom, I need my prom dress... the blue silk one with the silver belt. I think it's hanging in my closet. Can you look... NOW?"

"I can't right this second," I say.

"But Mom!" she interrupts, a refrain I suddenly realize I have missed these past few weeks. "I need it Saturday."

She has just been invited to her first college formal. I'm thrilled. But it's a quarter to five on Tuesday afternoon. Even if I find the dress, I won't make it to the post office before it closes at five o'clock.

I don't tell her I'm up to my elbows in noodles for the noodle kugels (puddings) that I'm preparing for the sixty-plus people I've invited for our Break-the-Fast dinner at the conclusion of the Yom Kippur holiday.

For an instant, my mind wanders back to the Sunday three weeks ago. Leaving Jill—and dozens of shoes, jeans, shirts, sweaters and most of the contents of her bedroom that she insisted she could not live without—at her college dorm was much more emotional than I had expected. The parent manuals do not prepare moms for that day.

My attention snaps back to the present situation.

"The short blue one, right?" I confirm, stalling for time, and beating the eggs that need to be added to the noodles draining in the colander. I'm following my Aunt Fern's noodle kugel recipe, wistfully remembering it's Jill's favorite.

"Yes! That's the one! Can you please look for it now?"

"Sure," I say. "I'll call you right back." I dump the noodles and eggs into the bowl.

"Thanks Mom. You're the best. I love you!"

My "right back" buys me the fifteen minutes I need to blend the sugar, vanilla and buttermilk into the noodles, pour the mixture into the already-greased pan, set the timer and pop the kugel into the oven.

For this instant, I'm still her best friend... I haven't been replaced by Carolyn, Scott, Stacy, Brian (who will become her husband), Joanne and the others who have punctuated her conversations each time she calls home. I'm thrilled she's made so many friends in the three long weeks she's been gone, but worry I might be losing her to the cornfields of Indiana.

I take the stairs quickly, but stop short of going into her room. Her bed's made. The dresser drawers are shut, without shirtsleeves or tank top straps dangling from them. I can see her rug. No jeans crumpled in a heap or flip-flops strewn about. Entering, I fight the urge to knock the *People* magazine and a stack of papers off her neatly organized desk.

I rummage through the rejects in her closet that didn't make it to college... her once favorite green T-shirt with COOL in sparkly letters, the brown suede fringed boots she absolutely had to have, the black cardigan with mother-of-pearl buttons from the GAP that she said I could borrow... left behind like me.

I call her back.

"Did you find it?"

"Yes, but it needs to go to the cleaners. There's a stain down the front."

"Can you take it NOW and get it back by tomorrow?"

I've already anticipated this request.

The yellow digital clock on the nightstand in her room screams 5:03. I do the math in my head. The kugel will come out of the oven at 5:35. I can get the dress to the cleaners before they close and plead with them to have it ready by four o'clock the next afternoon. I'll be able to get to the post office by five, send the dress Priority Mail, and, if all goes well, Jill will have her dress Friday.

This is my daughter, my first-born, away at college, and still needing me.

I remove the kugel from the oven, stopping for a moment to inhale the smell of brown sugar and vanilla oozing from the toasty brown cornflake-crumb topping blanketing the bubbling kugel, before racing to Dean Cleaners. Mrs. Kim assures me the dress will be ready the next afternoon.

I return home. The first of the three kugels I need to make has cooled. Without thinking, I put it in the freezer, which is very out of character for me. I prefer food to be served fresh, so I am puzzled that this first kugel is now in the freezer. But there is little time to put the puzzle pieces together. The dress distraction has set me back about forty-five minutes, and will set me back another forty-five minutes tomorrow when I need to zoom to both cleaners and post office.

By Wednesday afternoon at 3:45, the dress is ready. Back home, I find a box and pack the dress gingerly, so it won't wrinkle, or at least will wrinkle less. Then, much to my surprise, I find myself walking to the freezer, removing the frozen kugel, and wrapping it in aluminum foil and ice packs so it won't defrost, or at least will defrost less. I slip it into the box with the dress, the kugel sequestered into several heavy-duty plastic zippered plastic storage bags so that dress and kugel do not meet in their travels to the Indiana cornfields, and head to the post office.

It's her first Yom Kippur away from home. It's my first Yom Kippur without her. She wants the dress. I want her home. The kugel! The puzzle pieces begin to fit together.

The phone rings Friday afternoon.

"Mom, thanks so much. The dress is perfect for the formal tomorrow and everyone is soooooooo excited to have kugel to break the fast after Yom Kippur. I can't believe you did that!"

Her voice cracks. My eyes well with tears that, thankfully, she cannot see.

"I am your mother," I tell her. "That's what mothers are for."

"I love you," she says.

•••

April 2007.

The phone rings. It's my daughter Jill, calling from Denver where she, Brian and their two sons live.

"Mom, I need my prom dress… the blue silk one with the silver belt. Do you have any idea where it is?"

I'm in the midst of making matzoh balls for our Passover seder.

"No," I answer, about to ask why she needs her prom dress from twenty years ago.

"I just got invited to a Twentieth Reunion of our Senior Prom Party and we're all supposed to wear our prom dresses. If you can find it, will you mail it to me?"

"Sure," I say, recalling a similar request from two decades ago.

"Thanks Mom, you're the best. I love you!"

I smile. I didn't lose her to the cornfields of Indiana. Over the years we have become best friends. And although married with children of her own, she still needs me.

"I love you too," I say, hanging up the phone.

## Aunt Fern's Kugel

1 lb. wide noodles (cooked)
1 qt. buttermilk

4 eggs (beaten)
1/2 cup sugar
1 stick butter (room temperature)
1 tablespoon vanilla

Topping
2 cups crushed cornflakes
1/2-1 cup brown sugar
1/2 stick butter (melted)

Mist first six ingredients together in a large bowl.

Pour into 9 x 13 Pyrex dish.

Bake at 350 for 45 minutes and remove from oven.

Cover generously with topping mixture.

Bake at 350 for 15 minutes.

~Carol A. Boas

**Chapter 9**

# Food *and* Love

## Life Lessons in the Kitchen

*There are no mistakes or failures, only lessons.*

~Denis Waitley

# 83

# Everything I Would Need to Know

*There are some things you learn best in calm, and some in storm.*
~Willa Cather

My mother was the "different" mom. Rarely home, she more closely emulated the dynamic career women who would not become commonplace for another decade. The year I turned ten, Mom bought a deli and started her catering business in the back room. My friends arrived home from school to mothers in the midst of cooking dinner, eager to hear about their day. I often came home to an empty house and a dinner made by my grandmother or heated up in the oven by my sister or me.

I never liked school, but by high school I absolutely hated it. I used to fake all sorts of illnesses to get out of going. Mom had little energy left from her seven-day workweeks to argue with me. Her reputation as a caterer had grown. And impossible as it seemed, her work hours increased too, something I highly resented. Between designing wedding cakes, making entire meals and expanding deli hours to attract early commuters and last-minute evening shoppers, she was often on her feet a grueling seventeen hours a day. She simply had nothing left to deal with her willful fourteen-year-old. So she punished me the only way she could.

"I don't know what you're trying to avoid," she said. "But you're not going to stay here in bed all day if that's what you're thinking."

Impatiently, she sipped a cup of coffee while I showered and dressed.

Our first stop was Temmler's Bakery. At five-thirty in the morning, when the business district was empty and dark, the kitchen at Temmler's was brightly lit. We arrived at the back door as the men, all dressed in white, were just winding down from hours of mixing, baking and decorating. Business was about to shift to the front end of the building where the salespeople, including Mrs. Temmler, were sliding huge silver trays filled with sweets onto shelves in preparation for the arrival of hungry business people on their way to catch the train to Chicago.

Slouched atop a stool and holding a mug of steaming coffee, Mr. Temmler brusquely directed my mother to her orders through the ocean of sugary treats and racks of aromatic bread loaves. With his thick German accent, he sounded severe. But I noticed he always pointed her toward the best assortments. We lugged the heavy trays jammed with sweet rolls, cream horns, jelly doughnuts and coffee cakes out to her station wagon. Loaves of warm, unsliced bread were carefully placed into large brown bags and gently tucked into available nooks and crannies. A few miles away at her store, Mom parked the car on the empty street. We hauled everything inside to the deli's bakery section just beyond the front door where the appealing aromas would waken another set of early risers headed for the train.

I hated the deli business, with its unpredictable ebb and flow of demanding customers. I preferred the kitchen. At the back of the old narrow wooden building, the kitchen occupied an enormous space with twenty-foot ceilings that hoarded heat in winter but suffocated us with a thick blanket of warmth in summer. Rows of fluorescent lights suspended above the workspace cast a warm glow on the worn wooden floors and bounced light off metal prep tables. I was fascinated by the old Hobart mixer that stood nearly as tall as me. It was twice my age but its low-pitched motor whirred along reliably, mixing enormous bowls of ingredients into silken smooth cake batters. The big black pizza oven in the far corner looked like no oven I'd ever seen with its six-foot wide, one-foot high ovens stacked atop tall legs. But it effortlessly baked pies and cakes by the dozen.

My first job of the day was usually to make the doughnuts. Mom didn't trust me with the mix, so she prepared it herself. She poured it into the conical dispenser that hung suspended over the gurgling grease pit. I glided the dispenser over the sizzling pool, pressing the lever that dropped doughnuts one by one. The smell of fresh, hot doughnuts was at first inviting but eventually disgusting as the greasy fragrance permeated my clothes and hair. I swirled blistering hot doughnuts in pans of chocolate and vanilla glaze, then dropped them into huge tubs of brightly colored jimmies or fluffy coconut before settling them onto large silver trays like those from the bakery. I handled so many scorching hot doughnuts by the time I was fourteen, I swore my fingerprints had been permanently removed.

Mom might've been good at talking to me about my problems and the reasons I didn't want to go to school, but I wasn't listening. If we talked at all, it was usually a blazing verbal battle that got nowhere fast and ended abruptly with a slap across my face for some impertinent remark.

Ultimately, she gave up talking and just worked. And I worked alongside her. I learned to clean and prepare huge shrimp and make an attractive sandwich loaf layered with crabmeat or tuna and iced like a wedding cake with cream cheese and savory decorations of olives and chives. I stood for hours carefully cutting canapés from loaves of bread and learning to decorate them neatly. I noticed her attention to detail and the way she smiled and her posture straightened when customers praised her lovely presentations and the delicious flavors of her food. I listened to her conversations with the deliverymen. She knew everyone's name and all their stories. They looked forward to seeing her and sharing their lives with her. I saw how everyone respected and admired her. And I was proud she was my mother.

I scrubbed floors with a heavy rag mop and wiped down the equipment. I washed piles of pots and pans, and kitchen utensils. There was no electric dishwasher, only me. My back ached from standing over the old porcelain sink but I soon realized that if I hadn't been washing dishes, the person doing all the washing up would've been my mother. That was why she was always late for dinner or not home in time to eat at all.

In time, I understood her tenacity and determination to fulfill this dream. I loved how she brightened when we met the deadlines that constantly loomed over her, both from a production standpoint and a financial one. And I learned what price a dream can extract when, at the end of the day, she collapsed into bed knowing the routine would begin again within a few hours. But I saw how much she valued her dream and believed it worth that price.

Before I finished high school, I understood overhead costs and marketing, scheduling and payroll. But more importantly, I learned about faith and determination, hard work, responsibility and most of all, about caring. Mom and I never really had any of the conventional mother/daughter conversations you read about. But wordlessly, over pies and cakes, canapés and sandwich loaves, she explained everything I would need to know.

~Barbara Ann Burris

# My Bubbie's Bulkalah

*Learning is a treasure that will follow its owner everywhere.*
*~Chinese Proverb*

When I was nine or ten, my father would sometimes drop me off at my grandmother's house on Saturday morning when he went to work. Time spent with my bubbie meant one thing: baking. Mostly, though, she would bake while I would sit at the kitchen table and watch. Later, I'd get to sample the delicacies.

My grandmother had the heart, soul and hands of a baker. She could take everyday ingredients and somehow spin them into heavenly treats. Whenever I picture her, I see her with flour up to her elbows, rolling dough to make yet another kind of dessert.

My mother and sister liked my grandmother's roly poly, a rolled dough filled with raisins, Turkish delight, and nuts. Not me. I loved her cheese bulkalah, bite-sized pastries filled with an egg, cheese, sugar and raisin mixture, dusted with cinnamon.

I remember the first time I helped. She placed all her ingredients for the dough into a large bowl, plunged her hands into the bowl, and mixed everything together. "You see what I am doing?" she asked, bits of wet dough clinging to her fingers. "Sometimes it is good to get your hands dirty. You must be able to feel the dough. It is not enough to think; you must feel."

"Here, touch it," she said, once she had the right consistency. "That is what dough should feel like."

I patted the dough lightly, trying to imprint the texture on my mind.

Then, she tipped the dough out of the bowl and rolled it out on her counter until it formed a big sheet about half an inch thick, which she then cut into small squares. Once the dough was ready, it was time to make the filling and put everything together. Greasing several old, banged-up muffin pans, she placed a square of dough in each cup, forming a pocket with the corners sticking up.

"So, Harriet," she said, "do you think you can spoon out the mixture?"

Proud that I would finally be helping, I took a large spoon and dipped it into the bowl. I spooned a huge mound of cheese onto the dough.

"Not too much," she said. "Just a hint. Cheese is very expensive. Flour, on the other hand, is not. So, we hide the jewel in the middle, like a surprise when you bite into it."

I laughed at the thought of a jewel hidden in my favourite dessert. I removed half of the filling from the first pocket and put it in the next one. Then one by one, I carefully filled each dough pocket with a little filling, making sure to divide the raisins evenly among them.

My grandmother nodded her approval.

Once I had spooned on just the right amount, she took over. She pinched the four corners of each square together and then sprinkled cinnamon on top. After pinching the last one, she placed the muffin trays in the oven.

Over the next fifteen minutes, her kitchen filled with the heady aroma of cheese bulkalah.

"Is it ready yet?" I asked, five minutes after they'd started baking.

"Of course not, I just put them in. If I took them out now, they would not taste good. You must learn to be patient. Remember, good things take time."

I sighed and waited a few more minutes before repeating my question.

"Not yet," she said. "Soon. Soon. What did I tell you?"

"Good things take time," I repeated, not realizing I was learning much more than baking.

When she finally took the bulkalah out of the oven, their tops were lightly browned. Without thinking, I reached out for one and burned my finger on the hot pan. I screamed, more in surprise than in pain. My grandmother grabbed my hand and dragged me over to the sink where she ran cold water over my finger. "See what happens when you don't think?"

Disappointment overwhelmed me and tears flooded my eyes.

My bubbie turned off the water and looked at me. "It is only a little burn. Nothing to cry about."

I gulped. "That's not why I'm crying."

"So, what's wrong?"

"You'll think I'm stupid and not let me bake with you again."

My grandmother walked me over to the kitchen table and sat me down. Then she showed me her wrist, which had a long pink scar on it. "You see this? I burned myself three years ago. And I am not a little girl just learning to use a stove. It happens. You learn. That is life." She rubbed the scar. "And sometimes you have to learn more than once."

She went to the fridge and got me a large glass of milk. "Drink. The bulkalah will be cool enough to eat in about fifteen minutes. Since you were such a good helper, I will send you home with some. But," she paused, "you must share with your family, because the best part of cooking is sharing with others."

I nodded. "But you know, bubbie, they like your roly poly. I'm the one who really, really likes your bulkalah."

A hint of a grin played on her lips. "I know how much you like them, but you still have to share. However, that doesn't mean you can't eat a few extra before you go home."

Laughing, I sat at the table with my bubbie, eagerly awaiting my treats. Even now, a lifetime later, I remember the sweetness that filled my mouth when I took my first bite of the still-warm bulkalah. And I realized that if you're like my bubbie, you bake love into everything you make.

~Harriet Cooper

# The Gift that Keeps on Giving

*Food is our common ground, a universal experience.*
*~James Beard*

What do you give the woman who has everything? Every year our family has such a difficult time finding just the right gift for my mother.

My mother is eighty-two years young. There is nothing she wants that she doesn't buy for herself throughout the year. So, what do we do for the holidays, her birthday, and Mother's Day? What do we give to one of the most giving people on earth?

My mom begins asking all of us for our holiday wish lists in September. She has just so many days to shop and needs to get started early. She will not be in the malls in December during the flu season. When we ask what she would like, her standard answer is always "Nothing!"

We used to show up bearing the usual trinkets that had no place in her home or the piece of clothing that didn't fit and had to be returned. The grandchildren finally hit on the perfect gift — family photos, especially of the great-grandchildren and younger members of the family — but no frames, as she has enough to recycle. My sister and brother miraculously found that her garden was an untapped arena for gifts. They have purchased signs, statues, fountains, and of course, plants. They will all be able to milk these ideas for years to come. But what about me? I wanted something different!

One day, I asked my mom what she had been doing all day. She told me she was watching the cooking channel. Mom had always been a good cook and we loved to exchange recipes. In the past I had purchased special cookbooks for her from my travels. She would read them cover to cover like novels and then pass them on to other family members. Food was something she truly appreciated and, as I realized, a connection we shared.

For the next gift-giving occasion I gave my mom a certificate to a cooking class that she and I would attend together. It was a hit. I finally found the gift that keeps on giving. My mom and I have enjoyed many hours with special chefs and have now included my oldest daughter in our excursions.

During these classes we share techniques and ideas, making me realize that sometimes her old tried and true ways could have been lost to me, had I not initiated these classes. It has also made me aware that many of my mom's family specialties have never been written down. I have encouraged her to write down these recipes for all of us. So many of her best dishes were always "a little of this and a little of that." I couldn't risk that my "little" and hers would be different, so I had her include preparation instructions for perfect results in these recipes. Everything from her chopped chicken liver to something as simple as her deviled eggs—usually eaten before they were ever even brought to the table—could have been lost to us if we had not ventured down this path of cooking classes together.

We may not actually cook together, but through classes, recipes, menus, and diets, food has become a special bond we look forward to sharing.

~Kristine Byron

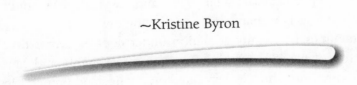

# 86

# Forgiveness Smoothies

*The best portion of a good man's life — his little, nameless, unremembered*
*acts of kindness and love.*
*~William Wordsworth*

Some foods, such as chocolate-covered strawberries, say, "I love you." Some foods say, "I'm sorry for your loss" — like the casseroles church members brought over after my dad's death. Some foods, like pepperoni pizza and chicken wings, say, "It's the weekend, the game's on and let's throw caution to the wind." Some foods, like chicken soup, say, "I hope you feel better." And some food says, "It's a new day, let's start fresh and make sure you're healthy and strong." That food would be my husband's strawberry smoothies, which I've secretly named "Forgiveness Smoothies."

I struggle with my weight. I have a wicked sweet tooth that rivals any celebrity's addiction ever splashed across the tabloids. If eating sweets were a crime, they'd definitely put me in jail and throw away the key. There'd be no need for a jury, judge or trial because everyone would already know I was guilty beyond a shadow of a doubt. I'm sure I'd never get paroled because no one (except my husband and my Weight Watcher's leaders, Amy and Gwyndolyn) would ever believe there was any chance of me changing my ways.

Sometimes I have my addiction under control. Other times it has control of me. But whether I'm acting reasonable and sane or coming home with chocolate smeared on my lips and French fries in my hair, my husband's Forgiveness Smoothies can always refocus my attention, help me move past my poor choices, and remind me of the person I want to be.

I want to be a person who loves herself and fills her body with wholesome nutrients like strawberries, yogurt, apple juice, protein powder and honey. I want to be a person who drinks one nice tall glass of smoothie and calls that a meal. I want to marvel at "how deliciously sweet strawberries are" rather than upping the sugar-shock value with more and more candy, looking for peace at the bottom of a one-pound bag of chocolate covered peanuts.

Sometimes I am the person I want to be! But sometimes I'm not... sometimes, I sit in my car and eat three candy bars and a piece of cake or a dozen cupcakes for no reason at all. When I sit in my car bingeing, I get a temporary high, but almost immediately I feel nauseated and disgusted with my destructive behavior. On these nights, I crawl into bed feeling like a slug and wonder if I will ever change.

This is where my husband's Forgiveness Smoothies come into play. My husband is naturally thin and he monitors what he eats without even really trying. He has a treat every now and then, but he never has five treats in one day. He's always looking for food that is both delicious and nutritious and he cares about my health enormously, so it's natural for him to say "Hey, do you want me to make smoothies for breakfast?" I always say "Yes!" because I feel like a champion when I'm drinking one of these smoothies. "Look at me," I think. "I'm doing what thin people do. I'm having a nice, healthy smoothie for breakfast. For this moment in time, I'm keeping pace with fitness gurus like Bob Greene, Richard Simmons, Kiana Tom and Arnold Schwarzenegger. I love it! I feel like a terminator!"

Drinking these smoothies restores me physically, mentally and emotionally. I feel like I'm being given a fresh start. Even if the day before was a disaster in terms of my food choices, I know at least for today—at least for this one meal—I am being good to my body and I am eating in a reasonable, sane, nutritious way.

Now, don't get me wrong—I don't think there's anything "bad" about having a decadent meal every now and then or splurging on a sinful dessert occasionally. I'm not talking about conscious, calculated decisions made because I really want Aunt Sally's macaroni and cheese or Mama's homemade lasagna. No one needs to be forgiven for eating things like that. But if, like me, you lose control sometimes, then you might be in need of a Forgiveness Smoothie too, so here's my husband's recipe. Bottoms up—it's a new day—a fresh start. This is indeed the breakfast of champions!

## Forgiveness Smoothie

Two smoothies:

1 banana
1 cup apple juice
1 cup low fat vanilla yogurt
1 scoop protein powder
2 cups frozen strawberries*
2 teaspoons honey

If you are only making one smoothie, just divide the entire recipe in half.

*When you use frozen fruit (instead of fresh fruit) there's no need to put ice in the blender—it's a handy trick that has worked well for me because the smoothies are cold without being watered down by ice cubes.

~Rebecca Hill

# 87

# Truly Appreciating Coffee

*No one can understand the truth until he drinks of coffee's frothy goodness.*
*~Sheik Abd-al-Kadir*

When I married Mike, I knew he came into the marriage as a full-fledged CA (Coffee Addict). It didn't bother me. I liked the smell of coffee and the yummy scents that came from the kitchen when he brought home specialty coffee beans like Kona and flavors like Irish cream, crème brûlée, English toffee, and amaretto. And yet, I had no desire to try it.

My husband offered me a cup every day with a smile on his face, claiming he'd wear me down eventually. My friends even tried to talk me into trying it. "I love having Maxwell House moments with my husband," one confided. I rolled my eyes.

Then Samuel James was born and life took a dramatic turn. Now the mother of two little ones, and far from family, I was exhausted. My husband's new job had him leaving at the crack of dawn and after several sleepless nights I could barely function. One morning, I stumbled downstairs and spotted the coffee pot still glowing, with one cup of coffee still warm.

A moment after I took my first sip it hit my bloodstream. My eyes opened wider, I walked faster, I smiled bigger, and it felt great. From that day on, I started drinking coffee in the morning, claiming that it was just to help me function after sleepless nights. The afternoon espresso was a little harder to explain.

Five months later, Sam was sleeping through the night. I was getting eight hours of sleep and still craving coffee in the morning. My husband smiled knowingly. "You like the stuff now, don't you?"

"All right," I cried. "Fine. I love the sheer variety of options — the syrups, the decaf, half-caf, the so-caffeinated-that-my-eyes-don't-blink-for-a-week, the lattes, the cappuccinos, iced, tall, grande! I love the Styrofoam cups with the sippy lids so I don't spill. I love that coffee and chatting go together so well! And fine! Maxwell House moments do exist and they are wonderful. I love wrapping my fingers around a big, beautiful ceramic mug and the warmth it brings me. And when I've had a really bad day, I can sneak a bit of whipped cream and chocolate syrup into my coffee and no one's the wiser."

I think my husband was a bit surprised. I think he was more surprised when, a couple of weeks later when Sam was sick, I told him that I believed a person couldn't truly appreciate the blessing of coffee until they'd been sleep-deprived at least once. So I gave him the wonderful gift of being on night-duty with Sam.

He didn't exactly thank me, but I think he did appreciate his coffee (and me) a lot more the next day. And that's all the thanks I need.

~Heather Humrichouse

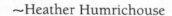

"We specially rigged the coffee maker; as soon as the baby starts crying at night, it starts brewing."

# The Path to His Heart

*Little children, headache; big children, heartache.*
*~Italian Proverb*

The difference between my son's behavior as a toddler and his behavior now as a teenager is negligible. As the years have passed, I have wondered why my son Keshav had not transformed from an active, cuddly, loving toddler to a competent, mature, loving teenager.

Then and now, the behaviors are the same. The idea of a shower has always led to resistance. As a toddler, I could pick Keshav up, kicking and screaming, and drop him in the bathtub. As a teenager, Keshav procrastinates, and an argument ensues.

A blank wall in the house provides fun for children of all ages. Years ago, it held Keshav's sprawling, colorful artwork. Now, it calls for a teenager's game of handball.

As a toddler, Keshav, with his heavy eyelids, insisted that he was not sleepy at bedtime. As a teenager, he argues that his mind is alert only after ten p.m.

However, there is one new behavioral trait that wreaks havoc on the household. Keshav now counts anger and rebelling as part of his daily routine. I am told this is "normal" behavior and it will help Keshav find his independence and his individuality. "It's a phase that will pass," other mothers have assured me. This phase has now extended for over four years, and in the middle of it there seems to be no place for his mother.

One day, I found hope. Posted on his Facebook wall, I read, "Just had the most awesome cauliflower curry for dinner... darn, can't think about that now. Must study for finals."

Wait! I thought. That was my cauliflower curry! I had unknowingly discovered the path to my moody teenage son's heart — it was through his stomach.

# Cauliflower in a Spicy Tomato Sauce

4 tablespoons vegetable oil
1 large yellow onion
2 medium ripe tomatoes
1/2 teaspoon turmeric
3/4 teaspoon chili powder
2 teaspoons cumin powder
1 tablespoon coriander powder
1/2 cup plain yogurt
2 teaspoon salt
1 medium cauliflower

Slice the onions and chop the tomatoes.

Heat half the oil in a large skillet. Add onions and sauté until they begin to turn light brown. Add tomatoes. Cover skillet and let the onions and tomatoes cook in the tomatoes' juices for 6 minutes. Add turmeric powder, chili powder, cumin powder and coriander powder. Mix.

Cover and cook for 3 minutes. Cool mixture. Place the mixture in a blender and liquefy. Add yogurt and salt. Blend again.

Cut cauliflower into medium sized florets. Wash and drain.

Heat remaining oil in the same skillet. Sauté cauliflower until slightly browned. Add yogurt mixture. Cover and cook for five minutes. Serve with roti, an Indian bread.

~Viji K. Chary

Editor's note: "Curries" in Asian culture do not require the spice curry to be added. The term refers to a wider range of dishes.

# Making Sherry Eat

*I cannot forget my mother. [S]he is my bridge. When I needed to get across, she steadied herself long enough for me to run across safely.*
~Renita Weems

I sat in the dimly lit lunchroom next to Becky Bailey. Neither of us spoke as the chicken gravy and peas on the tray before us cooled and glazed over. We could hear our first-grade classmates out on the playground. Their laughter and shouts drifted in through the open door of our elementary school and down the stairs to where we sat at our table in the basement. We could go outside, we were told, when we had eaten some lunch.

I had never been forced to eat anything. When it came to meals, my mother operated on a rule handed down from her father: If you have to make children eat, it doesn't do them any good. I had led a very happy existence at home for nearly six years before entering school, cheerily eating oatmeal and my mother's big puffy biscuits for breakfast, peanut butter crackers for snacks, and beans, potatoes and cornbread for supper.

In the summer, Mom let me have all the fresh lettuce I wanted and baked plenty of crunchy cornbread to eat with green onions and sliced tomatoes. She took me to the garden to pick corn and cucumbers and then let me help pick and break green beans, which I ate with enthusiasm. Whenever we got a watermelon, Daddy cut it in big, plate-size slices and sprinkled salt on top. I slurped it up. There were many foods I loved. Chicken gravy, however, was something I would not like to try, and canned peas smelled funny. Becky didn't like them either.

So there we sat day after day, Becky with her blond curls and me with my straight, dark hair, side-by-side, closed-mouthed and silent. We knew the routine. When the bell rang signaling the end of recess, we would be allowed to empty our plates and go to class, where Mrs. Williams would sigh over us in exasperation and turn to write on the board.

One fateful day, in complete frustration I suppose, Mrs. Williams stopped me on my way to the large gray trashcans where I would rake out my plate. Grabbing my fork, she scooped up some spaghetti and pointed it at my mouth. I was stubborn, but not usually disobedient. She had caught me off guard. Without thinking, I opened my mouth and in went the spaghetti, now cold and slimy from sitting on my plate for nearly an hour. In a very few seconds, the spaghetti came out again, and with it what was left of my biscuits and oatmeal. Mrs. Williams grabbed my plate. "Go to the bathroom," she barked.

The entire lunchroom staff was disappointed. I think they worried about Becky and me. We were both little girls from the mountain hollows. I lived on Skinfork, and she was from Turkey Creek. The good ladies in the kitchen seemed to feel that it was part of their job to get some nourishing food in us. They did not see our mothers preparing our breakfast in the pre-dawn darkness or know that they would have supper waiting for us when we got off the bus in the evening. No one at our school ever brought lunch from home. So we ate in the lunchroom — or sometimes didn't eat, much to the dismay of the adults. And now I had created a real mess. It made me sad when Mr. Webb, the custodian, a nice man I liked, was called to clean up after me. Although he whistled cheerily and gave me a big wink, I knew that the clean-up was not fun.

On the bus ride home I thought about it again: the slimy spaghetti hitting my tongue, the sudden warmth rising from my stomach, and Mrs. Williams' look of horror and disgust. It felt awful. After weeks of hiding in the cloakroom, I had finally learned to like school, and now it was going badly. I told the story to my mom at home, getting ready for bed. She didn't have a lot to say, just some questions as she poured hot water from a steaming kettle into the big round tub for my bath: "What happened then? Did you go to class? How do you feel now?"

In just a few days it was time for a meeting of the Parent-Teacher Association. My dad didn't like to attend these events, but I could count on Mom to be there. I was so proud of her. Mom was tall and slim, with black curly hair and a lovely smile. She was quiet and a little shy, and—I later realized—felt somewhat inadequate, but she had business to attend to at the PTA meeting, so she went.

At night the dreaded lunchroom was transformed into a meeting hall. A stage at one end provided a platform for programs and speakers. After hearing us sing "Smokey the Bear" and recite Joyce Kilmer's "Trees," parents were dismissed to classrooms where they met with our teachers. Mom and I looked around the room, oddly unfamiliar in the evening. We found my desk, and I showed off my colorful pictures and handwriting samples. Then it was Mom's turn to talk with Mrs. Williams. After only a minute or two, we were ready to go.

I rode the bus to school the next day, just like always. I wrote in my writing pad with my fat red pencil, went to the bathroom in a line to wash my hands before lunch, and picked up my tray from the counter by the kitchen just like always. But something had changed. When I sat down with my food, I ate the warm, yeasty roll that I enjoyed, stirred my mashed potatoes, and even sampled a few bites, but when the time came to leave, no one held me back. I was allowed to rake my uneaten potatoes and meat loaf into the trash can, run up the stairs and out into the sunshine with the rest of my class. My mother—my beautiful, quiet, smart mother—had been to school and had left clear instructions for everyone: "Do not try to make Sherry eat."

~Sherry Poff

# Love on the Menu

*Grandmother—a wonderful mother with lots of practice.*
*~Author Unknown*

"Mom! We've arrived!" I called, as I pushed open the screen door. After eight hours in the car, my husband, our six-month-old son and I had at last driven down the long driveway to my parents' home by the lake. The cool breeze from the shore and the shade of the tall pine trees offered relief from the heat of the summer day.

"Welcome!" my mother cried as she emerged from the kitchen and reached out to hold Timmy. "It's been three months since we've seen this little guy!"

Several months earlier, my husband and I had taken Timmy to visit my parents' home in Massachusetts. On that occasion, my brother and his wife had flown in from California with their new baby boy. The cousins met for the first time at Gramma's house. My mother had made grand preparations as two sets of inexperienced parents descended on her home with portable cribs, diaper bags, and baby toys. On the refrigerator door, she had written the words, "Welcome Andy & Timmy!" and she had used kitchen magnets to create a scene of diapers drying on a long laundry line.

Could two boys be more different? Andy was slender, Timmy was chunky. Andy whimpered gently while Timmy used his voice at full throttle to let the world know his needs. Both boys were teething and drooling, so Gramma produced frozen juice bars to soothe their gums. Now on this second trip to her home, Timmy already sported eight new teeth!

"Are you hungry?" Gramma asked Timmy as he squirmed in her arms, anxious to get on the floor and explore this new world.

"Thanks, but he can wait, Mom," I replied. "I just nursed him in the car. I brought some Cheerios and rice cereal with us for him."

I had only recently introduced Timmy to "real" food. The parenting magazines had warned me about introducing new foods one at a time, about avoiding foods like eggs and peanuts that might cause allergic reactions, about grinding the food carefully. I soon realized that my mother had not read those magazines.

When I got up after a brief nap, I found Timmy seated with my mother at the dining room table. Timmy was happily licking peanut butter off his fingers.

"He was hungry so I made him a little sandwich. I hope that was okay?"

"Er, fine," I replied. After all, what could I say? Short of pumping his stomach, there was nothing I could do. Trying to add authority to my words, I added, "Doctors say that peanut products could cause him to develop allergies later."

"Oh, he seems to be just fine. Children are very resilient. They survive an amazing variety of parenting styles."

Over the next days Timmy's menu expanded rapidly. Bananas, ham salad (never mind all the preservatives and nitrates), egg salad, honey, spaghetti and meat sauce. He gummed them all with gusto. My mother handed him the food and he figured out a way to get it down. Seeing the special bond forming between these two people I loved, I learned to relax and enjoy my son as much as he enjoyed stuffing his mouth.

Twenty-five years later Tim still has no sign of allergies. Gramma may not have followed doctor's orders, but she was right about one thing: Grandchildren are very resilient creatures.

~Emily Parke Chase

# Best Feeding

*With what price we pay for the glory of motherhood.*
*~Isadora Duncan*

Most women are walking refrigerators. No, wait, milk comes out warm, so they're more like walking ovens. Or walking stovetops. Whereas men are like table tops, ready to receive the food, women's bodies are fecund like farms, producing life-sustaining milk—nourishment for our children. We are walking, talking food makers.

I am not one of these women.

I used to be one of these women, or at the very least, I assume that I was one of these women before I started down the road of fertility treatments. The mandatory blood work each cycle checked hormone levels. Prolactin, the hormone associated with breast milk, was always in working order.

When we finally became pregnant with our twins, breastfeeding was the way I thought I would take back my body, the way I would learn to love it again after its wonkiness made me rack up enormous fertility-clinic bills. My breasts were going to produce milk for me, and I was going to forgive my body for letting me down in such a big way. The twins and I would be as peaceful as the woman and child on the nursing pillow tag: mother beatifically smiling down at her perfect baby, her modest nightgown hiding the majority of her perfect white breasts, her hair tidily back in a French twist.

The twins arrived and my milk didn't. I hadn't experienced

breast changes during pregnancy, but I had been assured that many women don't and this wasn't problematic. The twins were too small and premature to breastfeed, but I hooked myself up to a breast pump eight times a day, dutifully staring at the "breast is best" poster in the pumping lounge of the hospital.

Eight times a day the machine would hum, tugging at my breasts. And eight times a day, I would get only a few drops of liquid that looked suspiciously like boob sweat. After a few weeks, I became certain that if I hooked up the breast pump to my husband's chest, he'd be able to produce the same watery substance. It didn't help that across from the twins' NICU room was a family of triplets whose mother filled the NICU refrigerator with vial after vial of her rich, yellowish breast milk. She would close the refrigerator after putting in her pumping takeaway and inform me that she just didn't know what she'd do with "all that milk."

I did not look like the beatific woman on the nursing pillow label. My hair was not in a neat French twist, my boobs were red and raw from the machine, and the twins certainly weren't calmly suckling. At four weeks post-birth, we were a massive train wreck, both physically and emotionally. I had tried medications and sleeping more and sleeping less and drinking more water and eating more protein. I had been to several breastfeeding specialists, tried holding the twins' sleepy mouths to my breast prior to pumping or sniffing one of their spit-up-soaked burp cloths while on the machine—an idea, I was promised, that would trick my brain into producing milk.

I probably don't need to tell you that it didn't exactly work.

After four weeks, someone had the idea to test my prolactin levels, and lo and behold, the culprit for my lack of milk was found. I wasn't producing prolactin anymore, a possible side effect of the very treatments that brought me my twins. One month of useless pumping finally came to an end, at least physically.

Emotionally, I couldn't move on nor wrap my brain around the idea that once again, my body had failed to do what other women could do easily. It couldn't create a child without help, it couldn't carry said child to term, and now it couldn't even feed a child. This body that I had always loved and treated well certainly wasn't showing me the care I had showed it over the years. And beyond that, I had always been a nurturer, a cook. I was the person who always provided the food, who baked cookies for friends and held dinner parties and had worked her way through an entire cooking school textbook (with the exception of the forcemeats chapter, but I secretly believe that everyone would skip the forcemeats chapter if they could).

I was a woman: food was what we did. Not being able to feed my children in the way that I was led to believe was best from hospital posters and parenting books hit me in the very core of who I was as a person. Was I really the nurturer I saw myself as if I couldn't do this simple task?

One night, in the middle of yet another crying jag over the idea that I had failed so enormously at this whole make-and-keep-a-baby-growing thing, my husband gave me the solution I needed in order to take back that label of nurturer. He asked me to come up with another task equally as difficult as breastfeeding that didn't depend on my body to function in a certain way.

Making my own baby food instantly sprang to mind. Peeling all of those apples and pears, roasting butternut squash and deseeding it, pureeing steamed peach slices: all of these tasks were time-consuming and messy as opposed to simply twisting the top off a baby food jar. So we went to the supermarket and bought fruits and vegetables. We purchased dozens of ice cube trays and Sharpie markers for labeling. We set up marathon baby-food-making sessions after the twins went to bed, turning on some music and creating an assembly line of tasks until the last ice cube tray was in the freezer. And several days later, we did it all over again.

Making baby food for picky twins was a never-ending task. Instead of cracked nipples or mastitis, I had cuts on my fingers from the peelers and knives. Instead of searching for a discreet place to nurse in public, I was constantly seeking microwaves where I could heat-up our frozen baby food cubes when we were on an outing. And instead of feeding being a task solely on my shoulders (or should I say, my boobs), my husband was able to be an equal partner in not only the action of placing the food into the twins' mouths but creating it as well.

Our twins have had exactly one jar of store-bought baby food in their life, but it's not a fact that I hold over the heads of fellow mothers. I have come to realize that everyone has things they do well and things they don't; everyone has special ways they provide that others cannot, either due to time, inclination, finances or ability. There is no single way of feeding that is "best" in the grand sense of the term, but only ways that are best for each individual mother, each individual child.

I never got to be that beatific woman on the nursing pillow label, but like most advertising, I don't think her life was really like that anyway. Instead of a French twist, modest nightgown, and angelic child, I got a messy ponytail, jeans, and the Violent Femmes blasting from the computer while I made baby food, side-by-side with my husband. And that's a memory that is worth more to me than fulfilling someone else's idea of perfect motherhood.

~Melissa Ford

"My sister is one of those perfectionist moms. She not only makes her own baby food but also hand-draws the labels for each jar."

# In My Mother's Kitchen

*As a restaurateur, my job is to basically control the chaos and the drama.*
*There's always going to be chaos in the restaurant business.*
*~Rocco DiSpirito*

"Pick up!" I hear her scream from the kitchen as the bell chimes. Instinctively, my feet start to move across the tile floor, passing the bar on my left and the other servers moving swiftly, filling glasses and wiping counters. I turn left, into the bright lights of the kitchen.

In front of me is the rack where I pick up one bowl of pasta with pesto, lusciously green on a spotless white plate, and a steak, drizzled with chimichurri sauce and settled on French fries. I pull both plates down, one in each hand, and now I can see her. She is framed by the metal rack. Her hair is pulled back by a red bandana, but her gray roots are evident—unsurprising, since she hardly has time to eat, let alone color her hair. There is moisture on her face, a little sweat, and her eyeliner is smudged. Again, I am not surprised. I heard her put her make-up on at five o'clock this morning. We're well into dinner service now.

"Hot, hot, hot!" she yells, at no one in particular, as she hauls a sizzling pan from one burner to another. She is running on pure adrenaline and kitchen fumes at this point, and I hurry into the dining room, afraid of what exhaustion might bring out of her if I let the food get cold.

This is my mother.

Many peoples' moms cook for them, their families, and occasional guests. They make brownies for school birthdays and banana bread for bake sales. When I was very young, that's how it was. My mom didn't go to cooking school until after her divorce from my dad when I was seven, and so I have memories of broccoli steamed only for me, lasagna made just for our dinner, and Christmas cookies for holiday gifts instead of throngs of customers.

But that wasn't what my mom wanted to do. Cooking, she realized, was her gift, and it was one she wanted to give to more than just our little brood. She opened her first business, a bakery, when I was in high school, and there she made café food—egg sandwiches on fresh-baked croissants, simple salads, and omelets—while her partner handled the baking. I worked for her, enjoying the edges of the brownies and admiring the beautifully crafted pastries. Her partnership with the baker, however, was not so beautifully crafted, and she soon left the business.

Her next venture was her own restaurant—a place that was really hers. I remember spending hours in the space before it opened, watching it take form. The wall sconces, the artwork, the placemats. The glistening red bar with flecks that sparkled—just enough flare for it to belong to my mother. It was a sensuous place, dramatic and well made. It was my mom, in a restaurant.

I worked there too, but not willingly. By the time I was in college, I had realized that though I grew up in the restaurant business, I didn't love it. In fact, I hated it. I hated how my mom was never home and was always exhausted. I hated that our own refrigerator at our house was consistently bare unless she brought home leftovers. I hated the grueling pace of the restaurant, the customers with nothing nice to say, and the feeling that if I failed in the restaurant, then somehow I failed my mother too.

Because my feelings were so conflicted about her restaurant and her choices, and because I subsisted on leftovers and family meals at the café, I never cooked for myself. I didn't really want to. I had no desire to do what she did.

That changed when I moved into my first college apartment

with a kitchen. Wanting to save money and make what I considered a move into adulthood, I decided to cook something my mom always made—pasta with sautéed broccoli and sausage. A simple dish I figured I could make.

I boiled some water to blanch the broccoli, and got out my only cutting board. I began chopping the garlic, and something came over me—a strange, instinctual knowledge. I had never really done this before—chopped garlic—but how many times had I watched it done? How many nights had the scent of chopped garlic filled the kitchen while I did my homework? How often had I seen my mom or her employees fill plastic containers with garlic to use for dinner service? The answer was too many to count.

I looked down at my hand. I was holding the knife the proper way, lowering the blade front to back the way my mom always did. Why wouldn't I? Hadn't I sat on my mother's bed, quizzing her with flashcards on knife techniques while she was in cooking school? I was a good student. No matter how hard I had tried to stay away, somehow I had learned.

That night, I made a fine pasta dish. It didn't taste quite like Mom's, but I realized right away that I wasn't culinary-challenged. It came naturally to me to cook, and I did enjoy it. Since that night, I have done a lot of cooking, and especially baking. My mom, enamored with the hot line, didn't have time for slow, pretty decorations. I like to sit and decorate fluffy cupcakes, one by one, for an hour. You might call it a rebellion of sorts.

I tell people that I grew up in Connecticut, but I really grew up in the kitchen. For me, food is intertwined with love, but also loneliness, resentment, and forgiveness—blood, sweat, and tears. Food has made me cry, but food has also forced me to learn. Now, whenever I seem to feel, instinctually, that it is time to let the steak rest or take the chicken out of the oven, I know why and where those instincts come from. I am still learning from my mother. And my mother, of course, is still cooking.

~Madeline Clapps

# Pop-Up Thanksgiving

*One of the very nicest things about life is the way we must regularly stop*
*whatever it is we are doing and devote our attention to eating.*
~Luciano Pavarotti and William Wright, Pavarotti, My Own Story

What a year it had been! Our twelve-year-old daughter Sally had been diagnosed with leukemia in early winter, and we had all been thrown into a world that we did not know even existed: one filled with chemotherapy, complications, and hospitalizations.

When Sally developed a fever the week before Thanksgiving, we were all disappointed to go back to the hospital, but hopeful that she'd be home for the big feast we had planned. Her grandmother would be flying in from California and the menu had been developed and debated and amended on the phone by everyone in the family: Broccoli casserole or green bean casserole? How about both? Cranberry sauce with whole berries or jellied? Apples in the stuffing? Now the menu was on hold as we headed back to the pediatric ward.

The detour was easier to accept when Sally's hospital friend Mary, unlucky enough to have a fever of her own, was admitted to the room across the hall. Both girls were out of danger but needed to be monitored.

As the holiday got closer we could smell the homemade desserts in our minds, and picture the table laden with food and family, but going home seemed less likely. Then, on Thanksgiving morning, the doctors gave us great news: they would give Sally and Mary a "day pass" to David's House, the home-away-from-home for sick children and their families, next to the hospital. This felt like a "Get Out of Jail Free" card to all of us. Our two families hurried out in teams to the grocery store and to check out the cooking facilities.

David's House is a warm, welcoming place, and the kitchen is a cook's dream, with multiple ovens, range tops, refrigerators, and surfaces to prepare food, all in a light-filled space. Mary's parents and sister, my husband, and Sally's sister Kathleen pitched in to make the best meal ever. My mother arrived to the sounds of pots and pans and running water, and the smell of chopped onions and minced garlic, followed by the delicious scent of turkey just beginning to roast.

While the food cooked, I went to my car and pulled out all the decorations that had been planned for our home and had been riding around in my trunk since I bought them. Sally, Mary, and I set up multiple elegant tables to fit us all.

With so many handy cooks, the food all came out at the same time and we arranged it as a gorgeous buffet on the long counters. It looked like something from a magazine layout: the huge turkey with the crisp golden skin as the centerpiece, the roasted fall vegetables in beautiful shades of orange and yellow, the creamy gravy, and what seemed like every kind of cranberry sauce there is. What was even better was how it smelled—like home! The warmth and gratitude of this celebration that we had pulled out of nowhere seemed to mix with the rich smells of the food that we prepared all that afternoon.

Just then, the front door opened and an older couple and a younger man walked in, each wearing a look of shock and exhaustion. The young man explained that his wife had gone into early labor with their twins and needed to be hospitalized unexpectedly. He and his wife's parents had been directed to David's House as a place to stay for the night. Their plans had been to check in before going out to find a turkey sandwich somewhere. We led them into the kitchen where, to their great surprise, our beautiful homemade banquet was ready and hot. "Welcome!" we said, "to Thanksgiving!"

The three families sat down together for a meal that we would all remember long after Sally and Mary were cured. It was not the Thanksgiving that we had planned or expected, but it was one that we would never forget.

~Jane Brzozowski

Chapter **10**

# Food *and* Love

## Always Room for Dessert

*Dessert is probably the most important stage of the meal,
since it will be the last thing your guests remember
before they pass out all over the table.*

~The Anarchist Cookbook

# Cold Comfort

*Food is the most primitive form of comfort.*
~Sheila Graham

My teenage daughter was pregnant and the whole family was in turmoil. I was upset. My daughter was scared. My husband was furious. My older son was mad at his sister. And my ten-year-old son—well, he just stayed out of everyone's way.

I had plenty to worry about. But my immediate concern was mediating all of the emotions colliding under one roof.

One day, while cleaning the kitchen, I noticed a piece of paper lying on the table. Reaching for it, I recognized my younger son's handwriting. I started reading.

My jaw dropped and my heart stopped. I had to sit down. I put my hand over my mouth in an effort to hold back the ache growing in my throat as I read my son's troubling words:

*My life is very difficult for me. I'm always picked on by everyone except my mother. She is always kind to me. My sister is all right, but she's pregnant and you know how that can be. People don't know how I feel inside. Really, I am a hurt little boy.*

At the bottom of the page was a stick man whose outstretched arms begged for a hug. The giant teardrops flowing from his penciled eyes broke my heart. If the pitiful figure had worn a dress, it could have been me, for my own heavy tears were now steadily streaming down my face.

I was devastated. I felt so guilty. Had I had been so consumed by our family crisis that I had all but forgotten my youngest child?

"How do I kiss this hurt and make it go away?" the mother in me wondered.

A few days later I was driving through town when I noticed a fast food restaurant's enticing poster of a luscious bowl of ice cream. It triggered a childhood memory. I began reminiscing about a special time that brought me more joy than gifts at Christmas, hearts on Valentine's Day or chocolate bunnies at Easter. It was ice cream day.

Ice cream day didn't come around often, but my brothers and I knew it was on the horizon by the way my mother looked at my dad. As soon as we spied that spark in her eye, we knew we were in for a treat.

The scenario was always the same: My mother would bat her eyes at my dad and say, seductively: "Big John"—that's what she called my dad when she was trying to coax him—"How about let's go and get some I-C-E-C-R-E-A-M?" She spelled it out like a special code.

Of course, we could spell, and we would jump up and down, yelling, "Ice cream! Ice cream!" until my dad gave in.

My dad let us order anything we wanted. I always got a large, chocolate shake. It was chilly and smooth. Deliciously sweet. Slurping that scrumptious ice cream through a straw with my parents looking on made me feel special. I felt loved.

Remembering the way my mother looked at my dad on ice cream day made me smile. Her playfulness was contagious. Her love for him obvious. And on ice cream day, she showed us how to convert that love to quality time.

Watching my quiet son stare out the car window, I suddenly knew just what he needed. I glanced over at him with a gleam in my eye. "Hey, we need to spend some quality time together. How about let's get some I-C-E-C-R-E-A-M?" I asked, teasing him by spelling it out.

His eyes lit up and a big grin grew on his face. "Yeah, we need some quality time, Mom," he said, trying to be serious. But his smile revealed his delight.

We dipped into our treats of crushed cookies swirled in creamy, vanilla ice cream. I didn't mention his sad paper. The incredible combination of ice cream and my undivided attention seemed to be working its magic. I could see it written all over his face. He felt loved. He was happy.

As he got older, my son recognized times when I needed some attention. He'd look at me with that familiar twinkle in his eye and say, "We need some quality time, Mom. Let's go for ice cream." I was more than ready.

Over time, ice cream dates became a ritual. They didn't solve problems, but they satisfied cravings for love and attention. They always said, "You are special."

Now that my son is grown and life has settled down, I'm always on the lookout for the forgotten, mistreated or overwhelmed soul who might be longing for some attention. Right now it's my twelve-year-old granddaughter. She's a middle child, and you know how that can be.

When I realize some quality time might be necessary, I look at her with that comforting, grandmotherly gaze and suggest: "How about we go for some ice cream?"

"Sounds like a good idea," she always says, as her face lights up with a smile.

I let her order anything she wants. As we lap away at that delectable frozen treat, our cares seem to melt with each lick. We both feel better, but most of all, she feels loved.

My son's cry for attention made me realize that when life gets difficult, when the world is a hurtful place, we all need someone who will take the time to make us feel like the most important person in the world. We all need to feel loved. And as far as my family is concerned, love is spelled, "I-C-E-C-R-E-A-M."

~Teresa Anne Hayden

# Mom's Hot Chocolate

*Mother, the ribbons of your love are woven around my heart.*
*~Author Unknown*

One of my earliest memories is of waking up to the smell of camp smoke and my mother's hot chocolate. My parents were poor, and we lived in tenement apartments in the Portland suburbs. Dad worked two jobs and mom was disabled, but that didn't stop them from packing up our sometimes running station wagon and heading into the Cascade Mountains several times each year.

Dad would fish with remarkably poor results and Mom would read or knit.

Until I was old enough to garner my own interest in not catching fish, I would wander around the nearby woods pestering small animals and doing whatever it is that youngsters do to amuse themselves. Our gear was old and worn and our food was usually cheap and starchy. But no matter what, we always splurged on the ingredients for our traditional hot chocolate, a recipe that had been handed down from my grandmother to my mother.

There was no store bought, just-add-water powdered cocoa in our camp!

Mom would set the smoke-blackened and much-dented coffee pot at the edge of the fire and slowly warm the milk, adding chocolate and mints, and stirring until the steaming contents had become a thick, rich brown and the aroma of chocolate and mint mixed with the scent of Oregon pine to fill the camp. More than once I can remember folks that we had just met hours before wandering into our campsite with mug in hand to enjoy my mother's creation.

I remember blistering hot summer days, freezing spring mornings and torrential Pacific Northwest downpours that trapped us in our heavy canvas tent for days at a time, but I don't remember ever waking up in the woods without the beckoning smell of Mom's hot chocolate wafting into our tent.

Mom has been gone for a decade now. She went home years before I met my wife and started my own family.

Now, when we load up our car and head for the mountains, nestled among the air mattresses, fishing poles, and ultra-light sleeping bags, there are always Hershey's chocolate bars and Peppermint Patties. I still use that battered coffee pot, resting it over a portable camp stove now, and we always bring extra cups for the neighbors who will inevitably show up.

I've told my family a lot about Mom, her life, struggles and victories, and it seems like nothing brings back those warm memories better than sitting around the fire at night and sipping sweet hot chocolate.

## Mom's Hot Chocolate

1 quart of half-and-half
4 regular milk chocolate bars
1 large Peppermint Pattie bar

Bring milk to a very low simmer; add milk chocolate and peppermint patty. Mix all ingredients thoroughly.

Serve hot and enjoy the company.

~Perry P. Perkins

# 96

# Grandma's Recipe for Instant Stress Relief

*Grandmas never run out of hugs or cookies.*
~Author Unknown

The spoon is hot but I can't wait a moment longer. Gingerly, I pull the spoon's contents into my mouth with my teeth. The rich, creamy taste of sweet chocolate spreads across my tongue. The rough, rocky texture of oatmeal pleases my palate as I chew. Mmmm, instant stress relief. I close my eyes, lean against the kitchen counter, and savor my grandmother's answer to modern tranquilizers and antidepressants. The perfect cure for stress, grief, and anything else that threatens to ruin a perfectly good day—old-fashioned chocolate drop cookies.

What is it about these cookies that makes everything better? They have been working their magic in my family for generations. It's not just their sweet chocolate flavor or even the pleasure of eating them. For me, it is the memories associated with making the cookies that provide the cure. When the world knocks me down one time too many, decisions overload my brain, or disappointments threaten to overwhelm me, I head for the kitchen.

Dragging out my oldest, heaviest pan from the far back corner of the cabinet sets the stage for therapy to begin. A modern, nonstick, lightweight aluminum pan would never do—for the cookies to work their magic, an old, heavy pan is required. Mine was old when my mother used it twenty years ago. Somewhere along the way it lost its handle and the bottom is blackened, but no other pan makes cookies like this one does.

First, into the pan over medium heat goes one stick of butter. Not margarine, but real butter complete with fat and calories. "Never accept a cheap substitute when you can get the real thing," Grandma always said. "It might take a little longer to get, but the real thing is more satisfying and well worth the wait." Grandma never had much, but what she had was quality. Her hand-me-downs are still being enjoyed by her grandchildren and great-grandchildren.

Next, two cups of sugar and half a cup of cocoa are added to the pot. The sharp bitter odor of the cocoa fills my nostrils. It is a strong smell, a direct contrast to the sweet smell of the sugar. As the mixture begins to blend together, it reminds me of how strong grandma and all my ancestors before her were. They lived hard lives as frontier women. They faced danger, drought and disasters. They survived because they were strong. Simple pleasures like these chocolate drop cookies were enough to remind them of life's joy even in hard times.

Now into my pot goes half a cup of evaporated milk. Stir until everything is blended smooth, Grandma taught me. In life, focusing only on the good or bad times leaves life lumpy—unblended. A balanced life is blended with the realization that there will be ups and downs—it makes the mixture interesting and tasty rather than bland.

My mixture is bubbling, alive and active in the old pot. I quickly turn off the heat, add one teaspoon of vanilla for flavor, then three cups of uncooked oatmeal. Life needs a little flavor and crunch to stay exciting; nothing is quite so deadly as boredom. Perhaps I have been in the same place with the same people doing the same thing and facing the same problems in the same way for too long. I stir the mixture one more time then remove it from the stove. My life may need a little stirring too.

Now the fun begins—dropping the cookies one spoonful at a time onto waxed paper. Plop! That one is for the bills. Plop! That one is for the constant stack of dirty dishes in my sink. Plop! Plop!

Plop! Deadlines, grumpy people, fussy children. Halfway through the dropping of cookies, I start to smile. My kitchen smells sweet and cozy like the memory of my grandma's kitchen. I can imagine her here beside me. Her high musical laugh fills my ears as I continue to plop cookie mixture onto my frustrations.

Yes, the instant stress relief of chocolate drop cookies has worked its magic for me again. I can almost feel Grandma wiping chocolate from my chin with the corner of her apron. "Child, you can only do so much in a day," she often told me. "That's why God gives a new day every morning."

Grandma is right. I have done more than enough today. I think I'll turn off the phone and the computer and take a plateful of these cookies over to my neighbor Sheila's house. I bet she could use some stress relief too.

## Grandma's Chocolate Drop Cookies

2 cups sugar
1/2 cup cocoa
1/2 cup evaporated milk
1 stick butter
3 cups raw uncooked oats
1 teaspoon vanilla

Combine sugar, cocoa, milk and butter.

Cook over medium heat stirring occasionally until mixture starts to boil. Remove from heat.

Add oats and vanilla. Stir until blended.

Drop onto waxed paper by the spoonful.

~Sharon T. Hinton

# 97

# Fantasy Fudge

*There's nothing better than a good friend, except a good friend with chocolate.*
*~Linda Grayson*

Her Christmas fudge was a holiday tradition. She made it as gifts for neighbors, relatives, coaches, schoolteachers, business associates, and church families. Everyone, and I do mean everyone, looked forward to receiving a plateful. It was her specialty, and it came out perfectly—every time. It fully deserved its name: Fantasy Fudge.

In giggling stealth, the two of us stood in her pantry nibbling the last of her secret stash while our husbands and kids played table games downstairs.

"Is there a secret ingredient?" I licked a creamy smear from my fingertip.

"Nope." Vic laughed. "Nothing secret. I just follow the recipe on the marshmallow crème jar."

"Give me a break. It can't be that easy!"

"Yep. It's that easy." She looked at the empty candy plate, stuck it in the dishwasher, and tossed the used plastic wrap into the wastebasket. "Tell you what, let's make another batch and I'll show you."

"Now?"

"Now!"

And she did, in spite of our combined nine children romping through the house in joyous holiday confusion. Ignoring the clamor,

Vic did what she does best: whip up a batch of melt-in-your-mouth fudge.

She dissolved the grains of extra-fine sugar into a bowl of fluffy margarine and thick, evaporated milk, and then stirred the mixture on top of the stove with a wooden spoon.

My mouth watered.

"Take the butter wrapper and grease the pan," she ordered, probably to keep my nose away from her bubbly concoction. "And you can chop those pecans, if you'd like to help. Not too fine, though. Leave them a bit chunky."

Vic lifted the heavy pot off the burner. With a practiced hand, she added a generous slosh of real Mexican vanilla and a tumble of chocolate chips. I nearly drooled when she spiraled the hot spoon into the jar; marshmallow crème flowed out in a tidal wave.

"What next?" I asked.

"I stir like crazy." And stir she did, until the concoction was glossy. "Pour in the pecans," she said.

"How many?"

"As many as the fudge can hold."

She held the pot over the prepared pan. Lap upon lap of thick fudge flowed like rich, redolent lava. By twos and threes, a lip-smacking crowd of children and husbands followed the heavenly aroma into the kitchen singing out:

"What's that we smell?"

"Yum!"

"Can we have some?"

But her elder son twisted his lips. "Who's it for this time?"

"You'll see." In one smooth motion, Vic traded the woody evergreen on the center of the gnarled oak table for her steaming masterpiece. Her eyes crinkled at the corners.

"There's only one way to eat fudge," she announced. Dispensing a handful of spoons and ringing us around the table like a crew of wranglers at the chuck wagon, she invited: "Dig in!"

Dig in? Our eyes widened. We looked at each other in disbelief. My husband raised an eyebrow and nodded at the soup bubbling on a burner at the stove; each of us, even the youngest, knew it was time for lunch. Everyone hesitated—barely—before a symphony of thirteen spoons clinked and clanked against each other as they plunged around the fringes of warm Fantasy Fudge.

"Oooo."

"Ummm."

"Ahhh."

The hungry horde of us caroled the same, satisfied chorus.

My eyes met Vic's across the crowded table. And that's when I understood. Her recipe might have come straight from the jar, but there was a secret ingredient, too: Indulgence. Decadent, generous, unbridled indulgence.

Vic recognized that sometimes fudge should be made, and eaten, simply for the unrestrained pleasure of it. And, of course, for the warm memory years later.

~Carol McAdoo Rehme

# 98

# For the Love of Jell-O

*A winning effort begins with preparation.*
*~Joe Gibbs*

Jell-O is the official snack for the state of Utah, and it's reported that the state also holds the record for the highest per capita sales for green gelatin of any state in the U.S. But few people know the lengths that one woman went to in order to ensure that her family could continue to enjoy their favorite Jell-O dessert.

It all started back in November of 1985 when Leslie Austin, my mother, went grocery shopping. On her list was blackberry Jell-O, the necessary ingredient for the popular dessert Mom enjoyed taking to family parties, church cookouts and work dinners. She had looked for it at two different grocery stores only to find empty shelves. On a return trip to one of those stores, Mom discovered they no longer even had a tag for it. Suspicions mounting, she decided to find out why her favorite flavor was disappearing.

Someone finally had to call General Foods to find the answer. They were no longer going to make blackberry Jell-O. "What? No blackberry Jell-O?" Mom went into a panic.

Much like a dedicated environmentalist determined to preserve a species for the enjoyment of future generations, Mom began her own preservation efforts. She methodically searched the shelves of every grocery store in her area for her beloved flavor. When she found it, she bought it. All of it.

Storing the boxes in several different locations made it possible to disguise the actual numbers of the growing hoard. After a few months, however, Dad caught on. Mom recalls, "I really didn't know how much I had. I didn't start counting until Dad said, 'Don't you think you have enough?' 'No,' I said. To which he replied, 'Well, let's see how much you've got.' It was then that we realized I had spent a couple hundred bucks. But you know, if you're just buying six or ten boxes at a time, you don't realize that it's adding up."

Just what would motivate an otherwise sane woman to spend well over $200 on blackberry Jell-O, accumulating over 300 six-ounce boxes? I put the question to Mom. "I love it!" she said. "I wanted to make that Jell-O until I died."

It has now been over twenty-five years since Mom's search and rescue efforts. I asked her how many boxes remain. "Just four," she said. "I'm saving them so that you can serve my favorite Jell-O dessert at my funeral." (Mind you, Mom is nowhere near death's door.) Those may be her wishes, but unless she puts it in her will, I have other plans.

You see, just the other day as I was trolling the aisles at the grocery store, I noticed a new Jell-O flavor—blackberry fusion. Now that they've reintroduced a blackberry-flavored Jell-O, I'll use it in the Jell-O traditionally served at funeral dinners in Utah, and save the four vintage boxes to display near Mom's casket. In fact, I just might slip a box of blackberry Jell-O into the casket to be buried with her. That way Mom can enjoy her favorite Jell-O recipe in heaven!

## Mom's Heavenly Jell-O

2 6-oz. boxes blackberry Jell-O (or 4 3-oz. boxes)*
1 large can crushed pineapple, including juice
1 can blueberries, including juice (not pie filling)
1 8-oz. container sour cream
1 8-oz. package cream cheese
1/2 cup powdered sugar
chopped walnuts (optional)

Boil 4 cups water. Add Jell-O and dissolve. Pour into a 9x13 inch pan, adding scant 2 cups of cold water, pineapple and blueberries (with juice). Stir carefully. Let set in the refrigerator at least 4 hours or overnight.

Once set, top by mixing together sour cream, cream cheese and powdered sugar. (We like this topping lumpy.) Sprinkle with nuts and keep cold until ready to serve.

*If they discontinue making blackberry fusion Jell-O, you can substitute one 6-ounce box of raspberry Jell-O and one 6-oz. box of berry blue Jell-O.

~Christie A. Hansen

"When I found out they were discontinuing my favorite
Jell-O flavor, I stockpiled it. Then I found out the
old saying 'There's always room for Jell-O' isn't true."

# Butterfinger Baby

*Nobody better lay a finger on my Butterfinger.*
*~Bart Simpson*

My desire for Butterfingers overwhelmed me. I couldn't figure it out. Never one to drift toward sweets, I'd become obsessed with the flaky orange stuff coated in chocolate. I wondered if my husband could really be right when he insisted hormones gone wild were the reason. My insatiable compulsion confounded me. It had to be more than a normal gestational craving.

After approximately 150 of the "crispety, crunchety, peanut-buttery" treats during twenty-seven weeks of pregnancy, complications landed me in the hospital.

"It's gotta be the Butterfingers," my husband chided.

"Impossible," I replied. "Butterfingers don't cause bleeding. Besides, I eat healthy other than my once a day treat. You know I don't wallow in junk food or sugar. In fact..." I looked at the nutritional information on my dessert of choice. "Look! It even has four grams of protein."

My husband laughed and kissed me. "Well, they do make your lips tasty."

Being on bedrest wasn't easy. In fact, it was downright miserable. But that's when I realized the value of such an addiction. My daily Butterfinger allowance did more than please my pallet—it alleviated the boredom. Variety is, after all, the spice of life, and I found it in multiple ways.

First, variation came with size. On tough days, I indulged in a jumbo. Other days, I'd find satisfaction with the standard. Sometimes, I managed to limit myself to a "fun size." Who ever thought to call those tiny things "fun" anyway? The truth was, the bigger they were, the more enjoyment they brought.

I found diversity in opening the package. Sometimes, I ripped the paper off in one quick jerk. Other times, I carefully opened it and slipped the jewel out. Holding it to my nose, I inhaled the delicious scent. The fragrance made my tummy rumble as I pondered another choice — how to eat it. Would it be a day for devouring, or would I nibble it layer by layer? The decision had to be made fast, as the ambrosial aroma kicked my taste buds into overdrive. With every bite, the crackling sound filled me with joy, and to finish the feast, I licked the gooey mess from my fingertips.

My indulgence was the highlight of each day, topped only by feeling my son move inside me. Being bedridden, the biggest obstacle I faced was that I had to rely on others to fill my need. When my secret stash dwindled, thoughts of how to get more consumed me. Would my husband come through? Who would visit me and stop at the store on the way? If I didn't get one today, did that mean two tomorrow?

My husband took advantage of my weakness in several ways.

One day, he approached with tears in his eyes. "Please forgive me," he begged. "I know I messed up."

"Messed up?" I crossed my arms and glared. "You forgot about me on Mother's Day. You went fishing with a friend."

He clasped his hands together in prayer-like fashion. "I'm so sorry. I'll make it up to you, I promise." Then he got on his knees and handed me an entire case of Butterfingers. My anger dissolved into delight.

The delicacy became his bartering tool. He approached me one day holding three yellow and blue bags of something I'd never seen before. Chewing on his lip, he asked, "Baby, do you mind if I go out with my brother tonight?"

Excitement surged as I read the words on the package. "Butterfinger BB's? What are those?"

He smiled and wiggled his eyebrows. "They're new. What do you think?"

Eyes and mouth agape, I snatched the offerings. Anticipation pulsed through me as I tore the bag open and popped one of the round concoctions in my mouth. A familiar blessedness seeped through my body as I relished the bite-sized clone of the bar. "Mmm. My new love."

Many days, he'd approach with a mischievous smile and ask, "Do you know how much I love you?"

I'd cock my head and look into his eyes. "How much?"

With a wink and a kiss, he'd hand me a love note attached to the chocolatey gift.

Knowing I had his heart, I accepted his symbol of affection.

I continued to yearn for the delightful refreshment after giving birth. "See," I told my husband, "This isn't just a pregnancy craving. If it was, my urge for them would have gone away—but I still gotta have 'em."

Finally, when my son was two months old, I realized I'd gone three days without seeking gratification from the goody. What had changed? Understanding dawned on me as I fed my precious child from a bottle. In the process of weaning him from my milk, my ache for Butterfingers waned. The less I nursed him, the less I longed for them.

As my baby grew into a child, I noticed something curious—a fondness for Butterfingers. Whenever he received holiday candy, his Butterfingers always disappeared first. With his gone, he haggled for more. "I'll trade you anything I have for your Butterfingers," I heard him say to anyone that would listen.

Although I no longer pined for the snack myself, I understood my son's passion for them. And, being the great mom I am, I've been known to use the satisfying sweet to reward, bribe, and show affection on more than one occasion.

In the end, I'm left with a lingering question, as unanswerable as the old chicken or the egg dilemma. Did my hankering for Butterfingers while pregnant and nursing influence my son to love them, or was he the one who truly loved them before he was even born?

~Leigh Ann Bryant

"I'm eating a lot of vegetables while pregnant because I heard that helps your child develop a taste for them. I'm also trying to be a really good listener and to go to bed without throwing a tantrum."

# A Clump of Cake

*Never say, "oops." Always say, "Ah, interesting."*
*~Author Unknown*

I looked for the perfect cake recipe every day for an entire week, until I found it—chocolate espresso cake with a chocolate glaze. It was going to be the most delectable, rich, and perfect dessert for my boyfriend Logan's twenty-fourth birthday.

Unfortunately, that day was a busy one for me. Though we had time to eat brunch with Logan's friends in the morning, I was off and running as soon as I finished my French toast, making my way to rehearsal and other commitments. But I wouldn't be deterred—the cake would happen, and even though I wouldn't be able to start making it until eight o' clock, it would be delicious even if I served it at midnight.

I hightailed it out of rehearsal around seven and ran to the grocery store. Skimming the aisles, I shook off the idea of exhaustion. I couldn't be tired. It was Logan's birthday, and I didn't have the option to cancel on the cake. We were both low on money, scraping wages together to pay for rent and food every month and constantly trying to save, so this was his only planned present. I took a breath, reenergized, and plucked the espresso powder off the grocery store shelf.

Back at my apartment, I raced over to Logan, gave him a kiss, and got to work. First, I made homemade tomato sauce, because as much as I like cake for dinner, I knew he'd prefer something heartier. As that bubbled on the stovetop, I started the cake preparations. Mixing the ingredients, I was a little nervous. It was a new recipe, after all, and there's always a chance that new recipes will fail—or, more accurately, I will fail at making them. But I figured, worse comes to worst, the cake would be dry, or too moist, or too heavily coffee-flavored. No matter what, I knew we'd have cake.

Finally, the layers finished baking and I pulled them out of the oven. They smelled excellent, filling the apartment with the scent of chocolate. I let them cool for a moment while I worked on the frosting. In my apartment, the kitchen and living room were combined, so the whole time I mixed and cracked and sifted, Logan sat on the couch watching TV and plucking at his guitar.

The moment came when I was ready to try extracting the layers from the cake pans, and I was excited, knowing the end of my cake-making journey was nearing. I turned one over and tapped on the back. Nothing happened. I tapped it again and felt the cake loosen. It jumbled around, and then out fell a hunk of cake. Followed by another. And another. Minutes later, the same thing happened with my other layer. I looked down at a pile of crumbs.

At eleven p.m., with my cake in shambles and my kitchen a mess, I started shaking with sobs and throwing small objects.

"What's wrong?" Logan asked, as he came up behind me and wrapped me in a hug. I kept shaking, silently, until I could finally speak.

"The cake is ruined," I said, sucking in little spurts of air between choked sobs. "It completely fell apart. It's my... only birthday present for you... and it's ruined!" I threw my oven mitt onto the counter like a child having a temper tantrum.

"Shhh... shhh..." he said, pulling me around and forcing me to look at him. "Yes, I wanted a cake, but I didn't want this. You've been out doing things all day—things I know you had to do, and I'm not upset—but all I really wanted for my birthday was to be able to spend time with you. This whole time you've been working in the kitchen, and we've barely even spoken."

I realized he was right. I was so focused on being The World's Most Perfect Girlfriend and Human Being, I had completely ignored

Logan the entire night. I thought I could traipse in from rehearsing all day, snap my fingers, and make a cake. But sometimes the world has other plans, and the world had handed me cake mush covered in goopy frosting.

"Here, let's at least try it," Logan said, and we shoveled a piece onto a plate. Then I remembered.

"Oh God, we have to take a picture to send to your mom!" A fresh burst of tears and a whimper escaped my lips. Every year, Logan's mom made him a cake—nothing too fancy—but this year the duty was mine, and she had asked for a picture of the birthday boy with a slice of cake. She had specifically said the word "slice." This was most definitely a clump.

"Hey," he reassured me, "she doesn't care. Here, take a picture." I snapped a photo with his iPhone as he made a stupid face next to his clump of cake and I let out a little giggle. He took a bite.

"Wow. This is really good," he said. I grabbed his fork and scooped up my own bite. He wasn't lying. It really was delicious. It was a complete mess, dripping all over the counter and resembling an espresso-scented cow pie, but it was delicious. Really delicious.

He scarfed down his cake, let out a contented sigh, and then hugged me again. "Maddy," he started, "thank you for a great birthday. Now can you come over here and just sit on the couch with me?" I smiled a little, covered the cake with aluminum foil for the evening, and resigned myself to sitting on the couch, head on his shoulder, feet curled beneath a blanket.

The next day, I ate cake for breakfast. By the end of the week, every crumb of it was gone, devoured with forks right off the plate. Although that cake looked a lot like I did by the end of Logan's birthday—a complete wreck—inside it was every ounce of love and care I had for my boyfriend, and he could taste it.

~Madeline Clapps

# The Sweetness of Life

*Research tells us fourteen out of any ten individuals likes chocolate.*
*~Sandra Boynton*

It was Valentine's Day, the day we take the time to show our love with symbols and gifts. Ruth had them all: red balloons, cards filled with words of caring, large heart-shaped boxes of chocolates, her favorite music playing, and a gathering of her family and friends. Some had loved her for all her fifty-four years and some, like me, had known her for too short a time. But we were all there for the same reason, to celebrate her life and to say our last goodbyes. Ruth had died.

As the minister comforted us with his words, I thought back to the day Ruth walked into my life. It was the grand opening of our new business, Fitness Matters, later renamed Fit to Be ME. After months of planning, training and set-up, the big day had finally come and we were ready for the onslaught of eager members. Unfortunately, they weren't ready for us. Nobody came in for the first hour, or the second hour, or the third hour or the fourth hour.

It was early afternoon before I was startled by the bell on the door and the first person finally walked in. I jumped up from the desk and greeted her, while trying to remember the names of the machines and the names of the muscles they worked. I would have been happy to even remember my name.

Ruth giggled, a giggle that I would come to know well. "How about starting over," she said. "My name is Ruth. What is yours?"

"Cindy."

That was Ruth, making me feel welcomed in my own space. It was a gift she had and used generously. "Well, Cindy, I am glad to meet you. I see you just opened your exercise place and I am looking for a place to exercise."

I gained my first member and my newest friend at the same time. Ruth was quick with a pun and quicker with encouragement. When my newborn granddaughter would come to visit me, she would sit right on the floor in the middle of our small fitness circuit and play with her until she got her to laugh.

If you asked people to say one word that reminded them of Ruth, they would say, "chocolate." Dark chocolate to be exact. Ruth's love for chocolate was so well known that for every holiday, special occasion and birthday, she was showered with boxes and bags and bars of it.

It was the Monday after Easter that Ruth began a strange tradition for a fitness center—the reward of a piece of chocolate after every workout. Ruth had come in to exercise and when she was done, she counted the people that were still on the circuit and lined up a piece of chocolate on my desk for each of them.

"These are for all of you," she said.

"We work out and then eat chocolate?"

"One piece of chocolate didn't get you out of shape," Ruth said, "but one piece can sweeten your day or someone else's, if you'd rather pass it along."

So, Ruth would leave her chocolate encouragement every day and when her supply finally ran out, the tradition had been established. I continued it with a dish of chocolate by each door.

Ruth worked out every day. I teased her that if she ever wasn't going to make it, she should let me know or I would have to call 911 to check on her. It was funny until the day she didn't come in. It wasn't until the next day that I knew why.

Ruth had become ill and her sister had taken her to the emergency room. That night she was admitted to hospice. Ruth had acute leukemia and passed away less then forty-eight hours later. The news was shared with many tears. The sense of shock and loss were intense.

We closed our shop the day of the funeral. It was too quiet when I reopened. After a year of seeing and sharing with Ruth everyday, I expected it to be her every time the bell rang over the door. Of course, it never was.

Ruth's chocolate tradition continues. New members are often surprised when they notice the dish by the door, until I share her story. And every time someone takes a piece of chocolate, it is a toast to Ruth who reminded us to share the sweetness of life.

~Cynthia Hamond

# Afterword

*No matter what else they're doing, women are also always nurturing.*
*~Cokie Roberts*

I am writing this in southern Connecticut as Hurricane Irene rages outside. We have lost power, along with half the people in our state, but the generator has kicked in so we are able to use our computers and keep the refrigerator and well running. We have no cable TV, Internet, or phone service either, so we are using our cell phones and iPads to communicate and to check on the latest weather forecasts. The oldest of our four children is here with his girlfriend and dog, having elected not to spend a long weekend in Brooklyn in an apartment only two blocks from the mandatory flood evacuation zone.

What am I doing this weekend? I am editing this book and I am cooking up a storm. It is a normal human impulse, and a very maternal one too. The stores were packed with frantic shoppers as the hurricane approached, stocking up not only on water and milk and batteries, but on the less obvious items, such as food for a week, even though we were only going to be stuck inside for a day or two.

When we can't control the outside environment and how it affects our loved ones, we pour our feelings into what we *can* control—our sustenance. I am certainly not the only woman cooking like crazy this weekend. It's how we show our love for family and friends and create an environment of caring and stability during an uncertain time. And it sure feels wonderful to gather around a table with the wind howling outside and the rain pounding the windows and a pot of homemade stew bubbling on the stove.

Food and love are inextricably intertwined. Our memories of grandparents and parents, of favorite holidays, of family traditions, of first dates, of good times with friends, very often revolve around food. This book is all about the relationship between food and love, whether it is romantic love, the love between family members, or the love we show our friends when we invite them over and cook for them.

I hope you loved reading this book as much as we enjoyed creating it for you. You read funny stories about new wives learning to cook, stories about men learning to cook just one thing (and they seem to get a lot of credit for that), and stories where the food was terrible but the company was terrific. There were some stories that made me tear up and others that made me laugh out loud.

Whenever we found ourselves curious about the recipe for a dish that was mentioned, we asked the writer to share, so you'll find twenty-three recipes spread throughout the book as well. We were gratified that every single person we asked for a recipe agreed to share it with our readers, even if it was a "family secret." So now we are all family! We can't vouch for any of them as we do not have a test kitchen and we didn't have time to try them ourselves. But since they represent our writers' fondest memories and family traditions, my guess is that they'll be pretty good.

So what will we eat tonight? In deference to our two youngest children, who are vegan, even though they are weathering Hurricane Irene in other states, tonight will be a vegan night for us too. Our youngest introduced us to this absolutely delicious chickpea stew and I want to share it with you, because it was quite a revelation to us just how satisfying and filling a vegetarian dinner could be. I have made this for numerous meat-eating friends and family members and they have all loved it. Feel free to adjust the ingredients to your taste — like all stews, it is quite forgiving.

# Moroccan Chickpea Stew (vegan)

15 oz. can organic chickpeas or garbanzo beans, drained
    and rinsed
28 oz. can organic diced tomatoes
4-5 organic carrots, peeled and sliced in 1/2-inch rounds
2-3 small organic sweet potatoes or yams, peeled and cut
    in 1/2-inch rounds
1 large sweet onion, cut in pieces for sautéing
1 container organic baby spinach
2-3 garlic cloves, minced
olive oil for sautéing
8 oz. organic vegetable broth
2 teaspoons ground cumin
1 teaspoon ground cinnamon
1 teaspoon chili powder
1/2 teaspoon turmeric
1/2 teaspoon nutmeg
1/2 teaspoon kosher salt
1/2 teaspoon ground pepper

couscous
grated carrots
raisins or currants

Sauté onions and garlic in olive oil for ten minutes.

Add carrots, sweet potatoes, and diced tomatoes and simmer
for ten minutes.

Add vegetable broth, chickpeas, cumin, chili powder, turmeric,
cinnamon, nutmeg, salt and pepper. Simmer until carrots and
sweet potatoes start to soften.

Add baby spinach and simmer until potatoes and carrots are soft.

Serve over couscous. Add grated carrots and raisins or currants to couscous to make it more interesting. For a gluten-free meal, use rice instead of couscous.

Serves eight.

~Amy Newmark

# Recipes from Chef John

## Roasted Garlic Mashed Potatoes

### Ingredients
32 ounces Chicken Soup for the Soul chicken broth
5 cloves garlic, peeled
1 tablespoon olive oil
1 1/2 pounds russet potatoes
4 tablespoon unsalted butter
1/2 cup heavy or sour cream

### Directions
Preheat oven to 350 degrees. Wrap garlic cloves and olive oil in aluminum foil forming a pouch and bake for 25-30 minutes, or until golden brown and soft. Cut potatoes into even-size pieces (about 1-2 inches), peeled or unpeeled (your preference). In a 3-quart sauce pot, cover potatoes with Chicken Soup for the Soul chicken broth and simmer for about 25 minutes until very tender. Drain chicken broth into a bowl and reserve. Add garlic, olive oil, butter and cream (sour cream gives a nice tang) to potatoes and mash. Add back Chicken Soup for the Soul chicken broth as needed for preferred consistency.

# Thai Chicken and Shrimp

Serves 6

## Ingredients
32 ounces Chicken Soup for the Soul Thai-Style chicken broth
1 tablespoon oil
1 pound chicken, cut into 1-inch pieces
8 ounces peeled and deveined shrimp, split
1 teaspoon salt
1 medium onion, sliced
3 cloves garlic, chopped
1 red bell pepper, cut in matchsticks
1 cup sliced carrots
3 cups Nappa (or white cabbage), cut 1/2-inch thick
3 ounces vermicelli pasta or rice noodles

## Directions
Heat 1 tablespoon oil in a 12-inch/4-quart pan over high heat. Add chicken and shrimp and sauté lightly for 2 minutes. Add onions, garlic, red pepper, carrots, cabbage, salt and Chicken Soup for the Soul Thai-Style chicken broth. Mix all ingredients. Cover and gently simmer on the stove over low heat for 10 minutes. Add pasta and mix. Simmer for 5 minutes longer and serve.

# Beef Stroganoff

## Ingredients
2 cups Chicken Soup for the Soul beef broth
1 1/2 pounds beef tenderloin filet
salt and pepper
3 tablespoons butter
1/2 small onion, sliced
1/2 cup sliced mushrooms
2 tablespoons all-purpose flour
2 teaspoons mustard
1/3 cup sour cream
1 tablespoon olive oil or vegetable oil
1/4 cup coarsely chopped sweet gherkin pickles
1 pound extra wide egg noodles, cooked to package directions
chopped parsley leaves as garnish

## Directions
Slice meat into thin strips and season with salt and pepper. Heat a skillet over medium heat. Melt 3 tablespoons butter and sauté onions and mushrooms until tender. Add flour to mixture and cook for 1 minute. Whisk in the Chicken Soup for the Soul beef broth. Thicken for 1 minute. Stir in mustard and sour cream. Thicken 2 to 3 minutes. Remove from heat and season the sauce with salt and pepper. Heat a second skillet over high heat. Add 1 tablespoon oil. Add the meat and cook over high heat until brown on both sides for approximately 3 to 4 minutes total. Add the chopped pickles and combine with sauce. Arrange meat on a bed of egg noodles and top with parsley.

# Ravioli and Zucchini with Three Cheese Pasta Sauce

Serves 6

## Ingredients
25 ounces Chicken Soup for the Soul Three Cheese pasta sauce
1 1/2 pounds fresh zucchini
2 tablespoons olive oil
3 cloves of garlic, chopped
sea salt
24 fresh or frozen cheese ravioli
5 leaves fresh basil, chopped

## Directions
Put a large pot of salted water on to boil. Cut zucchini into 1/4-inch thick discs. In a 12-inch skillet, heat oil until it ripples and add cut zucchini. Season zucchini, add garlic and cook until lightly browned (about 4 minutes). In a medium pot, heat Chicken Soup for the Soul Three Cheese pasta sauce until just boiling. Cook ravioli according to the instructions, drain and put into a serving bowl. Spoon Chicken Soup for the Soul Three Cheese pasta sauce over ravioli and spoon zucchini over the pasta sauce. Sprinkle with chopped basil and serve.

# Chocolate Bread Pudding with Vanilla Sauce

Serves 6

**For the Bread**
4-day-old croissants, cut into 3/4-inch cubes
8 1/2 ounces bittersweet chocolate (preferably Valrhona), chopped

**For the Custard**
1 cup milk
1 cup heavy cream
1/4 cup granulated sugar
3 large eggs
1 teaspoon vanilla extract

**For the Vanilla Sauce**
8 large egg yolks
2 teaspoons vanilla extract
1/2 cup granulated sugar
2 cups milk
1 cup heavy cream

Preheat the oven to 400 degrees. Butter a 9-inch square (at least 2-inch deep) ovenproof ceramic or glass baking dish.

**To prepare the bread:** Place the cubed croissants on a cookie sheet and bake in the oven until lightly toasted, 4 or 5 minutes. Meanwhile, melt the chocolate in a metal bowl set over a saucepan of boiling water or in the top of a double boiler (or melt in the microwave for 35-40 seconds). Remove the croissants from the oven and, while still warm, toss them with the melted chocolate. Place in the buttered baking dish.

Turn the temperature to 325 degrees.

**To prepare the custard:** Pour the milk and cream into a saucepan, add 2 tablespoons of the sugar, and scald (bring to just below the boiling point). In a mixing bowl, whisk together the eggs, remaining sugar, and vanilla. Temper the egg mixture by slowly pouring in the scalded milk mixture while whisking vigorously. Strain into the buttered baking dish. Place the dish in a baking pan large enough to hold it. Create a water bath by pouring hot water into the baking pan until the water reaches halfway up the sides of the baking dish containing the bread pudding. Carefully place the pan in the oven and bake until the pudding is set, 50 minutes to 1 hour; the pudding is cooked when a toothpick inserted in the middle comes out clean. Remove the pan from the oven and let cool slightly, then carefully remove the baking dish from the water bath and set aside to let it cool completely.

**To prepare the sauce:** Prepare an ice bath. Place the egg yolks, vanilla and 1/4 cup of sugar in a mixing bowl and set aside. Pour the milk and cream into a sauce pan, add the remaining sugar, and set over medium heat. Scald the mixture (bring to just below boiling point), then temper the yolk mixture by slowly pouring in a little of the scalded liquid while whisking vigorously. Add the tempered yolk mixture to the saucepan and stir with a wooden spoon. Continue to stir over medium heat until the mixture is thickened enough to coat the back of a spoon, about 1 minute. Be careful not to let the mixture come to a boil. Strain the mixture into a metal bowl and transfer to the ice bath. Let cool completely, stirring occasionally, and transfer to a creamer.

**To serve:** Bring the dish containing the bread pudding to the table and spoon the pudding onto serving plates. Serve with the vanilla sauce.

# Recipes from Taste of Home

## Company Mac and Cheese

This is by far the creamiest, tastiest and most special macaroni and cheese I have ever tried. I'm not usually a fan of homemade macaroni and cheese, but when a friend served this, I had to have the recipe. Since it's so little fuss and well received, it's a terrific potluck dish. ~Catherine Odgen, Middlegrove, New York

Prep/Total Time: 30 minutes

**Ingredients**
1 package (7 ounces) elbow macaroni
6 tablespoons butter, *divided*
3 tablespoons all-purpose flour
2 cups milk
1 package (8 ounces) cream cheese, cubed
2 cups (8 ounces) shredded cheddar cheese
2 teaspoons spicy brown mustard
1/2 teaspoon salt
1/4 teaspoon pepper
3/4 cup dry breadcrumbs
2 tablespoons minced fresh parsley

**Directions**
Preheat oven to 400 degrees. Cook macaroni according to package directions. Meanwhile, melt 4 tablespoons butter in a large saucepan. Stir in flour until smooth. Gradually add milk. Bring to a boil; cook and stir for 2 minutes.

Reduce heat; add cheeses, mustard, salt and pepper. Stir until cheese is melted and sauce is smooth. Drain macaroni; add to cheese sauce and stir to coat.

Transfer to a greased shallow 3-quart baking dish. Melt remaining butter; toss with breadcrumbs and parsley. Sprinkle over macaroni. Bake, uncovered, 15-20 minutes or until golden brown. **Yield:** 6-8 servings.

# Everything Bread

I love to make bread from scratch and this has become one of our tried and true favorites to serve with any meal, casual or formal.
~Traci Wynne, Denver, Pennsylvania

Prep: 45 minutes + rising Bake: 25 minutes

## Ingredients
1 package (1/4 ounce) active dry yeast
3/4 cup warm water (110° to 115°)
1 cup warm 2% milk (110° to 115°)
1/4 cup butter, softened
2 tablespoons sugar
1 egg yolk
1 1/2 teaspoons salt
4 to 4 1/2 cups all-purpose flour
1 egg white
2 teaspoons water
1 teaspoon coarse sea salt *or* kosher salt
1 teaspoon dried minced onion
1 teaspoon *each* sesame, caraway and poppy seeds

## Directions
In a large bowl, dissolve yeast in warm water. Add milk, butter, sugar, egg yolk, salt and 2 cups flour. Beat on medium speed for 3 minutes. Stir in enough remaining flour to form a firm dough.

Turn onto a floured surface; knead until smooth and elastic, about 6-8 minutes. Place in a greased bowl, turning once to grease the top. Cover and let rise until doubled, about 1 hour.

Punch dough down. Turn onto a lightly floured surface; divide dough into thirds. Shape each into a 20-inch rope. Place ropes on a large greased baking sheet and braid; pinch ends to seal and tuck under. Cover and let rise until doubled, about 45 minutes.

Preheat oven to 375 degrees. Combine egg white and water; brush over dough. Combine salt, onion and seeds; sprinkle over bread. Bake 22-28 minutes or until golden brown. Remove from pan to a wire rack to cool. **Yield:** 1 loaf (25 slices).

# Simple Marinated Shrimp

Seafood is a staple here in Florida. This recipe is quick and easy to make and can be prepared well in advance. I always seem to get a lot of requests for the recipe when I make it for a party or special occasion.

Prep: 10 minutes + marinating

## Ingredients
2 pounds cooked medium shrimp, peeled and deveined
1 medium red onion, sliced and separated into rings
2 medium lemons, cut into slices
1 cup pitted ripe olives, drained
1/2 cup olive oil
1/3 cup minced fresh parsley
3 tablespoons lemon juice
3 tablespoons red wine vinegar
1 garlic clove, minced
1 bay leaf
1 tablespoon minced fresh basil *or* 1 teaspoon dried basil
1 teaspoon salt
1 teaspoon ground mustard
1/4 teaspoon pepper

## Directions
In a 3-quart glass serving bowl, combine the shrimp, onion, lemons and olives. In a jar with a tight-fitting lid, combine the remaining ingredients; shake well. Pour over shrimp mixture and stir gently to coat.

Cover and refrigerate for 24 hours, stirring occasionally. Discard bay leaf before serving. **Yield:** 14 servings.

# William Tell's Never-Miss Apple Cake

I bake my family-favorite fall cake to usher in this abundant season.
It looks so luscious that eating one piece is nearly impossible.
~Jamie Jones, Madison, Georgia

Prep: 40 minutes Bake: 50 minutes + cooling

**Ingredients**
1 package (8 ounces) cream cheese, softened
2 cups sugar, *divided*
4 eggs
1 cup canola oil
2 cups all-purpose flour
2 teaspoons baking powder
2 teaspoons ground cinnamon
1 teaspoon salt
1/4 teaspoon baking soda
2 cups chopped peeled tart apples
1 cup shredded carrots
1/2 cup chopped pecans

**Praline Icing**
1/2 cup packed brown sugar
1/4 cup butter, cubed
2 tablespoons 2% milk
1/2 cup confectioners' sugar
1/2 teaspoon vanilla extract
1/4 cup chopped pecans, toasted

**Directions**
Preheat oven to 350 degrees. In a small bowl, beat cream cheese and
1/4 cup sugar until smooth. Beat in 1 egg; set aside.

In a large bowl, beat oil with remaining sugar and eggs until well blended. Combine flour, baking powder, cinnamon, salt and baking soda; gradually beat into oil mixture until blended. Stir in apples, carrots and pecans.

Transfer half of the apple batter to a greased and floured 10-inch fluted tube pan; layer with cream cheese mixture and remaining apple batter.

Bake at for 50-60 minutes or until a toothpick inserted near the center comes out clean. Cool 10 minutes before removing from pan to a wire rack to cool completely.

In a large saucepan, bring the brown sugar, butter and milk to a boil. Cook and stir 1 minute. Remove from heat; whisk in confectioners' sugar and vanilla until smooth. Drizzle over cake. Sprinkle with pecans. **Yield:** 12 servings.

# Meet Our Contributors

**Georgia Aker** grew up in rural and small-town New Mexico. She has taught in a one-room school. Georgia has had several articles published in devotion magazines. At ninety-six she still does some gardening, in Oregon, where she lives with her daughter and son-in-law Marty and David Magee.

**Barbara Blossom Ashmun** gardens on an acre in Portland, OR. She's written six garden books, most recently *Married to My Garden*, about her love affair with plants. A garden columnist for the *Portland Tribune* since 2004, she's also contributed to magazines and anthologies. She blogs at blessingsfromthegarden.blogspot.com.

**Suzanne Baginskie** lives on the west coast of Florida with her husband, Al. In between volunteering for the local sheriff's office and her community, she writes and sells short mystery stories, flash fiction and writing articles. She is currently penning a legal thriller novel. Visit her website at http://mysite.verizon.net/resv10om.

**Celeste Barnard** received her Practical Theology degree from Christ For The Nations with a third-year advanced study in Youth Ministry. She is currently a contributing author for Destiny in Bloom, an online magazine. She plans on doing more writing and speaking in the future. Learn more at celestebarnard.wordpress.com.

**June Harman Betts** is the author of three books in *The Echoes in My Mind* series: *Father Was A Caveman*, *We Were Vagabonds*, and *Along Came*

A *Soldier*. Her story, "The Christmas Present," was published in *Chicken Soup for the Soul: Thanks Dad*. Learn more at www.authorsden.com/junehbetts.

**Lil Blosfield** is the Chief Financial Officer for Child and Adolescent Behavioral Health in Canton, OH. She loves writing and tries to capture her own photo album in words of many life experiences. Lil enjoys music and laughter or, in other words, karaoke! She adores time spent with friends and family. E-mail her at LBlosfield40@msn.com.

**Carol A. Boas** is a retired teacher and children's book author. She loves cooking, walking, hiking and traveling. Her four grandchildren love taking her to school for show-and-tell on visits to Chicago and Denver. She lives in Connecticut with her husband, renowned proofreader Rick. E-mail her at cboas4@gmail.com.

**Heather Brand** is a graduate of Shorter University in Georgia and is currently pursuing a Master of Education. Her newly acquired cooking skills have been challenged since becoming gluten intolerant. When not experimenting in the kitchen, Heather enjoys traveling with her husband, volunteering, performing in community theater productions, and teaching creative writing.

**Sandra D. Bricker** is an award-winning author of laugh-out-loud fiction for the inspirational market. She has fifteen novels and devotionals in print with several more slated through 2013. Sandie resides in the Tampa area and would love to hear from her readers through her blog: sandradbricker.blogspot.com.

**Cynthia Briggs** embraces her love of cooking and writing through her story-filled cookbooks *Pork Chops & Applesauce* and *Sweet Apple Temptations*. She enjoys speaking to women's groups, critiquing and reviewing books, and writing for various publications. Coaching budding authors is her most recent passion. E-mail Cynthia at info@porkchopsandapplesauce.net.

**Debra Ayers Brown**, a marketing professional, received her B.A. with honors from the University of Georgia and her MBA from The Citadel. She loves traveling with her daughter Meredith, eco tours, Zumba, and living life on the Georgia coast. Link to her blogs at www.DebraAyersBrown.com or e-mail her at dabmlb@comcast.net.

**Leigh Ann Bryant** is a wife and mother of three sons. She received her BSN from the University of Texas at Arlington. She loves the Lord and is very active with the youth at her church. She loves to write, travel, and watch her sons do gymnastics. E-mail her at bryant_leighann@msn.com.

**Jane Brzozowski** comes from a family of writers, including her husband Steve and her daughters Kat and Sally. This is her first published work. Her sister, Lava Mueller, got her hooked on the *Chicken Soup for the Soul* series and she also has a story in this book!

**Barbara Burris** lives with her husband Bruce in a log home set in the middle of three acres of informal cottage and woodland gardens. These gardens serve as inspiration for Barbara's photographs and watercolor paintings. Her future plans include a series of stories about summers at her grandmother's cottage. E-mail her at bbburris@tds.net.

**Kristine Byron** worked as a trainer for Tupperware and in later years as an interior designer. She loves to cook and entertain. Kristine also loves to travel with her husband and spend quality time with her five grandchildren.

**Barbara Canale** is a freelance writer and columnist for the *Catholic Sun* in Syracuse, NY. She has been published in several *Chicken Soup for the Soul* books. She is the author of *Our Labor of Love: A Romanian Adoption Chronicle*. She enjoys biking, skiing, and gardening.

**Sandy McPherson Carrubba** stopped teaching first grade for full-time motherhood. She's written for children and adults. Her essays have appeared in *Voices of Alzheimer's*, *Voices of Lung Cancer* and the *Chicken Soup for the Soul* series. Her poetry chapbook, *Brush Strokes*, was published by Finishing Line Press.

**David Chalfin** is a native New Yorker living in Los Angeles as a television and film editor. He received his B.A. from the University of Pennsylvania and an M.A. in Media Studies from The New School. He lives for a good slice of NY pizza. E-mail him at dchalf@aol.com.

**Viji K. Chary's** passion for writing stories began in elementary school and has evolved into teaching and coaching children in various activities including gymnastics, classroom activities and creative competitions. Her stories have been published in *Highlights for Children*, *Ladybug* magazine and many more. E-mail her at vijikchary@gmail.com.

**Emily Parke Chase** speaks at conferences and retreats and has authored six books, including *Help! My Family's Messed Up* (Kregel 2008) and *Standing Tall After Falling Short* (WingSpread, 2011). She enjoys reading, cooking and spoiling her grandchildren. Visit her at emilychase.com.

**Robert Chrisman** took early retirement from his thirty-two-year career as a civil servant to spend the rest of his life writing. He has published several short stories, with more in the works. He teaches writing practice at a local writing center. He enjoys reading and eating out.

**Madeline Clapps** lives in Brooklyn, NY, and is an actor, singer, and editor at Chicken Soup for the Soul. She recently edited *Chicken Soup for the Soul: Just for Preteens* and *Chicken Soup for the Soul: Just for Teenagers*. She also designs the monthly communiqué for Chicken Soup for the Soul contributors.

**Courtney Conover** exists in what she calls a mixed marriage: She is a vegetarian, but her husband Scott, a former NFL football player turned professional chef, is a proud meat-eater. This is Courtney's sixth contribution to the *Chicken Soup for the Soul* series. Learn more about her at www.courtneyconover.com.

**Harriet Cooper** is a freelance writer who specializes in creative non-fiction, humor and articles. Her topics often include health, exercise, diet, cats, family and the environment. A frequent contributor to the *Chicken Soup for the Soul* series, her work has also appeared in newspapers, magazines, newsletters, anthologies, websites and radio. E-mail her at shewrites@live.ca.

**D'ette Corona** is the Assistant Publisher for Chicken Soup for the Soul Publishing, LLC. She received her Bachelor of Science in business management. D'ette has been married for nineteen years and has a fourteen-year-old son.

**Michael Coscia** is a screenwriter and lyricist living in Los Angeles, CA. He believes in the power of words, and chooses to use them wisely. In his spare time he loves to cook, read, travel, and laugh. E-mail him at michaelcoscia@mac.com.

**Priscilla Dann-Courtney** is a freelance writer and clinical psychologist living in Boulder, CO with her husband and three children. Her book, *Room to Grow*, is a collection of personal essays previously published in national newspapers and magazines. Her passions include family, friends, yoga, running, skiing and baking.

**Stephanie Davenport** is a wife, mom and currently the pastor of The Vineyard Church in Bloomington, IL. Stephanie was previously a newspaper columnist and correspondent, and her writing has appeared in several national magazines. She also enjoys time in the kitchen with her family. E-mail her at stephaniedavenport08@gmail. com.

**Judy DeCarlo** is employed as a registered nuclear medicine technologist but is at heart a writer. She resides in Northeast Pennsylvania and is a married mother of two adult daughters. Judy enjoys reading, all outdoor activities, and traveling (particularly planning trips). E-mail her at superrep1@aol.com.

**Lola Di Giulio De Maci** contributes regularly to Chicken Soup for the Soul. Her now-grown children and former students inspire her children's stories, some appearing in the *Los Angeles Times*. Lola has an M.A. in education and English and writes from her loft overlooking the San Bernardino Mountains. E-mail her at LDeMaci@aol.com.

**Jeannie Dotson** is a middle school language arts teacher in Powell County, KY. She enjoys writing nonfiction and is currently working on a nonfiction picture book for children.

**Shawnelle Eliasen** and her husband Lonny raise their five sons in Illinois. She home teaches her youngest children and writes about their adventures. Her stories have been published in *Guideposts*, *MomSense*, *A Cup of Comfort*, *Christmas Miracles*, *Christmas Spirit*, *Chicken Soup for the Soul* books and more. Find her blog at Shawnellewrites.blogspot.com.

**Melissa Face** teaches and writes in Virginia. She lives with her husband, son, and dog and enjoys spending time and traveling with all three of them. E-mail Melissa at writermsface@yahoo.com.

**Melissa Ford** is the author of the award-winning website Stirrup Queens (www.stirrup-queens.com), as well as the novel *Life from Scratch*. Melissa completed her MFA at the University of Massachusetts. She lives in Washington, DC, with her writer husband, Joshua, and their twins.

**Sally Friedman** has been writing about the sounds of her own family life for four decades. An honors graduate of the University of

Pennsylvania, Sally's works have appeared in *The New York Times*, *The Philadelphia Inquirer*, *AARP The Magazine* and numerous publications around the country. E-mail her at pinegander@aol.com.

**Beverly Golberg**, of St. Paul, MN, began writing after retirement from paralegal work. Her essays have appeared in the literary journals *ARS Medica* and *Willard & Maple*, *Cottage Life* magazine, the St. Paul *Pioneer Press*, and various anthologies. She reads her work at the Wild Yam Cabaret in St. Paul.

**Gina Guilford** received her master's degree in Screenwriting at University of Miami in 2003. She has published articles in national magazines and has written an original sitcom based on her blended family. Her screenplay, *The Sweet Spot*, won various awards, including first place in All She Wrote. Learn more at gleesganders.blogspot.com.

**Cynthia M. Hamond, S.F.O.**, is in over 100 publications including magazines, and Bible study aids. She's received several writing awards. Two stories have been made for TV. Cynthia enjoys speaking and school visits. She is founder of Joyful M.O.M. (Moments of Ministry) and co-founder of Grandmas in Pajamas. E-mail her at Cynthiahamond@aol.com.

**Christie Hansen** lives with her husband, three children, two cats and dog on Belly Acre Farm in Northern Utah. She teaches seventh grade English and language arts and delights in finding ways to use squeaky rubber chickens to enhance student learning. E-mail her at bellyacrefarm@gmail.com.

**Teresa Anne Hayden** is a writer who lives in Cayce, KY, with her husband Mike and their dog Tweeter. They have three children and six grandchildren. Her work has appeared in several publications including *Chicken Soup for the Soul: A Book of Miracles*. E-mail Teresa at hayden5765@bellsouth.net.

**Karen R. Hessen** is an author and speaker. She has been published in *Chicken Soup for the Soul: Divorce and Recovery*, *Guideposts*, *Vista*, *Seeds of...* and others. She and her husband Douglas live in Forest Grove and Seaside, OR. Karen can be reached at karenwrites@frontier.com or visit her website at www.karenrhessen.com.

**Miriam Hill** is a frequent contributor to the *Chicken Soup for the Soul* series and has been published in *Writer's Digest*, *The Christian Science Monitor*, *Grit*, *St. Petersburg Times*, *Sacramento Bee* and Poynter Online. Miriam's manuscript received Honorable Mention for Inspirational Writing in a Writer's Digest Writing Competition.

**Rebecca Hill** and Tom Caufield live in Los Angeles. She and her friend Dominique work at Channel Road Inn and the Inn at Playa del Rey. Rebecca's stories have appeared in previous *Chicken Soup for the Soul* anthologies and in *Redbook* magazine. Her novel is entitled *Confessions of an Innkeeper*.

**Sharon T. Hinton, RN, MSN, FCN**, is an educator, consultant, national speaker and writer specializing in faith community nursing and spiritual journaling. She is completing a Doctorate in Global Health focusing on how stories can heal. Sharon lives in Texas. E-mail her at hinton.sharon@att.net.

**Heather Humrichouse** is a freelance writer who starts each day with a cuppa. Her hubby used the same technique to win her over to hot sauce, red wine, and onions. Her palate will never be the same. They celebrate each day with their three children. Join them on CreativeFamilyMoments.com.

**Pauline Hylton** is a freelance writer living in Florida. She specializes in humor or anything else you will pay her for. She loves the Lord, her family, and dark chocolate. (Not necessarily in that order.) Feel free to read her blog, send an e-mail, or mail her dark chocolate at paulinehylton.com.

**Mary Potter Kenyon** cooks up soup and words in the Manchester, Iowa home she shares with her husband David and four of their eight children. Her writing appears in magazines, anthologies and the local newspaper. She is working with her agent on a book about couponing and blogs at marypotterkenyon.wordpress.com.

**April Knight** spends her days riding horses and her nights writing mystery novels. She also writes a newspaper column and novels under her tribal name Crying Wind Hummingbird.

**Miranda Koerner** is a writer living in Texas with her husband Ben and two Chihuahuas, Bitty and Bear. After getting her B.A. in Journalism, she worked as a children's magazine editor and reporter. Now, she teaches creative writing classes and writes stories for children and adults. For more, visit www.aduckinherpond.com.

**Mitchell Kyd** wrapped up a thirty-year career as a Fortune 500 PR professional and is enjoying life as a wordsmith and storyteller. Her stories often reflect the joys and poignant moments of small-town living and she is a frequent contributor to the *Chicken Soup for the Soul* series. Visit her at www.mitchellkyd.com.

**Patti Lawson** is an award-winning author and lawyer. Her first book, *The Dog Diet, A Memoir: What My Dog Taught Me About Shedding Pounds, Licking Stress and Getting a New Leash on Life* won the Dog Writers Association of America Maxwell Award for Humor. Learn more at www.thedogdiet.com.

**Andrea Lehner** is a freelance writer with a master's degree in Creative Writing and a bachelor's degree in English Writing. In addition to writing, she has a passion for cooking new and traditional recipes that fill her home with the kind of love that connects generations. E-mail her at aclehner@gmail.com.

**Beth Levine** is a veteran health and humor writer. She lives in

Stamford, CT, where her family's new favorite restaurant is The Fez. (Order the Fez Burger—you won't be sorry.) Learn more at www. bethlevine.net.

**Nikki Loftin** writes in the Texas Hill Country, surrounded by dogs, chickens, and small, loud boys. She studied fiction writing at The University of Texas at Austin (M.A. '98). Her first novel, *The Sinister Sweetness of Splendid Academy*, will be published by Razorbill/Penguin in Summer 2012. Learn more at www.nikkiloftin.com.

**Barbara LoMonaco** has worked for Chicken Soup for the Soul as an editor and webmaster since 1998. She has co-authored two Chicken Soup for the Soul book titles and has had stories published in various other titles. Barbara is a graduate of the University of Southern California and has a teaching credential.

**Donna Lowich** works as an information specialist, providing information to people affected by paralysis. She enjoys writing about her family and personal experiences. Other hobbies include counted cross stitch and reading. She lives with her husband in New Jersey. E-mail her at DonnaLowich@aol.com.

**Carrie Malinowski** is a first grade teacher and reading tutor. She has a degree in psychology. She wrote her first story at the age of five and has been writing ever since. She loves to write picture books. Ms. Malinowski lives in Arizona with her husband, son, and dog Chester. Please visit her at www.carriemalinowski.com.

**David Martin's** humor and political satire have appeared in many publications including *The New York Times*, the *Chicago Tribune* and *Smithsonian Magazine*. His latest humor collection, *Dare to be Average*, was published in 2010 by Lulu.com. David lives in Ottawa, Canada, with his wife Cheryl and their daughter Sarah.

**Lynn Maddalena Menna** is a freelance writer and former educator.

She's a columnist for *Main Street Magazine*, and writes for *NJ Education Now*. Lynn lives in Hawthorne, NJ, with her husband, Prospero. Sadly, Toonsie passed on a few months before this book was published. E-mail Lynn at prolynn@aol.com.

**Esme Mills** has two lovely boys and a sweet little girl, all of whom love cookies. Esme loves family, slow food, writing, crafting and, yes, cookies too! Feel free to connect with her on Facebook to find out more.

**Lava Mueller** is grateful to be a frequent contributor to the *Chicken Soup for the Soul* series. She lives in Vermont with her very cute husband Andy and their two children, Sophie and Max. Lava is also a fiction writer and is working on a novel for young adults. E-mail her at lavamueller@yahoo.com.

**Lauren Murray** is a writer and knitting aficionado who lives in the Rocky Mountains of Alberta, Canada. She's older than she looks — really — and younger than she feels — most of the time — and she loves to explore women's journeys in her stories. Visit her at www. laurenhawkeye.com.

**Alice Muschany** is close to retiring after working forty years for the same company. She hopes to find more time to hike, swim, bike and play. Photography and writing are her passions and her eight grandchildren make wonderful subjects. E-mail her at aliceandroland@gmail.com.

**Irena Nieslony** was born in England, but now lives on the island of Crete, Greece. She studied English and Drama at University of London and graduated in 1982. Irena enjoys reading, traveling and walking her dogs. She plans to write mystery novels. E-mail her at irena_nieslony@hotmail.com.

**Marc Tyler Nobleman** is the author of more than seventy books including *Boys of Steel: The Creators of Superman* and one due out in 2012 about the "secret" co-creator of Batman. His cartoons have appeared in more than 100 international publications. At noblemania. blogspot.com, he reveals the behind-the-scenes stories of his work.

**Kimberly Noe** studied journalism at Oklahoma State University and currently works as advertising director at a suburban weekly newspaper in central Oklahoma. She and her nine-year-old daughter love to travel and play with friends and family. Kim often writes personal columns and is working on her first novel. E-mail her at kimnoe@ gmail.com.

**Linda O'Connell** teaches in St. Louis, MO. Her humorous and inspirational essays have been published in twelve *Chicken Soup for the Soul* titles and many other regional and national publications. When Linda is wrist-deep in flour and sugar, she is knee-deep in thought. Linda blogs at lindaoconnell.blogspot.com.

**Caitlin Q. Bailey O'Neill** has been previously published in *Chicken Soup for the Soul: Empty Nesters* and *Chicken Soup for the Soul: Thanks Dad*. A freelance editor and writer, she can be reached at PerfectlyPunctuated@yahoo.com. This story is for Kathy Bailey — who still loves seeing her daughter's name in print.

**Robin O'Steen** is sixteen years old and lives in Boulder, CO. She is currently working on her first novel.

**Lisa Pawlak** is a creative writer of nonfiction who enjoys coffee, traveling, and being married to Geno. She received a B.A. in Communication from the University of California, San Diego, and now works in the non-profit world. This is her second story in the *Chicken Soup for the Soul* series. E-mail her at lisapawlak@hotmail. com.

**Saralee Perel** is a national award-winning columnist. Her book, *The*

*Dog Who Walked Me*, is about her dog, who became her caregiver after her spinal cord injury, the initial devastation of her marriage, and her cat, who kept her sane. E-mail her at sperel@saraleeperel.com or www.saraleeperel.com.

Novelist, blogger, and award-winning food writer, **Perry P. Perkins** is a work-from-home dad living in the Pacific Northwest. Perry has written for hundreds of magazines, from *Writer's Digest* and *Guideposts*, to *American Hunter* and *Bassmaster Magazine*. He's the author of two novels, four cookbooks, and numerous short stories.

**Jami Perona** received her degree in Education from Pittsburg State University. She is currently an elementary teacher. Jami enjoys spending time outside with her family. She plans to keep writing and would like to have a book published. Check out her blog at jamidawnperona. blogspot.com.

**Sherry Poff** grew up in southern West Virginia and currently lives in Ooltewah, TN. In addition to baking pretty good biscuits, she enjoys gardening, writing, and teaching high school English. E-mail Sherry at poffmeister@comcast.net.

**Felice Prager** is a freelance writer and an educational therapist from Scottsdale, AZ. Hundreds of her essays have been published locally, nationally, and internationally in print and on the Internet. She is the author of *Quiz It: Arizona*. Please visit www.QuizItAZ.com or e-mail her at felprager@cox.net.

**Tim Ramsey** is a school administrator by day and a college instructor by night in Avondale, AZ. He has been an educator since 1983 and a writer since he could first hold a number two pencil. He lives with his wife, daughter and six cats. E-mail him at tkramsey59@msn.com.

**Virginia Redman** received her B.A. in English from Loyola Marymount University in 1970. She received her M.A. in English from San Diego

State University in 1990. Virginia is a retired English teacher and lives in Southern California. She is writing her first young adult novel.

**Carol McAdoo Rehme** values food and friendship—and the bonds they forge. An award-winning author, editor, and ghostwriter, she examines life through the lens of a wordsmith, focusing on memory-making moments. Carol writes from her window-banked home office along the Front Range of the Colorado Rockies.

**Jacqueline Rivkin** lives in New York with her teenage daughter, Natasha, also a writer. Jacqueline has a master's degree from the Columbia University Graduate School of Journalism and has contributed to publications including *Newsday*, *Self* and *Jet*. Her essay "Bean Soup" appeared in *Chicken Soup for the Soul: Grieving and Recovery*.

**Sallie A. Rodman** has contributed to numerous *Chicken Soup for the Soul* anthologies, magazines and *The Orange County Register*. She earned her Certificate in Professional Writing from Cal State University, Long Beach. Sallie enjoys writing about true events in her life that have shaped her character. Catch her at sa.rodman@verizon. net.

**John Scanlan** is a 1983 graduate of the U.S. Naval Academy and a retired Lieutenant Colonel from the U.S. Marine Corps. He is currently pursuing a second career as a writer and can be reached using ping1@hargray.com.

**Deborah Shouse** is a speaker, writer, editor and vegetarian. She loves helping people write books and facilitating creativity and storytelling workshops. Deborah donates all proceeds from her book, *Love in the Land of Dementia: Finding Hope in the Caregiver's Journey*, to Alzheimer's programs and research. Visit www.thecreativityconnection.com and read deborahshousewrites.wordpress.com.

**Diane Stark** is a former elementary school teacher turned stay-at-home mom and freelance writer. She is a frequent contributor to the *Chicken Soup for the Soul* series. She is the author of *Teachers' Devotions to Go*. E-mail her at DianeStark19@yahoo.com.

**Linda St.Cyr** is a writer, blogger, activist, and short story author. When she isn't writing or raising her kids with her life partner, she is busy being vocal about feeding the hungry, sheltering the homeless, and bringing attention to human rights violations all over the world.

**Annmarie B. Tait** lives in Conshohocken, PA, with her husband Joe Beck and Sammy their Yorkie. Annmarie has contributed to several *Chicken Soup for the Soul* books, *Reminisce* magazine and the *Patchwork Path* anthology. Annmarie also enjoys cooking along with singing and recording American and Irish folk songs. E-mail her at irishbloom@aol.com.

**Becky Tidberg** is a frequent contributor to Focus on the Family's *Thriving Family* magazine and she enjoys speaking to women and parents. Becky is a mom of two and extra mom to over 100 foster children. She and her husband just celebrated fifteen years of marriage. Contact her at www.BeckyTidberg.com or campfireministries@yahoo.com.

**Lisa Tiffin** is a freelance writer from upstate New York, where she lives with her husband and twin sons. She has a weekly column in the Rochester *Democrat and Chronicle* and has had a variety of essays, magazine articles and short fiction published. Learn more at www.lisatiffin.com.

**Elaine Togneri** has an M.A. in English from Rutgers Graduate School. She and her husband are enjoying early retirement in their home in Central Florida. For more information on her published stories, visit her website at sites.google.com/site/elainetogneri/home.

**Stefanie Wass's** stories have been published in the *Los Angeles Times*,

*The Seattle Times, Christian Science Monitor, Akron Beacon Journal, Akron Life &Leisure, Cleveland Magazine, The Writer, A Cup of Comfort* and *Chicken Soup for the Soul* books. She is currently seeking representation for her middle grade novel. Visit www.stefaniewass.com.

**Linda C. Wright** is an award-winning freelance writer and lives in Viera, FL. She's had many of her personal stories anthologized. Linda enjoys traveling, reading and photography. She is working on her second novel. E-mail her at lindacwright@ymail.com.

**Helen Zanone** lives in Pittsburgh with her husband and three children. She is on the board of St. Davids Christian Writers' Conference. Helen is active in her writers' group and fulfilling her love for writing. She has several stories in the *Chicken Soup for the Soul* series. E-mail her at hzanone@yahoo.com.

# Meet Our Authors

**Amy Newmark** has been Chicken Soup for the Soul's publisher, coauthor, and editor-in-chief for the last six years, after a thirty-year career as a writer, speaker, financial analyst, and business executive in the worlds of finance and telecommunications. Amy is a Chartered Financial Analyst and a *magna cum laude* graduate of Harvard College, where she majored in Portuguese, minored in French, and traveled extensively. She and her husband have four grown children.

After a long career writing books on telecommunications, voluminous financial reports, business plans, and corporate press releases, Chicken Soup for the Soul is a breath of fresh air for Amy. She loves creating these life-changing books for Chicken Soup for the Soul's wonderful readers. She has coauthored and/or edited more than 100 Chicken Soup for the Soul books.

You can reach Amy with any questions or comments through webmaster@chickensoupforthesoul.com and you can follow her on Twitter @amynewmark or @chickensoupsoul.

**Catherine M. Cassidy** is Editor-in-Chief of *Taste of Home* (tasteofhome. com), overseeing the creation of all branded media, including *Taste of Home*, the number one food and entertaining magazine in the world, and its website, social media, special interest publications and cookbooks, as well as *Simple & Delicious* magazine. Catherine has toured the country as the face of *Taste of Home* for national and local TV, radio, and newspaper interviews in support of the bestselling *Taste of Home* cookbooks and magazines.

Prior to joining *Taste of Home*, Catherine served as Editor-in-Chief of *Prevention* magazine, the nation's largest health publication, at Rodale, Inc. Catherine joined Rodale in 1986 as an associate editor in the book division, and was later named Executive Editor of Rodale's Custom Publishing division. She started her career at *Runner's World* and *Fit* magazines in Mountain View, California. Catherine lives in Milwaukee, Wisconsin with her husband, Steve.

After twenty-three extraordinary and fulfilling years at The Waldorf-Astoria as Executive Chef, **John Doherty** has aligned with Designer Mark Zeff to create Merchant Hospitality in New York. He recently developed and opened Porto Vivo restaurant in Huntington, NY; The Astor Room in Astoria, NY; and Diamond Mills Hotel & Tavern in Saugerties, NY. Currently, he is Chef of Innovation and Recipe Development for Chicken Soup for the Soul Foods, a national food product line launched in August 2013.

Voted student most likely to succeed from the Culinary Institute of America, Chef John went on to become Executive Chef at The Waldorf-Astoria at age twenty-seven. He was the youngest person ever named to the position of Executive Chef in the New York landmark's notable history. After more than twenty-three years at his post, Chef John holds the distinction of having cooked for more presidents, royalty and heads of state than any other chef in the country. Chef John elevated the quality of food to a level that positioned The Waldorf as one of New York's dining hot spots. He released *The Waldorf-Astoria Cookbook* in 2006, featuring over 120 recipes.

Chef John is a frequent guest speaker at national culinary and hospitality colleges, and industry events. He has been awarded an honorary doctorate degree from Johnson & Wales, an honorary master's degree from the Culinary Institute of America, and a Food Industry Leadership Award from Niagara University as well as Food Arts magazine's Silver Spoon Award.

# Thank You

We owe huge thanks to all of our contributors. We know that you poured your hearts and souls into the thousands of stories that you shared with us, and ultimately with each other. As I read and edited these stories, I was truly inspired, excited about trying your recipes, and impressed by your willingness to share your favorite meals and personal anecdotes.

We could only publish a small percentage of the stories that were submitted, but we read every single one and even the ones that do not appear in the book had an influence on us and on the final manuscript. We owe special thanks to our editor Barbara LoMonaco, who read every submission to this book and narrowed the list down to a few hundred finalists, and then did the final proofreading of the manuscript. Madeline Clapps did the first round of editing, selected most of the quotations at the beginning of the stories, and shaped the manuscript into chapters. Our assistant publisher, D'ette Corona, worked with all the contributors as kindly and competently as always, obtaining their approvals for our edits and the quotations, and also obtaining their special recipes. And editor Kristiana Glavin performed her normal masterful job of coordinating our production process for this book.

We also owe a special thanks to our creative director and book producer, Brian Taylor at Pneuma Books, for his brilliant vision for our covers and interiors. And speaking of creativity, we were fortunate to once again have the talented writer and cartoonist Marc Tyler Nobleman custom-create all the cartoons you see in this volume.

~Amy Newmark

# Sharing Happiness, Inspiration, and Wellness

Real people sharing real stories, every day, all over the world. In 2007, *USA Today* named *Chicken Soup for the Soul* one of the five most memorable books in the last quarter-century. With over 100 million books sold to date in the U.S. and Canada alone, more than 200 titles in print, and translations into more than forty languages, "chicken soup for the soul" is one of the world's best-known phrases.

Today, twenty-one years after we first began sharing happiness, inspiration and wellness through our books, we continue to delight our readers with new titles, but have also evolved beyond the bookstore, with wholesome and balanced pet food, delicious nutritious food that makes it easier to bring people together around the table, and a major motion picture in development. Whatever you're doing, wherever you are, Chicken Soup for the Soul is "changing the world one story at a time.®" Thanks for reading!

# Share with Us

We all have had Chicken Soup for the Soul moments in our lives. If you would like to share your story or poem with millions of people around the world, go to chickensoup.com and click on "Submit Your Story." You may be able to help another reader, and become a published author at the same time. Some of our past contributors have launched writing and speaking careers from the publication of their stories in our books!

We only accept story submissions via our website. They are no longer accepted via mail or fax.

To contact us regarding other matters, please send us an e-mail through webmaster@chickensoupforthesoul.com, or fax or write us at:

Chicken Soup for the Soul
P.O. Box 700
Cos Cob, CT 06807-0700
Fax: 203-861-7194

One more note from your friends at Chicken Soup for the Soul: Occasionally, we receive an unsolicited book manuscript from one of our readers, and we would like to respectfully inform you that we do not accept unsolicited manuscripts and we must discard the ones that appear.

# Chicken Soup for the Soul®

Delicious, nutritious food
that makes it easier to bring
people together around the table.

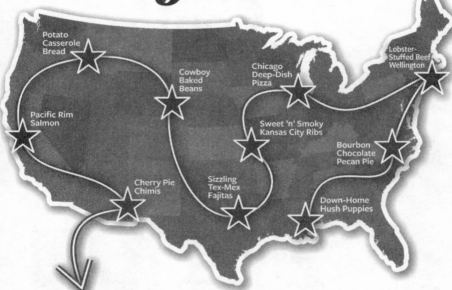
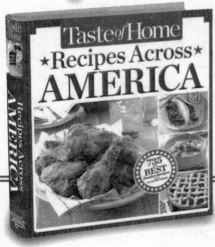

# Our Commitment to Great Taste...
# Tetra

## Taste Quality

We chose to package our products in Tetra Pak cartons because they allowed us to deliver our food tasting the way it was originally intended. So you can have the same fresh, homemade taste that we do in our kitchens!

## Smart Choice for You and the Environment

Tetra Pak cartons are easy to store in the pantry or fridge. And you get the peace of mind from knowing that they are a smart choice for the environment, with 60% less landfill waste. Tetra Pak cartons are made from 70% paper — a renewable resource.

If you want to learn more about Tetra Pak cartons,
visit becartonsmart.com.

www.chickensoup.com